EXPLORATIONS

FOR EARLY CHILDHOOD

Lalie Harcourt

CONSULTANTS

Betty Coombs
Jennifer Travis

ADDISON-WESLEY PUBLISHERS

Don Mills, Ontario • Reading, Massachusetts • Menlo Park, California
New York • Wokingham, England • Amsterdam • Bonn • Sydney
Singapore • Tokyo • Madrid • Bogota • Santiago • San Juan

Explorations for Early Childhood

Editorial Development
Dianne Goffin
Ricki Wortzman

Editorial Consultants
Roberta MacKean
Bill Nimigon
Nancy Wannamaker

Copy Editor
Karen Kligman

Design, Art Direction and Illustration
Pronk&Associates

Line Master Art
Graham Bardell
Barbara Massey

Line Art
Iris Ward

Silhouettes
Kim LaFave

Photography
Birgitte Nielsen

Acknowledgements

The authors and publishers would like to express their appreciation for the invaluable advice and encouragement received from educators during the development of this program. We particularly wish to thank the following people:

Peter DePratto, Margaret Jenniex, Eileen Mansfield, Linda McCrudden, Shelagh Simpson, and Yvonne Simpson. We would also like to thank Jennifer Travis for contributing the annotated bibliography.

In addition, we would like to say a special thank you to the staff and students of Blessed Sacrament, St Fidelis School, and St Mary of the Angel, Toronto; Brookmill Boulevard Junior Public School and Burrows Hall Junior Public School, Scarborough; Cedarvale Community School, Cherrywood Alternative Program, Humewood Community School; and The Hugh MacMillan Centre School, Toronto; and William Berczy Public School, Unionville.

Canadian Cataloguing in Publication Data

Harcourt, Lalie, 1951–
   Explorations for early childhood

Bibliography: p. 223
ISBN 0-201-19106-7

1. Mathematics — Study and teaching (Preschool).
I. Title.

QA135.5.H37   1988   372.7   C88-093116-7

ISBN 0-201-19106-7

Printed and bound in Canada by The Bryant Press Limited.

H —BP— 95 94 93

Table of Contents

Explorations for Early Childhood: The Theory and the Practice

Explorations for Early Childhood is an activity-based mathematics program designed for use in kindergarten and pre-kindergarten classes. It provides a solid base that leads naturally into any child-centered first grade mathematics program such as *Explorations 1* or *Math-Quest 1*. This program makes it possible to put the solid theoretical underpinnings of experiential learning into practice. Activities are carefully designed and spiralled to promote repeated exposure to concepts in each of these main strands of primary mathematics: Problem Solving, Number, Geometry, and Measurement.

Theory

Because most children in the primary grades are at a pre-operational stage of development, they learn mathematics best by manipulating concrete materials and interacting with their environment. A carefully planned environment fosters thinking, security, and the development of mathematical concepts.

Practice

Children explore sorting concepts using a variety of concrete materials. Routines have been carefully established and reinforced so that the children clearly understand procedures and expectations . Note that the materials are easily accessible and labelled so that the children can pursue the task independently.

Theory

Play is recognized as an important factor in the development of the whole child. It is through play that the child acquires and confirms knowledge of the environment. It is also through play that the child has an opportunity to express and represent what he or she knows or imagines.

Practice

The teacher sets the stage for meaningful play experiences by creating a safe environment and by selecting materials that spark the children's curiosity, observations, and thinking. Careful observations and knowledge of the program will assist the teacher in determining when, how, and whether to intervene, modify, or extend a child's play.

Theory

Children must manipulate materials and verbalize the results of their activity to develop a solid grasp of mathematical concepts. Only after children have participated in a wide range of activities, using a variety of materials, and have had frequent opportunities to discuss their observations and discoveries will they have an understanding of the concepts. At the appropriate time, symbols can be modelled and introduced as one way to label or represent a concrete activity. Introducing symbols as a tool to represent concepts rather than to teach them reflects the belief that learning proceeds in a continuum from concrete to pictorial to symbolic.

Practice

Children have created sets concretely to show the different ways of creating a number under consideration. The children are encouraged to describe the combinations they create. The dot card and numeral card are displayed to act as models of other ways the number can be represented.

Theory

Experiences and learning styles of children vary considerably. Activities must be designed to accommodate individual needs.

Practice

Children work side by side at the same center but at their own level. One child is exploring the properties of sand, while the other child is comparing the capacity of the 2 containers.

5

Theory

Children should be encouraged to think and to engage in tasks that motivate as well as challenge. Problem-solving skills and strategies should be integrated into all facets of your program.

Practice

Children have many opportunities to develop the problem-solving skills of observation, sorting, patterning, seriation, and graphing. Problem-solving activities are interwoven through each strand: Number, Geometry, and Measurement. Children are shown here using their sorting skills as they predict whether objects are longer than, shorter than, or the same length as a given object. They then check their prediction by measuring.

Theory

The internalization of mathematical concepts and the development of language skills are two aspects of a child's intellectual growth that can and should reinforce each other. Activities should offer children opportunities to discuss their discoveries and questions.

Practice

Children have many opportunities to verbalize as they engage in observation during the Circle Activities. The children are encouraged to report the results of their activities to their classmates and to interact freely as they pursue different tasks at the centers.

Theory

Mathematics is an exciting and far-reaching element of the child's world with relevance to virtually every aspect of that world. It is important to encourage the children to search their environment for examples of concepts under consideration and to place mathematical experiences in practical and meaningful situations.

Practice

The Dramatic Play Center offers a practical setting for many meaningful mathematical experiences. This child is practicing one-to-one correspondence as she sets a place for each person.

Theory

Children's feelings about themselves as learners and about their experiences with mathematics can greatly influence their success with the subject. By providing an environment that is accepting, encouraging, stimulating, and enjoyable, a program can foster a strong self-image and a positive attitude towards mathematics.

Practice

Current topics of interest or study offer a motivating context for many experiences. These children are ordering themselves by height as part of their investigation related to an All About Me theme.

A Guide to Explorations for Early Childhood

In designing *Explorations for Early Childhood,* utmost consideration was given to making the book as inviting and easy to use as possible. It has been organized into 6 units: Circle Activities, Activity Centers, Theme Activities, Daily Routines, Home Projects, and Finger Plays.

It is not intended that these units be followed sequentially, but rather that they serve as a resource from which you can select activities that meet the needs of your children as well as your own teaching style.

Circle Activities

This unit offers a selection of brief activities for each of these main strands of mathematics: Sorting, Patterning, Number, Graphing, Geometry, and Measurement. You may select, adapt, or extend these suggested activities to meet the needs and interests of your children and your teaching style when planning a program. Circle Activities provide an opportunity to:

- expose children to a concept, skill, or problem
- model language and procedures
- promote discussion and sharing
- introduce activities that can be established at a center

These points should be kept in mind when using the Circle Activities:

- Not all activities are to be completed; rather the ideas, sequencing, and questions should act as a planning resource and guide.
- A strand is not intended to be presented and developed from beginning to end but should be spiralled throughout the year.
- Activity selection should complement curriculum objectives.
- These same ideas or activities can be reinforced and pursued at a center or centers.
- These instructional activities can be implemented in small or large groups.

Activity Centers

This unit features activities for each of these centers: Math, Sand, Block, Art, Dramatic Play, Water, and Science. The activities are organized according to sets of materials and then listed by mathematical strand.

It is the child's thinking and imagination, coupled with your insight and initiative, that unlock the potential of these materials and open the door to a wealth of learning experiences. Activity Centers provide an opportunity for:

- free exploration of materials, ideas, and relationships
- fostering social, emotional, and intellectual growth
- child initiation as well as teacher initiation of activities
- the exploration, reinforcement, and extension of ideas presented in the Circle Activities
- building on the mathematical potential of a child's play, interests, questions, or discoveries

To assist you in maximizing the potential of each center, a wealth of information and suggestions are offered under these headings:

- Mathematics at the Center
- Vocabulary
- Suggested Materials
- Setting up the Center
- Recording at the Center
- Free Exploration with the Collections of Materials
- Extending Free Exploration
- Activities with the Collections of Materials

Theme Activities

This unit features reinforcement and application of ideas presented through 5 themes: All About Me, Special Days, Colors, Seasons, and Animals. The suggested activities of each theme are organized according to mathematical strands and are intended to act as a springboard for planning mathematical activities for these and other topics.

Daily Routines

Incidental experiences in mathematics often take place during daily classroom routines. By highlighting and labelling these experiences as mathematics, you can help the children to increase their awareness of the relevance of mathematics. This unit features 2 daily routines: Snack Time and Calendar Time. Activities that reinforce mathematical ideas and skills can be implemented during these times.

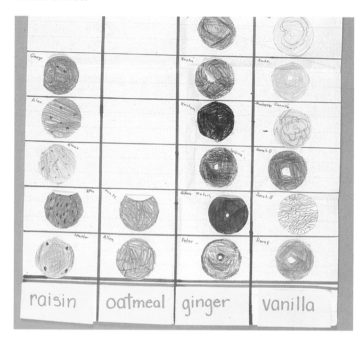

Home Projects

Parents of young children frequently want to be involved in their children's education. To encourage and facilitate interaction between the home and school, this unit features suggested home involvement tasks. Optional home activities and brief descriptions of mathematical experiences are described in sample letters to parents.

Finger Plays

Many of the rhymes that children typically listen to and recite reflect mathematical ideas and language. This unit presents a variety of counting finger plays. There are suggestions provided on how to integrate these finger plays into your mathematics program.

Mathematics and the Young Child

When one observes a young child's environment and her or his natural curiosity, it becomes apparent that the child has already engaged quite naturally in a wide range of mathematical activities before entering school. Mathematics has been an integral and incidental part of most of the play and activities in which preschool children have typically been involved.

Infants are beginning to understand spatial relationships when they maneuver themselves into a position from which they can grab an attractive toy or kick at their mobile. When toddlers climb, crawl, and walk over, under, and around objects and stack their rings and blocks, they discover more about the shape and size of the world in which they live. Young children are also naturally drawn to adult activities. They ask to be involved in such daily routines as sorting laundry, setting the table, and measuring baking ingredients. These experiences involve them in sorting, matching, counting, and measuring in natural situations. Whether the young child is digging in a sandbox, pouring water from one container to another in the bath, balancing on the teeter-totter with a playmate, or trying on clothes to see what still fits, he or she is experiencing new ideas that form the basis for developing mathematical concepts.

It is important that we recognize the young child as someone who has already learned a great deal independently and be mindful that the learning has taken place because the child was able to manipulate materials, to observe the results of the actions, and to think about the meaning of the observations at her or his own level of understanding. If we recognize that the child has made tremendous strides in learning before entering school, it makes sense to consider setting up an environment similar to the home setting. Therefore, the Dramatic Play Center, the Sand Center, and the Water Center provide a natural extension of this home setting for the children to continue their learning.

As children continue to experiment with materials, discuss their observations with adults and classmates, and make choices, they progress in their mathematical thinking. By encouraging the children to talk about their ideas and observations, we can gain insight into their level of understanding. You can enhance the child's mathematical understanding by providing appropriate feedback. When a child is in the process of creating something, the most appropriate feedback may be silence or simply recognition of the activity: **You've worked especially hard to make a very tall tower with the blocks.** There are also moments when a nudge, be it a question or gentle challenge, will naturally extend the child's activity without forcing the child in a new direction. A healthy balance between child-initiated and teacher-initiated activity should be an integral part of a good early childhood program. When the child shows interest in your questions or comments, a dialogue will begin. During this discussion, you can naturally draw out the mathematics inherent in the activity. The child who has built a bridge and road with blocks may be interested in describing how he or she moves the cars in, out, over, under, or around the blocks. The child might respond enthusiastically to a challenge such as, **I wonder how you could build a road around the bridge.** Not every child will respond in the same way or be ready for the same type of nudge or question. The child's imagination, interests, ability, and experiences will directly affect each interaction. Teachers of young children must be prepared to be flexible and responsive to unanticipated, as well as expected, responses.

It should be noted that a child's development of concepts does not take place in a linear fashion. Therefore, even though one can analyse the steps or levels of complexity for a given mathematical concept, it would be a mistake to assume that a child should only be exposed to activities at the particular level at which we assess her or his development to be. Rather a child should be surrounded by experiences at many levels and will glean from these experiences whatever is appropriate to her or his particular needs (often much more than the adult observer realizes).

In summary, then, it is evident that young children are naturally curious and eager to investigate their environment. In so doing, they are continually gaining new mathematical insights and refining their concepts of number, geometric relationships, and measurement. It is your role to provide a stimulating, positive, and secure environment, in which the children's natural enthusiasm for solving problems will be fostered, and to encourage them to describe their discoveries.

Free Exploration

Free exploration plays an important role in the intellectual and social growth of the child. The opportunity for exploration and experimentation should be an ongoing focus in planning your program for young children. Free exploration offers many benefits:

- The self-directed nature of play is a motivating and enjoyable stimulus to learning.
- Children make discoveries as they explore and manipulate the selected materials.
- Children can explore and test information and ideas they have gained through other experiences.
- Children have opportunities to represent ideas, knowledge, feelings, and past experiences in different ways.
- Children become familiar with the materials before they are used in a specific activity or task.
- Free exploration allows for interaction and sharing.

- You can become acquainted with the child as a person as well as a learner through silent observation and interaction.
- Opportunities arise in which you may choose to draw from the child's experience to extend or discuss the learning and thinking taking place.
- Free exploration provides an opportunity to establish and reinforce effective routines.

During free exploration, your role becomes that of observer, facilitator, and catalyst. Many situations will arise from which you can gain insight into the children's thinking by observing their behavior and actions and listening to their interaction. A child's activities, questions, comments, or interests can be used as a basis for stimulating further mathematical learning. You should watch for these opportunities, but also be sensitive and selective about when and how to initiate interaction. At times a child may respond to the gentle nudge of a question or comment, and at others he or she may choose to ignore the nudge and continue along a chosen path.

Problem Solving

Problem-solving skills and strategies are best developed in a classroom that is supportive and responsive. Practical mathematical problems should be presented in a motivating and challenging manner to encourage children to think and to apply the mathematical skills they have already developed. Children must be encouraged to try new approaches, to take time, and to take risks. Children have to see that it is acceptable not to have an immediate answer, that often there may be more than one answer as well as several different ways of solving a problem. This insight comes if you provide time for the children to investigate, encourage them to persevere, applaud when they take risks, and ask them to explain their answers and, just as importantly, how they arrived at them.

Activities and discussions that encourage children to think and become confident problem solvers are integrated throughout this program. Five basic problem solving skills are emphasized in this program: Observation, Sorting, Patterning, Seriation, and Graphing.

Observation Skills

The development of observation skills provides a foundation on which other mathematical skills can be built. Observation activities promote:

- identification of attributes using all the senses
- language acquisition and development
- the making of comparisons
- logical thinking

Initially children should be encouraged to use their 5 senses to observe and describe the obvious characteristics of an object. Objects can be selected to focus children's attention on a particular attribute, e.g., color, shape, or texture, and to promote the related vocabulary. Over time, children should be encouraged to look beyond the obvious and to make comparisons, predictions, or generalized statements about an object. For example, the children may have generated many observations about the appearance of an apple. They then might be asked to compare it with another apple, to predict whether it will roll, or to generalize whether it is bigger or smaller than most apples. To promote comparisons and comparative language, children should be given opportunities to observe and describe 2 (and then more) objects at one time.

You might consider asking any of these key questions to initiate discussion and observation activities:

- **Tell me about it.**
- **What else did you notice?**
- **How is this the same as _____ ?**
- **How is this different from _____ ?**
- **What else is the same color as this?**
- **How are these the same? Different?**

Sorting

Sorting is a basic thinking skill that helps us organize and understand our surroundings. By labelling and discussing everyday sorting experiences as they happen, children can be guided to see the relevance of sorting in their everyday life. Sorting also forms the basis for patterning and graphing skills and provides a way to distinguish and display materials in geometry and measurement.

In sorting, children must focus on the specific property or attribute that defines their set. For this reason, it is recommended that observation activities be introduced prior to and in conjunction with sorting activities to promote children's vocabulary and awareness of different attributes. By providing appropriate materials and guided activities, you can stimulate the children to develop and refine their sorting skills. Sorting skills follow a developmental sequence:

- Initially, a child isolates a set from a collection. For example, the child forms a set of black buttons.

- At the next level, the child sorts a collection into subsets based on an attribute, e.g., size.

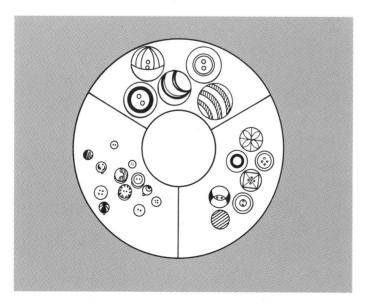

- As the child gains more experience, he or she realizes that a collection can be sorted in more than one way, e.g., by color, features, texture, or size.

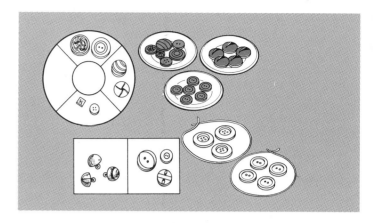

By encouraging the child to explain her or his sorting rule and to re-sort the collection in as many ways as possible, you can stimulate logical, analytical thinking.

When observing children, it is important to keep in mind that a child's level of thinking and observation skills influence the sorting of a collection. For example, 2 children can bring a different level of thinking to a collection of materials even though both isolate only 1 set. At a simpler level, a child isolates a set from a collection of odds and ends by an easily distinguishable attribute, e.g., white things. At a more complex level, a child isolates a set based on a more abstract attribute, e.g., things used in the kitchen.

It is also important to observe whether a child can identify the sorting rule for a given set or sets. One child may be able to identify a sorting rule but not be able to sort consistently on her or his own, whereas another child may be able to sort a collection but not be able to identify the sorting rule for given sets.

It is suggested that sorting activities be continued over the course of the year. The Sorting Circle Activities, pages 44 to 47, offer a variety of ideas for the various levels of sorting. All of the Activity Centers also feature a selection of sorting activities, with a particular emphasis found in the Math, Science, and Dramatic Play Centers.

When selecting sorting materials, consider that concrete materials vary in their level of sorting potential and level of sophistication.

While the children are sorting, you can pursue an individual's thinking or assess knowledge by asking any of these key questions:

- **How are these the same?**
- **How are these different?**
- **Why does this belong in the set?**
- **Should this object be a member of your set? Why?**
- **Does anything in this set not belong?**
- **Which set does this object belong in? Why?**
- **What is your sorting rule?**
- **Can you please show me another way to sort these materials?**
- **What name can you give this set?**

Patterning

Patterning, the repetition of a sequence, is a skill that touches virtually every aspect of a child's life. When infants recognize the human face as a regular arrangement of eyes, nose, and mouth, they are beginning to see pattern. The toddler who automatically brings a storybook at bedtime has recognized (or is seeking to establish) a pattern.

The recognition of pattern has been an ongoing process for the young child and will continue to be a requisite skill throughout the child's academic life. Mathematics, literature, the arts, and the sciences all demand the recognition and creation of patterns.

There are several points to consider when planning patterning activities:

- Children should experience visual, auditory, and kinesthetic patterns.
- Observing and sorting materials give children the opportunity to focus on interesting characteristics of the materials. Some children may pattern spontaneously in the course of free exploration or play.
- Children should have opportunities to read patterns in many different ways. Reading patterns aloud helps children focus their attention on the pattern, provides a way of checking the pattern, and is especially beneficial for auditory learners.
- Children should have many opportunities to identify, copy, and describe simple and complex patterns using concrete materials, sounds, actions, and pictures.
- Children should be encouraged to extend patterns.
- Children should have opportunities to create patterns with many different materials at both the concrete and pictorial levels. The patterns created may be as simple or as sophisticated as the child's abilities and imagination dictate.

When selecting a patterning activity, one should consider these points:

- It is important to be aware that some children may be able to create their own pattern but not be able to extend a given pattern. This is understandable when one considers the analytical thinking required to interpret the elements of a given pattern.
- It is also important to be aware of the complexity of the pattern presented or created. For example, consider the number of different elements used to create the pattern. A 2 element pattern (ab) pattern is simpler than one with 3 or more elements (abb, aab, abc, aabb, etc.).
- It is also important to observe the complexity of the attributes selected to present or create the pattern. For example, a color pattern such as red, red, blue is simpler and more easily distinguishable than a position pattern such as straight, straight, diagonal.

Patterning Circle Activities, pages 48 and 49, provide many activities that can be used and adapted throughout the year. In addition, other patterning activities are interspersed throughout the program.

These key questions can be asked frequently as the children work with the materials in individual or group assessment situations.

- **How could you read this pattern?**
- **What is another way to read the pattern? Another way?**
- **What would you put next in this pattern? And after that?**
- **Show me more of this pattern.**

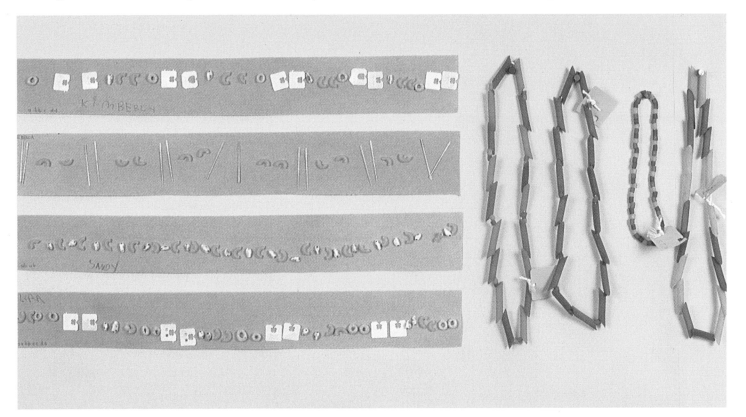

Seriation

Seriation is an ordering process that draws on the children's observation and sorting skills and lays a foundation for more formal work with measurement and number. Seriation involves the creation of a logical sequence for a set of objects or pictures by observing and distinguishing slight variations of a specific attribute and ordering the objects according to a graduated sequence. The children should participate in these experiences:

- comparing 2 items and then identifying and describing which exceeds the other according to an observable criterion, e.g., louder/ softer, taller/shorter
- comparing 3 (or more) items by a selected criterion and then ordering and describing the sequence, e.g., loud/louder/loudest or softest to loudest
- inserting an item into an existing sequence at either end or in the middle

When the children are engaged in activities, you should circulate among them and, when appropriate, pursue an individual's thinking by asking key questions such as these:

- **Which is rougher? Which is smoother?**
- **Would you like to order these objects by (size), please? Tell me about your order.**
- **Can you order these items in another way? Tell me about your order.**
- **How have you ordered the _____ ?**
- **Where would you place this one in your order? Why?**

Graphing

Graphing is a useful recording device frequently used in problem-solving situations as a means of organizing and presenting information. As a direct extension of classifying and comparing skills, graphing presents and clarifies the relationship between groups through a visual display. The prerequisite skills of classifying objects and comparing sets should be addressed before graphing experiences are presented.

Graphing activities should result from spontaneous questions and situations arising in the classroom. Meaningful experiences should occur frequently to provide the children with a realistic impression of the purpose and usefulness of graphing as a recording and organizational tool. Sample questions are provided in the Graphing Circle Activities, pages 68 and 69, and are interspersed throughout the other sections of the program.

The graphing experiences of young children should mainly involve creating and interpreting concrete graphs. Through these experiences, the children can develop an understanding and appreciation for the usefulness and purpose of displaying information on a graph. The concrete graph does, however, have these limitations:

- Often the materials cannot be displayed permanently.
- Many questions do not lead naturally to concrete materials being displayed.
- Concrete graphs usually require a large physical space.

For these reasons, the pictograph is a very useful type of graph. Each picture on a pictograph represents a concrete object. To understand this connection, the children should participate in creating pictographs for the same information that is displayed on a concrete graph.

To assist in leading a discussion about a graph, you might consider any of these key questions.

- **Do you think there are more (less) _____ than _____ ?**
  (This should be asked before beginning to create a graph.)
- **Which column has more (less, most, least)?**
- **Are any columns the same? What does this mean?**
- **Are there more (less) _____ or _____ ?**
- **What does this graph tell us?**
  (This question should be asked after the children have interpreted a number of concrete graphs.)
- **How many more (less) _____ are there than _____ ?**
- **How many children have _____ ?**

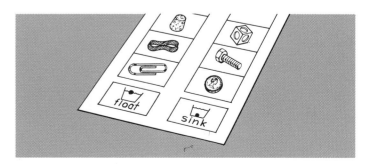

Number

Number is a fundamental strand in the primary mathematics program. Unfortunately, erroneous assumptions about number have often lead to poor programming decisions. When a child counts without hesitation, it is often assumed that this reflects a solid grasp of number. However, a closer analysis often reveals that the young child who counts quite fluently is simply a mimic with a good memory.

A child does not truly understand the number concept 3 until he or she understands these ideas about 3:

- There is a one-to-one correspondence between each number name and an object in the set being counted. That is, in counting a set of 3 toothpicks, the child points to toothpicks, in turn, as he or she says, **1, 2, 3.**
- The number name, 3, applies not only to the last toothpick named, but also to the entire set of toothpicks.
- 3 toothpicks are 1 more than 2 toothpicks.
- There is the same number in a set of 3 toothpicks as in a set of 3 trees or of any other 3 objects.
- The number of toothpicks does not change if we vary their arrangement. Although the sets may look very different, each has 3 toothpicks.

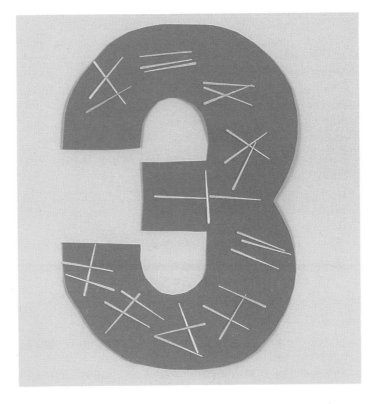

It is important for children to have many opportunities to match, sort, compare, order, recognize, describe, and manipulate sets in order to develop conservation of number.

In this program, number activities are designed to cover these concepts:

- more/less/same
- quantity
- counting
- numeral recognition

More/Less/Same

One-to-one correspondence is an essential prerequisite to the understanding of number. A young child who can recite number names in sequence will still be unable to count the number of objects in a set until he or she recognizes that there must be a one-to-one correspondence between each number name spoken and an object in the set.

The concept of one-to-one or one-to-many correspondence is established concretely by physically matching the objects in 2 sets. Comparisons between the sets can then be made without the use of numbers in response to questions such as: **Is there an egg for each egg cup? Are there as many forks as spoons? Are there enough paint smocks for each child? Are there more crayons or more pencils?** In this way, the children acquire the concepts and vocabulary that form the necessary groundwork for a true understanding of number.

As you circulate among the children, these key questions can form the basis of discussion:

- **Are there as many _____ as _____?**
- **Are there enough _____ for _____ ?**
- **Show me another set with as many as this set. And another set.**
- **Do you think there are more (less) _____ than _____ ? How could you find out? Show me.**
- **Show me a set with more (less) than the set you just made.**

Observe the children as they participate in the matching activities to gain insight into their level of thinking. It is important to ascertain whether children are conserving number. To do so, ask a child to create a set equivalent to the one given. Ask, **Are there as many white counters as there are blue counters?** If the child responds, **Yes,** continue the task by spreading out one of the rows of counters. The non-conserver will see one row as longer and conclude that it has more. This child considers the length of the row as an indicator of number. The conserver knows that the number has remained constant even though the arrangement has changed.

Many opportunities arise in daily classroom routines, e.g., handing out work, supplies, or notes, that lead naturally into a discussion of whether there is enough/not enough, as many/not as many, etc. Children should be involved in such discussions as often as possible. Activities in the Math Center, pages 76 to 99, provide more directed experiences in comparing quantity. As well, many sorting activities can be extended to include a comparison of the quantities of the 2 sets created. As children continue to engage in sorting activities, they should be encouraged to consider whether the sets created have an equal number of members or whether one set has more or less members than the other.

Quantity

It is advisable to develop the concept of a particular number by first focussing on the relationship of the new number to familiar numbers through the notion of 1 more. Children should then explore and describe arrangements and combinations of this number by manipulating a variety of objects. It is important that many sets of familiar objects be arranged and rearranged so visual patterns and combinations of the number can be discovered and discussed. This manipulation and discussion heighten the child's understanding that quantity does not change when the set takes on new configurations.

In addition to the verbal labelling of the number, a model of the visual symbol might be provided during these early stages. In this way, the child can begin to understand that verbal descriptions and symbols are different ways of labelling quantity.

As you circulate among the children, these key questions can form the basis of discussion or assessment:

- **Show me a set of (3).**
- **How many do you have?**
- **If you add 1 more, how many will you have? Add 1 and find out.**
- **Show me (3) another way.**

There are many ways a child can label and/or record her or his work. For example:

- A concrete or pictorial set can be glued down to make a permanent record.
- A dot card, picture card, or numeral card can be used to label a concrete set.
- A numeral can be recorded by or for the child to label a set.

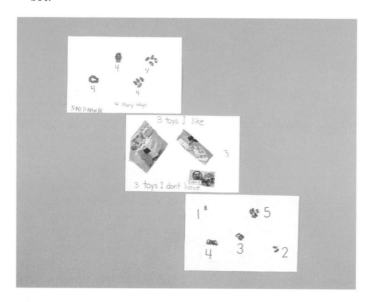

Counting and Numeral Recognition

Suggestions for counting and numeral recognition activities are featured in the Circle Activities, pages 53 to 57. These experiences are not intended to be the focus of number study but should be brief ongoing experiences that are interspersed throughout the year.

Geometry

Children enter school already having discovered through play a great deal about the geometric properties of 2- and 3-dimensional objects. The children's knowledge has been acquired by interacting with the most visible strand of mathematics in our natural world — geometry. To continue the development of the children's spatial ability and to enable them to acquire the fundamental concepts that underpin geometry, it is essential that the early childhood mathematics program have a strong focus on geometry activities.

One should consider these points when planning geometry experiences:

- Initial instruction must provide many experiences with concrete materials. Only by manipulating and discussing models of geometric solids and figures can children acquire an understanding of relationships and properties.
- Children should be encouraged to relate real-world objects to both geometric solids and geometric figures.
- The appropriate vocabulary should be modelled when referring to either geometric models or figures.

Many suggestions for manipulating concrete materials and relating real-world objects to geometric solids and geometric figures are presented in the Geometry Circle Activities, pages 64 to 67. In addition, the Block Center and the Art Center provide natural settings for many geometry activities.

Evaluation may be accomplished largely by observing and listening to the children as they manipulate the materials. These key questions can form the basis of discussions while children work with geometric solids.

- **Can you place together all the other things that have the same shape as this?**
- **How are these alike (different)?**
- **What does this look like?**
- **What else has the same shape as this?**
- **Which of these do you think rolls (slides, stacks)?**
- **Does this roll, slide, or stack? Show me.**
- **What else could you make with this?**

While the children are working with geometric figures, you might ask any of these key questions:

- **Show me all of the triangles (circles, squares, or rectangles).**
- **Tell me about the different shapes you have used.**
- **Why do these figures belong in the same group? What else belongs?**
- **How are these figures the same? How are they different?**
- **What can you find in our room that has the same shape as this?**

Measurement

Adults frequently estimate and measure objects in order to understand and describe their environment. Measurement is one of the strands that most obviously connects mathematics to our environment.

The measurement of length, mass, capacity, temperature, time, and area should be part of primary mathematics instruction. In all of these aspects of measurement, the following developmental sequence should be considered when planning activities and observing the children.

- Children should have many opportunities to make direct and indirect comparisons without measurement tools.
- Only after many comparing activities should children be asked to measure with non-standard units. These experiences will lay the foundation for future measurement experiences with standard units.
- To develop measurement concepts, children must participate in many measuring activities and use and compare a variety of materials of different sizes and shapes. They should be encouraged to estimate before they measure.

Capacity activities are presented primarily in the Sand and Water Centers. Mass is a natural focus for the Sand Center, the Science Center, and the Math Center.

Time and temperature suggestions are offered in the Measurement Circle Activities, pages 70 to 71, as well as in the Daily Routines section under Calendar Activities, pages 202 to 205. Seriation activities offer many prerequisite experiences for linear measurement, pages 50 to 52. Once children have had many opportunities to compare the size, width, and height of different sets of objects, introduce them to comparison of length using any of the suggested activities in Measurement Circle Activities, pages 71 and 72 or the suggestions presented throughout the Activity Centers.

To assess the children's knowledge and vocabulary development in the various aspects of measurement, you might ask any of these key questions:

Length
- Which is longer (shorter)? Show me.
- Show me something longer (shorter) than this.
- Where does this belong in the order?
- Read this order aloud.

Mass
- Which do you think is heavier? Lighter?
- How can you find out? Show me.
- What did you find out about these things when you put them on the balance?

Capacity
- Which do you think holds more (less)?
- How can you find out? Show me.

Money
- Show me a penny (nickel, dime).
- Sort these coins. How did you sort them?

Time
- Will it take a long time or a short time to do that?
- Which will take you longer (shorter) to do, _____ or _____ ?
- What happened first? Second?
- What did you do before (after) recess?
- What do you think happened next?
- What do you think took longer? Why?
- Did it take more or less time?

Temperature
- Which is hotter (colder)?
- Find one that is colder than this.
- Where does this belong in the order?

Area
- Is this _____ completely covered with the blocks?
- Do you think it will take more squares to cover the _____ or the _____ ?

Implementing the Program

To successfully implement an activity-based program, it is essential to provide an organized environment that is rich in materials and experiences. Careful planning is necessary to ensure that your classroom provides such an environment. Here are some questions you will want to consider.

How do I use *Explorations for Early Childhood* as a resource?

Explorations for Early Childhood is not a program to be implemented from the first page to the last in a given order. The number of different teaching styles and personalities is reflected in the number of different ways this program can be implemented.

This program has been developed to act as a resource for teachers to implement local curriculum objectives and guidelines in a manner that is consistent with the way their children learn and with their own teaching style.

It is you who must play the most significant role in planning, implementing, and evaluating this mathematics program. The main goal of *Explorations for Early Childhood* is to surround children with a mathematical concept by providing frequent experiences that allow them to encounter the same idea in different contexts. This continuous exposure allows children to absorb and test an idea at their own pace so that it can be used and built upon in subsequent experiences. Planning a mathematics program is an ongoing process. The program should be developed at your discretion in light of your teaching style, knowledge, and observations of your children.

The selection of specific activities should be based on long-term learning curriculum goals and short-term programming. The latter develops in conjunction with a knowledge of curriculum and child. The process can be described as follows:

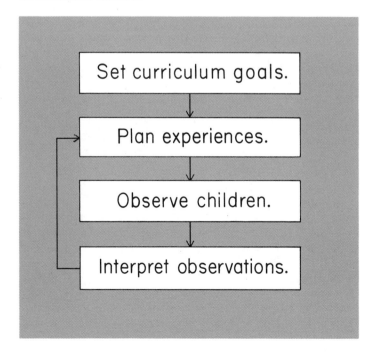

Line Master 1 can be used as a weekly planner for Circle Activities and Activity Centers.

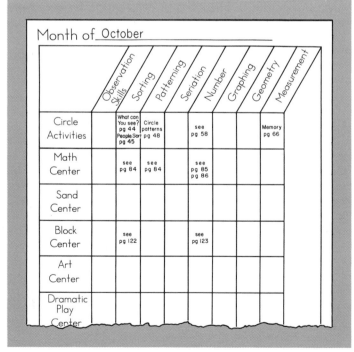

In this example, a selection of Circle and Center Activities has been identified that can be used to introduce and explore the concept of more and less. The Circle Activities were selected after examining and adapting the ideas on pages 58 to 60. To provide further exposure to these ideas, 2 centers were selected to reinforce and extend the concept.

Line Master 2 can be used to plan a month's activities. The Scope and Sequence chart, pages 32 to 35, can be used to locate and select appropriate activities.

How do I establish centers in my classroom?

It is common for early childhood education teachers to establish several learning centers in different areas of their room. The size of some materials defines the location and establishes the area as a permanent center.

On the other hand, the Math Center, Small Block Center, and Science Center can be established in the same manner or can be portable. Portability is achieved by placing the related materials and activities in labelled containers and placing them in an accessible area. These containers can be transported to a work space, thus making any area a center.

It is suggested that related centers be positioned closely together so that the materials and activities can complement one another. For example:

- Dramatic Play and Blocks
- Sand and Water
- Mathematics and Science
- Art and Writing/Book Making

The degree of noise and mess generated by work at a center should also be considered when arranging your room.

Centers can be added and removed throughout the year. There are simple systems that can be introduced so that small groups of children can proceed independently to work areas. For example:

- Limit the number of centers at the beginning of the year and introduce new ones gradually. If you have not established centers before, have reasonable expectations of yourself and the children. In your first year, you may wish to establish only an effective Math Center.
- Take the time to establish and reinforce routines and guidelines for use of space, noise, storage, and handling of materials. Consistency is essential to create a secure environment where children know what the expectations and limitations are.
- Ensure that the materials are clearly labelled and stored for easy access and cleanup.
- Ensure that the children are given the responsibility for the care, handling, and cleanup of the materials.
- Limit the number of children at the center. For popular or new centers, you may wish to provide a set of clothespins or necklaces that define how many children can be there. Children take 1 as they enter the center and wear it until their work is completed. Alternatively, a sign with a numeral and a picture set can be posted to identify the number of children permitted at a center.

How can I keep track of children and their work at the various activities or centers?

There are many different ways of keeping records of the children's activities. You may wish to choose from the following suggestions:

Activity Board

This can be used to record the center that the children decide to attend. Each child places her or his name card into the selected center pocket. The center pockets can be created using cutouts from Line Master 3.

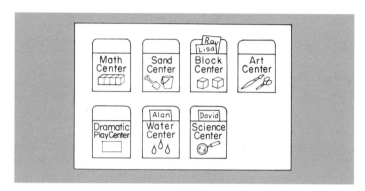

Name Board

This can be used as an alternative to the activity boards. Place sets of activity cards cut from Line Master 3 at the centers to identify how many children can attend. The child places 1 of these activity cards in the name pocket for the duration of her or his time at the center.

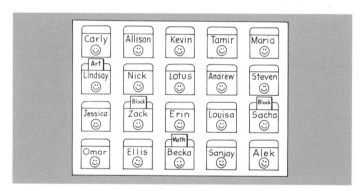

Pocket Chart

This chart is a useful scheduling device. The center cards can remain fixed while the children's name cards are posted by the children themselves or by you.

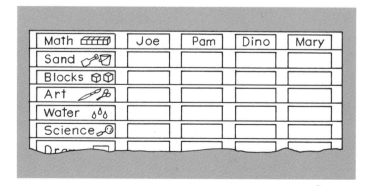

Rotation Wheel

A fixed inner circle identifies the activities or centers. The outer circle rotates. The children's names are affixed to it with clothespins. This allows you to easily change the group members.

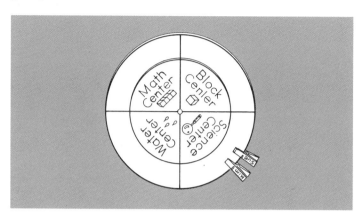

Sign-up Sheet

This chart lists the different centers in operation and is another way to keep track of children's activities. The children can select the center of their choice or you may determine their placement.

	Monday	Tuesday	Wednesday	Thursday	Friday
Math	Zoe Jane				
Blocks	Leslie Kyle Elsa				
Water	Valerie Riva				
Science					

Individual Activity Record

This record sheet can be made using the same format as the sign-up sheet. It can be secured to a child's file folder. Once a child completes an activity, the work is discussed with you. Comments or a symbol indicating that an activity has been completed can be recorded on the sheet.

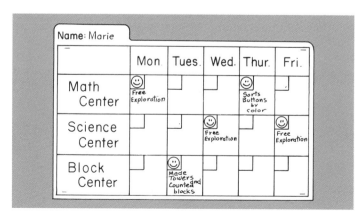

Scrapbook or Notebook

This book can be used to record the center, date, and any work or pertinent observations. If center labels cut from Line Master 3 are kept at the center, a child can glue 1 into her or his scrapbook and date stamp the page. You might wish to record comments or observations or have the child glue in a piece of completed work.

Tracking Sheet

Line Master 4 can be used to record the centers the children visit during a week. You can transfer the information collected using any of the suggested tracking methods daily or weekly to create a cumulative record.

Name	Center	Comment
Alexis	Math Water	-made set cards for 4 and 5 -free exploration with collection A
Debbie	Math	-made set cards for 4 and 5 -patterns made with shells -read patterns well
Donnie	Water	-free exploration with collection A
Elena	Water Block	-found two containers that held same amount -free exploration
Greg	Math	-sorted buttons according to color -enjoyed making patterns with buttons -made abb color patterns
Micah	Dramatic Play Block	-sorted boxes, arranged shelves -free exploration with blocks
Michael	Block Math	-counted blocks in tower -sorted shells according to type

How can I establish effective classroom routines?

Well-established consistent routines are essential to the management of any classroom. An activity-based program promotes more movement, verbal interaction, and materials than are found in traditional programs. Attention must be devoted to establishing classroom procedures and routines early in the year. Expectations must be clearly stated and consistently reinforced. Teachers often comment on how hard they work on establishing routines in the early months of the school year. These same teachers also comment on how independently the children work from then on. As with any new skill, routines take time, experience, and practice before they are understood and consolidated; be patient, consistent, and positive.

Here are some simple devices you may wish to use to help establish routines:

Work Mats

These are useful devices for establishing children's work space. In some cases, the mats will be specific to the area, e.g., sorting, graphing, or ordering mats. In other instances, an appropriately-sized sheet of construction paper or newsprint can be used. Discuss with the children the need to respect others' work areas, and how they would feel if another child walked over their work space.

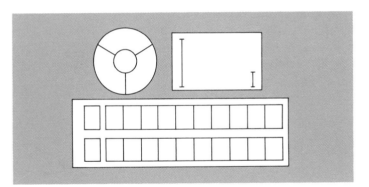

Tidy-up Timers

Timers can be used to encourage the children to tidy their work space quickly and efficiently. A homemade sand timer works well because you can adjust the amount of sand to allow a reasonable time for children to complete the task. You may wish to record the results of each day's efforts by making a simple chart. Color in 2 squares if the children beat the timer, 1 square if they took the same time as the timer, and none if they were too slow.

Boundary Lines

Secure masking tape to the floor to help define the circle for Circle Activities or identify the work space for activities such as block building.

Name Labels

These can be made available for children to label finished work or activities before they pursue a new task. This labelling can be a useful management device for several reasons:

- It allows you to work with an individual or group without frequent interruptions.
- It avoids the long lineups of children waiting to share their work with you.
- It encourages children to use their time constructively.
- It provides you with a record of the tasks completed by the children with whom you may not have conferenced. It also allows you to acknowledge your awareness of their efforts.

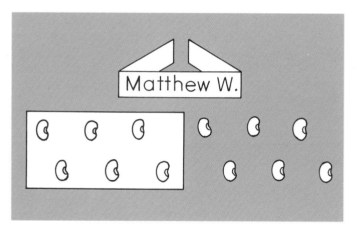

Work Files

These files can be used by the children and you to store samples of complete (or incomplete) work. They should be accessible to the children. By placing a stamp pad near by, the work can be dated before it is filed.

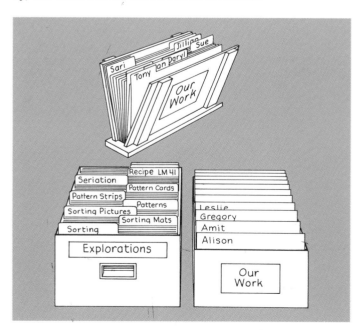

How do I assess the children's progress?

The main assessment tool for the teacher at the early childhood level is observation. Observe the child under consideration while he or she works at an activity to identify strengths, weaknesses, interests, work habits, and learning needs. These observations should be recorded to establish a continuous record of the child's development and progress. It is important that the actual observed behaviors be recorded, not inferences you may draw. These observations are most useful as they help chart behavior patterns, attitudes towards work and towards other children, interests, difficulties that have been overcome, and areas of success and weakness. It is important to remember that recorded observations are not an end in themselves, but merely provide a window into the child's thinking processes and how he or she relates to the program of instruction. Observations provide a basis on which to plan an appropriate program to meet the children's needs.

You should spend much of the student activity time circulating, observing, questioning, assisting, fostering inquiry, and recording observations. You may wish to observe children silently or engage them in discussion.

Encouraging the children to verbalize their ideas and discoveries enables you to develop a clearer picture of the children's thought processes and to become aware of confused perceptions which, if not explored further, can contribute to misunderstanding. It is also important to acknowledge and explore all children's responses. Often an answer may not be the one expected or even, perhaps, considered appropriate. Further investigation of the child's unusual answer will often reveal an interesting, creative response and may initiate further discussion and investigation. When responses are acknowledged and discussed, children receive the message that their ideas and discoveries are valued. This perception promotes an enthusiastic attitude towards learning and develops self-esteem. Many children will think of new ideas and questions that will result in self-motivated activity as they listen to their peers explain their discoveries.

To assist in this task, suggestions for observation and evaluation are included in the discussion of Mathematics and the Young Child, pages 11 to 19.

In addition, a list of key questions is provided to assist in assessing a child's grasp of a specific objective. When appropriate, an informal evaluation task for individuals or small groups is described. When asking questions or initiating evaluation tasks with an individual or small group, the format should be as follows:

test or question –>teach–>test or question

This format provides further insights into a child's understanding of the concept and helps bring to light, rather than perpetuate, any misconceptions.

How can I record my observations?

Recorded observations should be brief and to the point to avoid suffocating in a welter of paper. These records can be kept in a variety of ways. Here are some suggestions:

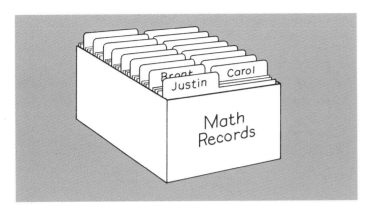

File Cards

Cards may be kept in a box. Regular dated entries should be made. Cards may be added as required.

Record Book

A 3-ring binder or an exercise book clipped at the edge for easy indexing may be used. Allow 2 or 3 pages per child. Observations should be added regularly and dated.

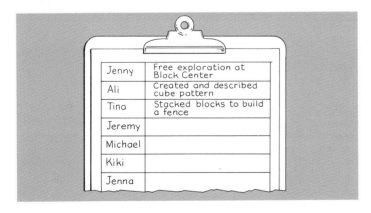

Clipboard and Pad

A chart may be placed on a clipboard and used to record observations as you circulate and interact with the children. Observations may be transferred to permanent records later.

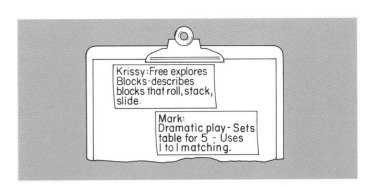

Individual Files

Comments can be recorded on self-adhesive papers or paper squares as you circulate and interact with the children. These observations can then be secured to individual files and date stamped.

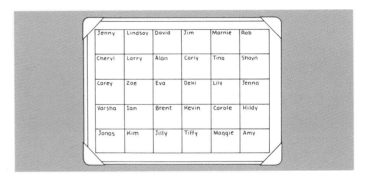

Desk Pad

Put the children's names on a chart on your desk, leaving space in which to jot observations. This will allow you to see at a glance who has not been observed recently.

Observations may be rewritten in permanent records or cut and pasted. Blank peel-off stickers are a convenient way to transfer records from the chart to your record book.

Anecdotal Comments			
Name			
Date	Situation	Observations	Program Plans

Anecdotal Record

Line Master 5 is provided to assist you in recording your observations of an individual. Keep in mind the whole child when observing: her or his actions, responses, interests, comments, approaches, reactions, interactions, and preferences. Key questions are interspersed throughout the program to serve as a resource for initiating interaction or further activity. Be selective in your questioning. Young children may retract or withdraw when presented with too many questions.

How can I modify the program to meet the children's needs?

Your observation of a child working with materials and concepts plus the discussion that takes place are important sources of information for determining growth and deciding on future learning possibilities. By establishing centers, you are free to:

- interact or silently observe an individual or small group
- work with an individual to modify, extend, or clarify an activity
- establish open-ended activities with materials that allow children to work side by side at the same center but at their own levels. For example, as children sort materials or create patterns, it is their individual abilities and imagination that help to determine the complexity and creativity of their activity. Similarly, different children can work with the same materials at number centers as each explores arrangements of a different number.
- provide a variety of materials so that different levels of complexity are provided for the same task
- offer nudges or questions that may initiate further activity or investigation

Repeatedly exposing children to the same ideas in different ways allows for different rates of learning as well as different learning styles. By asking a range of questions related to a given discussion or task, it is possible to challenge children at a variety of levels.

How can I encourage children to verbalize their thinking?

You should encourage language development through appropriate modelling and by providing many opportunities for your children to informally interact with their peers and adults. Both the Circle Activities and Activity Centers provide suggested key questions to guide you in initiating discussion with an individual or small group. The activities facilitate and encourage group interaction and interplay.

Setting aside a time in the children's day for sharing work and experiences gives children an opportunity to identify, describe, explain, and/or reflect upon their feelings or discoveries.

As children listen to you and to their peers, they hear many different ways to express an idea. It is important that the children be exposed to a variety of language patterns to express a mathematical idea or to describe the result of an activity. The variety of language patterns enables the children to see concepts in a broader scope. For example, the word "big" is refined to mean heavy, long, tall, etc. Gradually the children become conversant in the language of mathematics—a rich and expressive language which can bring clarity to their thoughts.

What materials will I need?

A comprehensive list of suggested materials is provided on pages 29 to 31. However, do not feel that you must collect each and every item listed. Feel free to substitute materials with those available to you. Generally speaking, it is not the particular material that is essential, but that the children have the opportunity to manipulate concrete objects. For example, children can sort or pattern with buttons, shells, keys, bottle caps, lids, or any other set of objects with distinguishing characteristics, as long as they have many opportunities to sort and pattern. Similarly, it is not the type of small object—plastic animal, toy car, counter, or finger puppet—that is important when children act out number stories, but that they use the objects to create and show their stories.

How can I obtain the materials?

The materials listed on pages 29 to 31 fall into 3 categories: materials which can be collected, those which can be prepared, and those which are available commercially.

Collected Materials

Obtaining a sufficient quantity of collected materials is a manageable task if you enlist the help of the children and their parents. As children contribute materials to a classroom, they develop an awareness that the classroom belongs to them and that they have responsibilities to it. Children also become aware of the mathematics surrounding them as they search their environment for appropriate materials. As the materials are collected, you may wish to record the type of materials contributed by each child on a class graph. This acts as a check on the kinds of materials that still need to be collected and as an ongoing motivator. You will find it helpful to distribute a letter to parents outlining your requirements several times throughout the year. Sample letters are provided in the unit on Home Projects, which you may wish to use as models.

Prepared Materials

Here, too, you should enlist the help of parent volunteers as well as older children. Many of these materials (numeral cards, story boards, etc.) can be made more durable by laminating them.

Commercially Available Materials

Your supply of these materials can be built up over a period of time. Many of the materials may already be available in your school. Make arrangements to borrow appropriate materials from other classrooms for specific time periods to augment your own classroom supply. You should also note that prepared materials can be substituted for some of the commercial materials. Some teachers may wish to equip the classroom immediately with all of the items listed. To facilitate this, a comprehensive kit, *Math Manipulatives Kit (K)*, is available from the publisher.

How should I store the materials?

Materials that are clearly labelled and stored openly allow children to proceed to activities independently. There are many different types of containers you can use to store materials. A variety is shown here. Covering containers with wrapping paper, wallpaper, shelving paper, or construction paper helps brighten drab storage areas.

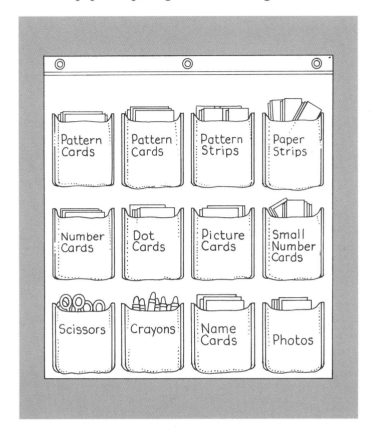

Materials that everyone will be using can be stored conveniently in a hanging shoe bag.

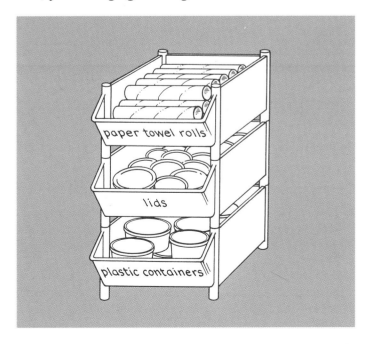

Stackable vegetable bins make convenient containers.

Pizza boxes stack nicely in a larger box.

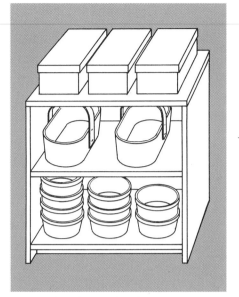

Many shoe boxes, baskets, or plastic food tubs fit on a shelf.

Milk cartons can be cut down and stored in a larger box; the small individual cartons are easily removed and replaced.

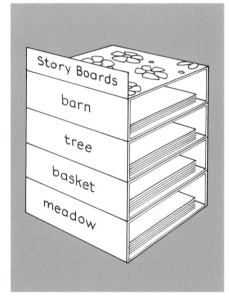

Large detergent boxes (with the tops removed) can be stacked and taped to store papers.

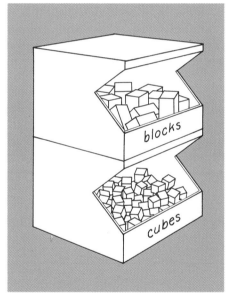

Large boxes can be cut so that they are easy to grip, carry, and stack.

Materials that are not going to be used can be placed out of sight in a cupboard or filing cabinet. However, it is beneficial to display many materials as children will naturally discover numerous valuable uses for them and will often think of ways to use them in their activities.

Before placing materials on shelves, you should label not only the container but also its storage place. Large containers should be labelled with a list of all the materials contained. These procedures enable children to develop an awareness of where materials belong. Children are then able to take responsibility for the orderliness of their classroom. Encourage children to participate in planning new organizations for centers and to suggest improvements on the existing plan.

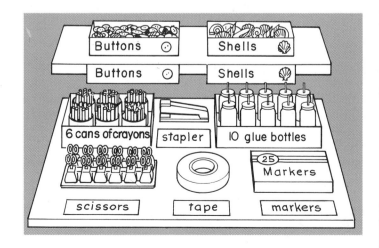

Suggested Materials

Collected Materials

- *Egg cartons, plastic food containers, boxes, cans, paper rolls, clear plastic containers, and lids*

- *Old magazines, catalogues, and old wallpaper books*

- *Toothpicks, popsicle sticks and/or tongue depressors, straws, pipe cleaners, and stir sticks*

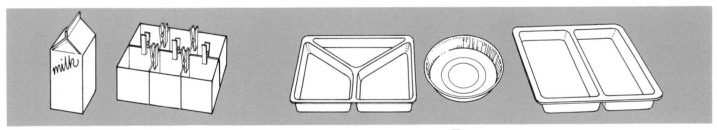

- *Milk cartons cut down*

- *Trays*

- *A variety of materials to use for sorting and patterning and as counters*

Lids | Puzzle Pieces | Pebbles | Packages | Toys | Odds and Ends | Keys | Bread Tags

Bottle Caps | Buttons | Shells | Nuts and Bolts | Plastic Animals | Seeds | Pasta | Paint Chips

Prepared Materials

- *Sorting mats made on large sheets and laminated*

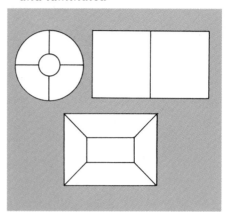

- *Pattern Block puzzle cards*

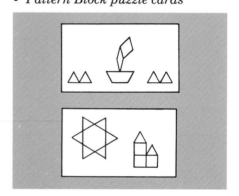

- *Number strips*

- *Pattern cards*

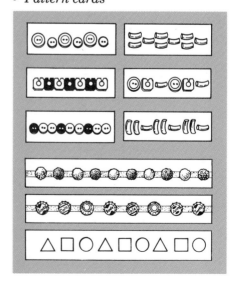

- *Balances*

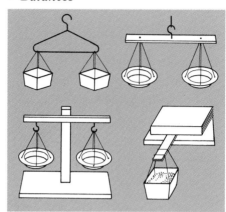

- *Counting boards*

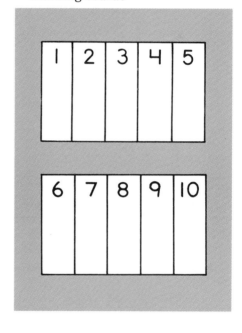

- *Game boards*

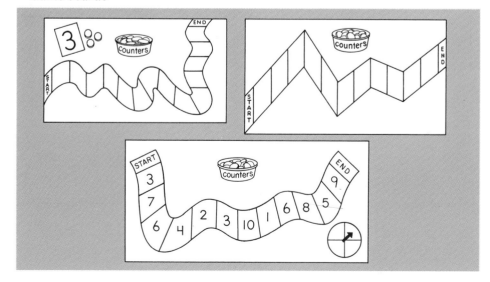

- *Timers*

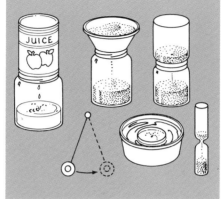

- *Large and small graphing mats drawn on large sheets of mural paper or a plastic sheet sectioned off with masking tape*

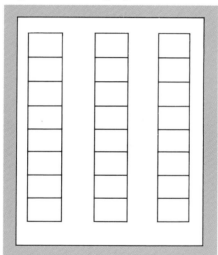

Commercially Available Materials

• *Multilink cubes*

• *Wooden Pattern Blocks*

• *Beads and laces*

• *Double-sided counters and bingo chips*

• *Primary balance*

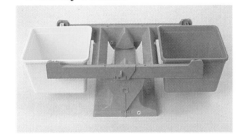

• *Wooden geometric solids*

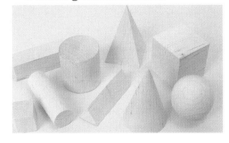

• *Related Attribute Blocks*

• *Geoboards*

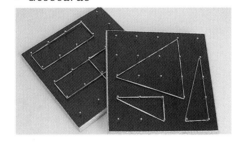

• *Play money*

• *Buttons and sorting animals*

• *Sand kit*

• *Sand/water mill, water kit, water pump, waterfall glasses*

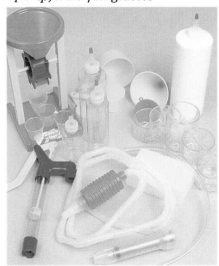

Scope and Sequence

Problem Solving*

	Circle Activities	Activity Centers**	Themes	Daily Routines	Home Projects
Observation Skills					
Observing and describing objects using the 5 senses	38-43	M92, M97, B122, A131, W160, SC169	180, 184, 188	198	213
Identifying likenesses and differences	40-43	M97, B122, W160, SC169	188, 192		
Sorting					
Sorting a collection	44-46	M84, M92, M97, S110, B122, A131, DP142, DP146, W157, W160-161	178, 183, 184, 190, 194	198, 205	210
Sorting and re-sorting a collection	44-46	M84, M92, M97, B122, A131, DP142, DP146, W160, SC169-170, SC173	176, 180, 187, 188, 192		211
Identifying the sorting rule	47	M97, A131, W161, SC169	176, 183		214
Patterning					
Identifying and describing patterns	48-49	M84, M92, M97, S110, A132, DP142, SC173	180, 184, 188	205	209
Extending patterns	48-49	M84, M92, M97, S110, A132, DP142	180		
Creating patterns		M84, M92, M97, S110, B122, A132, DP142, DP146	183, 184, 187, 190, 192, 194		211
Seriation					
Comparing 2 objects	50	B124			
Ordering 3 (or more) objects	50-52	M85, M93, M98, S115, B122, A133, DP142-143, DP146, SC173-174	176, 184, 188, 192		
Graphing					
Creating and interpreting a concrete graph	68-69	M88, W162	176, 180, 188	200	
Creating and interpreting a pictograph	69		176, 178, 180, 187, 188, 190, 194	200	

*It should be noted that **Problem Solving** is interwoven throughout the program. Referenced here are those skills that are emphasized in the program.

**Page references identify the specific center as follows:
M—Math, S—Sand, B—Block, A—Art, DP—Dramatic Play, W—Water, and SC—Science.

Number	Circle Activities	Activity Centers	Themes	Daily Routines	Home Projects
One-to-one Correspondence					
Matching items one-to-one	58	M85, M98, DP143	176		210
Creating an equivalent set through matching	59	M85-86		200	
Matching to determine equivalent sets	58-59	M85-86, M98, DP143			209
Counting*					
Counting forward	53-54	DP146		204-205	
Counting backward	54			204	
More/Less/Same					
Estimating and identifying a set with more/less/same	58-60	M86, M93, B123, DP144	180		
Creating a set with more/less/same	59-60	M85-86, M93, B123, DP144			
Sets to 10					
Creating a set to 10	61-63	M86-88, M93-95, M99, S113, S115, B123, A133, DP144, W162	180, 183, 190, 192	200	211, 214
Identifying ordinal positions to fifth	64				210
Numeral Recognition					
Printing numerals to 10		M98, SC173	176	204	
Recognizing numerals to 10	55-57	M87, M99, S113, DP143, DP146		203	209, 213
Labelling a set to 10	61-63	M86-88, M93-95, M99, DP146	183, 190		
Story Problems					
Creating and solving story problems	59-60	S115	180		

*Note that the finger plays found on pages 216-222 can be used to develop counting skills.

Measurement

	Circle Activities	Activity Centers	Themes	Daily Routines	Home Projects
Length Estimating and comparing length	50-52, 71-72	M89, M95, S108, S111, B124-125, SC174	176, 180, 194	199	209, 211
Ordering objects by length	50-52, 71-72	M95, S108, B124, A135			
Mass Estimating and comparing mass		M89, M95, S108, DP147, SC170, SC173	180, 188		214
Capacity Estimating and measuring capacity		S106-107, S110-111, S113, S115, DP144, W154-155, W157-158, SC171		200	
Money Identifying penny, nickel, dime	73	DP147			
Time Comparing and describing time; sequencing events	70	A133, DP144, SC173-174		199	
Estimating and measuring time in non-standard units	70	S113, W158			
Identifying months of the year from a calendar				202-205	
Identifying days of the week; yesterday, today, tomorrow				202-205	
Temperature Comparing hot/cold objects	71	SC171			
Area Estimating and comparing area		B125, DP144			

Geometry	Circle Activities	Activity Centers	Themes	Daily Routines	Home Projects
Spatial Relationships Comparing positional relationships		B124	176		
Geometric Solids Observing and describing 3-dimensional solids	64-65	M89, S111, B124, A134			
Sorting geometric solids	65	S111, B124, DP146			209, 214
Relating real-world objects to geometric solids	65	B124, A134, DP146	192		
Geometric Figures Observing and describing geometric figures	66-67	M95, A135, DP144			
Sorting geometric figures	66-67	M95, A135		200	
Relating real-world objects to geometric figures	66	A135	190, 192	200	209, 211, 213

Circle Activities

The Circle Activities are organized according to these mathematical strands: Observation Skills, Sorting, Patterning, Seriation, Number, Geometry, Graphing, and Measurement. Although each set of activities is presented in a developmental sequence, it is not our intention to prescribe a program sequence. Instead, the range of activities is designed to act as a menu from which you can make selections based on the needs and interests of the children.

There are many ways to sequence the concepts presented in the Circle Activities. Some teachers might decide to engage the children in an activity from a different strand each day. Others will prefer to focus on a particular strand, e.g., patterning, for a week.

Day	Strand	Activity
Monday	Sorting	What If...?
Tuesday	Number	Number Path
Wednesday	Patterning	People Patterns
Thursday	Geometry	Memory
Friday	Graphing	Shoe Graph

Day	Strand	Activity
Monday	Patterning	Circle Patterns
Tuesday	"	Circle Patterns
Wednesday	"	Read the Patterns
Thursday	"	Read the Patterns
Friday	"	People Patterns

You will undoubtedly decide to initiate many of the Circle Activities with the whole class at one time. However, there will also be occasions when you'll decide to invite a smaller group of children to participate in an activity. For example, many of the number activities encourage each child, in turn, to describe the set he or she creates. To ensure participation in these activities, you might limit the number of children in your circle to 8.

Most of the Circle Activities require few, if any, materials. Activities which require materials for each child are carried out most effectively in a smaller group so that you have an opportunity to observe how each child is using the materials.

As you engage in the Circle Activities, you will notice a range of responses to both the direct and open-ended questions that you ask. Acknowledge all responses, no matter how unusual or unexpected they may be. Many children may have difficulty expressing themselves. Ensure that they are given time and support to verbalize their thoughts. Some responses may indicate that a child does not understand the mathematical concept you are presenting. This is not the time to instruct a particular child. You might decide to repeat the activity at another time on a one-to-one basis with the child who appears confused. At that time, you might discover that the child has little difficulty with the concept and engages readily in the activity. This may indicate that he or she was inattentive, or perhaps distracted, as a member of the large group. On the other hand, you might discover that indeed the child does not understand the concept under consideration. It is important to remember that, at times, the most appropriate response on your part may be no response. The child may simply not be ready developmentally or have had enough incidental exposure to the concept to be able to participate successfully in a particular activity. Do not rush the child. Rather, consider

what this information tells you about the child, and try to incorporate the information in future programming plans. For example, if you assessed an individual who does not conserve number, continue to invite that child to Number Circle Activities but also ensure that he or she is given time to manipulate materials and explore number as suggested at the different centers.

When the children respond enthusiastically and confidently during Circle Activities, you might encourage them to pursue a particular concept further at a center. For example, if the children had suggested several sorting criteria for a collection of objects, you might place the collection at the Math Center and have the children pursue the sorting activity independently.

When you call the children to the Circle Activities, use the term "math circle." This helps the children to establish a context and purpose for the activity. It also gives them a label so that they can communicate with you and other adults. You will start to hear, **We haven't had math**

circle today. It is also worthwhile to tell the children the name of the activity you are playing. They then can request favorite activities. For example, **Can we play Rolling and Showing in math circle today?**

Remember to consider an appropriate amount of and an opportune time for Circle Activities. The activities should be brief to ensure that the children are attentive throughout. The time of day will probably vary. Your children may be ready to sit for a Circle Activity first thing in the morning or perhaps after recess. This will undoubtedly vary throughout the year.

One of the main objectives of the Circle Activities is to introduce and reinforce math concepts. It is equally important to foster a positive and enthusiastic attitude towards mathematics. The tone of the Circle Activities should therefore be supportive and responsive. Encourage participation and applaud risk taking. The most important thing you can instill in your children is an enjoyment of mathematics.

Observation Skills

Initial observation activities should provide the children with opportunities to explore, identify, and describe various attributes of objects so that they can make comparisons and identify similarities and differences. Focussing the children's attention on attributes and promoting their vocabulary will assist them in other areas of mathematics.

Come to the Circle

Invite the children to the circle or gathering area by naming a color or attribute. For example, **Everyone who is wearing red, come to the math circle. Everyone who has squares on their clothing, ...**

Stop, Look, and Find

Have the children move slowly and quietly around the room until a leader calls out an attribute (color: red). The children locate something in the room which is red then stand very still, pointing to or touching the object.

I See

- Objects that reveal an attribute to be examined (interlocking cubes to represent color)

Give the children a selection of objects that reveal an attribute to be examined. For example, if you were focussing on the attribute of color, you might state observations about the classroom that refer to color. For example, **I see a blue box.** Ask, **What color do I see?** The children hold up the blue cube in response. Have a volunteer repeat what was said and add a new color by following the same procedure. **Miss Lee saw something blue. I see a brown chair. What color do I see?**

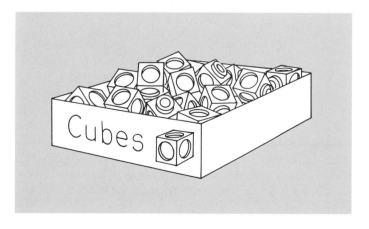

What Did You See Today?

- Interlocking cubes

Have the children identify specific items from their environment that correspond to a given attribute. For example, if you were focussing on color, you might ask, **What did you see on the way to school today that was red? What else did you see?** If you wish to create a graph or keep a record of how many different red things the children saw, you might link a cube of that color together for each item identified. Save the cube tower so that after 2 colors have been considered, the height of the blocks can be compared. Encourage the children to suggest the next color to be considered and to predict if they will find more (or less) items of that color than they found of red items. You might then ask:

- **Which tower is taller?**
- **Which tower is shorter?**
- **Why do you think the red tower is taller?**
- **Why do you think the blue tower is shorter?**
- **What would we have to do to make both towers the same height?**

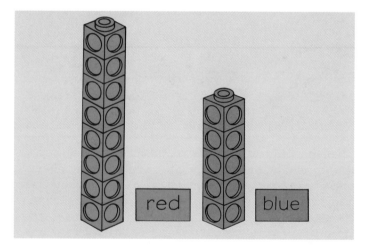

I Spy with My Little Eye

Emphasize different attributes by playing I Spy with My Little Eye with the children. You might say, **I spy with my little eye something that is round.** A child may guess the ball in the picture. If that wasn't what you were thinking of, recognize the child's response and add another characteristic. **The ball is round, but it's not what I spied. I spy with my little eye something that is round and black and white.** Continue the procedure until the item is identified. Once the children are familiar with the game, invite them to do the spying.

Tell Me About It

- An object of the day (apple, orange, pineapple, sock, mitten, key, candle, pasta, etc.)

Present an object of the day, pass it around the circle, and ask the children to examine it (using all senses) carefully and silently. Then ask each child to tell something about the object. Assist the children, when necessary, in observing an attribute by asking a guiding question. For example, **What color is it? What can you say about its size?** Encourage the children to look at the object in different ways by considering less obvious characteristics. You might say, **What does it smell like? Tell me about the sounds it makes. Where would you find this? Where else? What else would you find there? What is it used for? What else? What else is used for the same thing?** Reverse the direction in which the object is being passed if you wish the children to offer a second observation. Repeat the process with different items.

Tell Me About It can be played throughout the year following a similar procedure. These suggestions provide one method of developing the game:

- After the children have examined 4 different objects, select 2 of them and pass them around together for the children to compare. Repeat by substituting other familiar objects.

Tell Me About It

- Pass a bottle around the circle using the same procedure. Then pass 2 different-shaped bottles around the circle for the children to describe and compare.
- Pass 2 similar bottles filled with different levels and colors of water.

What Do You Hear?

Have the children close their eyes and listen to identify common sounds around the classroom. Change the location so that other sounds can be compared: library, school playground, office, etc.

Who Said It?

Identify a phrase or sentence to be spoken, and then have the children close their eyes. Tap a child on the shoulder. That child then says the phrase or sentence. The other children try to identify the speaker.

Tape It

- A tape recorder and blank tape

Tape each child saying a common phrase or sentence. Play the tape and have the children identify who is speaking.

Once the children have learned to use the tape recorder, they can tape various school, neighborhood, or home sounds to play for the others to identify.

Sound Tray

- A variety of items (bell, clock, drum, paper, cotton balls, box of paper clips, etc.)

Place a variety of items on a tray, and have the children discuss and compare them. Questions such as these can be used to stimulate discussion:

- **What can you tell me about the sound each of these makes?**
- **Can the noisy ones be silent? How?**
- **Can the quiet ones be noisy? How?**
- **Can the noisy ones be made to sound loud? Soft?**

You may wish to have the children sort the items in a variety of ways. You might also consider leaving this sound tray on display so that the children can examine the items further and add to it.

Shake It

- A sound container

Have the children close their eyes. Shake a sound container rapidly and say, **How am I shaking it? Tell me about the sound it makes.** Repeat, shaking the container slowly.

What's Inside?

- A sound container

Have the children take turns shaking a sound container and identifying what they think might be inside. After the children have predicted, open the container to check.

What's Inside?

Sound Containers

- Sound containers

Prepare about 5 pairs of sound containers by placing 5 different types of materials, e.g., pebbles, counters, rice, sand, and paper clips, in covered containers so that they will create distinctive sounds when shaken. (Containers do not need to be more than a quarter full.) Have the children find the matching pair.

You may wish to take one set and have the children order the containers from loudest to softest.

After the children have had many experiences, select materials that will produce less distinctive sounds. Later, children may wish to make sound containers for other children to use.

Find the Pair

- Objects that come in pairs (shoes, mittens, boots, etc.)

Place objects randomly in the middle of the circle, and have the children find the matching pairs. This activity can be repeated many times using different collections of paired items.

- **Tell me something that is the same about these 2 things. Can you tell me something else?**
- **If you were blindfolded, could you find the pairs? Why? Why not?**
- **Is there anything different about the 2 things in this pair?**

Gradually, increase the level of difficulty by presenting items that are similar but not identical, e.g., upper and lower case letters, number cards (Line Masters 6 to 13), or 2 shades of the same color.

Color Match

- Pairs of colored paint chips, spools of thread, or fabric swatches

Present pairs of objects in the same color tone. Have the children find the matching pair. Ask, **How are these the same? Are they different in any way?**

Match Up!

- Lids and containers

Have the children match each lid to a container. Repeat this same activity matching lids to boxes or cards to envelopes.

Smelling Containers

- Smelling containers

Prepare about 5 pairs of smelling containers by placing 5 different distinctive smells, e.g., perfume, garlic, cheese, vinegar, and peanut butter, on or under cotton or paper towelling. Have the children find the matching pairs. Encourage the children to describe the smells and any similarities and differences they might detect.

Sharing Similarities and Differences

- Concrete objects or pictures from home

Encourage the children to select 2 items from the classroom or their homes to share with their classmates. Have the children compare the 2 items by identifying at least one way in which they are similar and one way in which they are different.

Look at Each Other

Have each child identify another child who is like her or him in at least one way. Ask the child to identify how they are different also. Encourage the children to explain these similarities and differences.

Likenesses and Differences

- A set of objects or pictures that reflect several similarities and differences

Present a set of objects or pictures in clear view of the children.

Ask, **What is the same about all of these pictures? What else?** Once the children have identified as many similarities as they can, ask, **What is different about these pictures? What else?**

Which One Am I?

- A set of objects or pictures that reflect similarities and differences

Present a set of objects or pictures in clear view of the children.

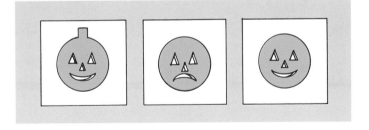

Give a series of clues. For example:

- **I am round.**
- **I do not have a stem.**
- **I am smiling.**
- **Which one am I?**

After each clue, eliminate possible choices by asking, **Can it be this one? Why not? Can it be this one? Why?** Repeat this procedure using a new set of clues. For example:

- **I am orange.**
- **I am smiling.**
- **My eyes are triangles.**
- **I have a stem.**
- **Which one am I?**

What Am I?

- A classroom object

Describe a classroom object and have the children identify it. For example, **My length can change from long to short, but I always stay thin. I am always hard and most often made of wood. People use me in their hand. What am I?** (A pencil)

This activity can be played and extended throughout the year. For example:

- Present clues related to a familiar object that is not visible from various places. You might say, **I have 2 main colors: brown and green. The long rough parts of me are brown. Many small green parts are found at the top of me. What am I?** (A tree)
- Present a collection of pictures that span different categories, e.g., places, animals, flowers, people, or vehicles. Have a child give clues related to one of the pictures. **I'm an animal that gives milk. What am I?**
- What Am I? can be played with Attribute Blocks or geometric or real-world solids.
- Have children make up and present What Am I? clues.

What Could It Be?

- A variety of objects

Display a variety of objects in front of the children, and tell them you will present a clue to help them guess which item you are thinking about. For example, **I am thinking about something that is made of wood. What could it be?** Children will volunteer the possible answers. **It could be the pencil, the block, or the stick.** Continue to present clues until only 1 possibility is left.

Mystery Bags

- An opaque bag (cloth or plastic)
- An object with a distinctive shape, smell, and/or sound

Place the object in the bag. Pass the closed bag around the circle, and have the children touch and smell it silently. Ask the children to volunteer what they think is in the bag and why they think that. Try to ensure that the children give the rationale for their predictions.

How Are They the Same?

- Objects for comparison

Present 2 objects for the children to compare. Initially the objects should be fairly similar, e.g., a plastic food tub and a plastic jar, a pen and a pencil, or a greeting card and a letter. Ask, **How are these 2 things the same?**

Once the children have had many opportunities to compare similar objects, present objects that do not have such obvious similarities, e.g., an apple and a chestnut. At other times, How Are They the Same? should be adapted so that the children can consider how the objects are different.

What's on the Tray?

- Objects on a tray

Place 5 or more objects on a tray, and have the children observe the items silently for a brief time. Cover the tray and ask, **What's on the tray?** After the children have had time to share their observations, lift the covering to reveal the objects.

Children will enjoy setting the tray to present to the group. From time to time, you might focus on similar items that vary by 1 attribute, e.g., color, shape, texture, or size. Over time, increase the number of items displayed. You might like to keep a record of how many items the children can remember.

What's Missing?

- Objects on a tray

To vary What's on the Tray? remove an item from the covered tray while the children cover their eyes. Reveal the objects on the tray and ask, **What's missing?**

Over time increase the number of items removed and/or use items that vary slightly in appearance.

Which Am I Thinking About?

- A variety of objects (perfume bottles, blocks, lids, toy cars, pencils, etc.)

Display a set of about 5 objects, and tell the children you are thinking about one of them. They can ask only identifying questions that can be answered with a yes or a no. Children who think they know the answer may signal in some way, e.g., by crossing their arms.

How Can It Be Different?

- A common item that can be seen in many forms (apple, water, lemon, wood, paper, etc.)

Present the apple and have the children identify the different ways and forms it can be seen, felt, and smelled. Have the list develop over time as children observe or think of new forms.

I Wonder

Present situations that can be discussed. For example, place a balloon in the middle of the circle and say, **I wonder how many different ways there are to make a balloon stay up in the air. I wonder what some of them might be.**

You could also place a child's possession out of reach and say, **I wonder how many ways there are to get Samuel's shoe off the top shelf.** Or, **I wonder why a shoe might be on the shelf.** Encourage the children to think of as many different ways as possible to solve the problem.

What Can It Be Used For?

- A common object (string, can, paper, stick, etc.)

Pass around the string, and have the children examine it in silence. Encourage the children to give a suggestion for its use. This activity provides a wonderful opportunity for creative thinking.

How Did It Happen?

- 2 clear containers

Present the 2 containers half filled with ice. One container should have been placed on its side in the freezer so that the ice forms as shown in the container on the left.

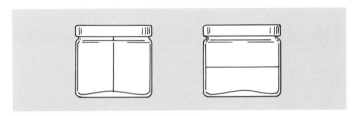

Have the children observe, describe, and compare the containers of ice. Give them time to consider how the ice formed on only one side of the one container and not on the other. Have the children assemble later in the day to share their ideas. At that time, observe the changes that have taken place in the containers of ice.

What Am I Thinking About?

Sorting

Children need many and varied experiences in sorting different materials. For this reason, a variety of sorting activities is featured here. It is intended that favorite activities be repeated often with different types of materials. Sorting activities should be continued throughout the year and integrated into other areas of your program whenever possible.

What Can You See?

- A hoop or a loop of wool
- A collection of materials

Once the children are comfortably settled in a circle around the hoop, spread the collection of materials around the outside of the hoop. Hold up an item, e.g., a red ribbon, and chant this rhyme:

What can you see
That looks like me?
What can you see
That's red?

As children identify items for the set, have them place the items in the hoop. Engage the children in a discussion about the set created. Any of these questions could be used:

- **How are these the same?**
- **How are these different?**
- **Why does this belong in the set? Does anything else belong in this set?**
- **Is there anything in this set that doesn't belong?**
- **What is the sorting rule? Did we sort by color, size, shape, or type?**
- **How else could we sort these materials?**

Repeat the procedure using a new sorting criterion. Also present What Can You See? using materials and pictures that appeal to a variety of senses. Introduce some of these criteria and vocabulary: hard/soft, light/dark, hot/cold, thick/thin, wide/narrow, old/new, rough/smooth, or tall/short. You may wish to use pictures to label the sets.

This Hoop? That Hoop?

- 2 hoops of different colors
- A collection of materials (boxes, lids, etc.)
- Interlocking cubes

Provide each child with 2 interlocking cubes that match the colors of the 2 sorting hoops used, e.g., blue and white. Display a collection of materials. Place at least 3 items in each hoop as you describe your actions. For example, **I'll put this box here because it's big. I'll place this box here because it's small.** Hold up an object so that the children can see it clearly and chant this rhyme as you move the object over each hoop:

This hoop? That hoop?
Which hoop
Is the right hoop?

The children answer your question by displaying either their blue or white cube. You respond by saying, **This box is big. I need to put it in the set of big boxes.** Repeat the procedure. Identify the new criterion. For example, **We sorted the boxes by size. Now we can name the sets. What can we name this set? And this one?** Repeat This Hoop? That Hoop? many times, focussing on different attributes by presenting different collections of materials.

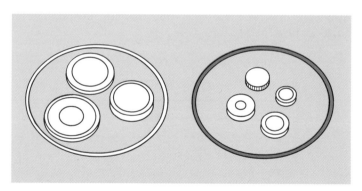

What Is This Set Called?

- A collection of materials (toys, buttons, straws, keys, shells, etc.)

Present a collection of toys and ask, **What do you see that is the same about some of the toys in this collection?** In response to a volunteer's suggestion, ask the children to assist in isolating a set of these toys, e.g., toys with wheels. Ask, **What is the same about these toys?** Pointing to the 2 sets of toys, ask, **If this is a set of toys with wheels, what can we call this collection of toys?** Restate the labels: **We sorted a set of toys with wheels and that left a set of toys without wheels.**

Daily Sorting Opportunities

Take advantage of sorting opportunities as they arise in the classroom. For example:

- If materials have become mixed together, bring the collection to the circle and use it to initiate a sorting activity. Provide the appropriate labelled containers to hold the sets. (Asking children to tidy materials independently also reinforces the natural sorting experience.)
- If there is a classroom lost and found box, bring it to the circle and have the children sort the items before they claim their missing belongings.
- Before new collections of materials are presented for use at a center or an activity, or when they have been brought in from home, have the children examine, discuss and suggest ways of sorting the items.
- A sorting criterion can be used to collect or put away equipment in the gym or on the playground.
- If the children are bringing in special items to share with their classmates, sorting activities can be easily integrated into this activity. For example:
  - A sorting criterion can be given to focus the type of item to be shared for a given time, e.g., books that are funny, things from nature.
  - A record can be kept classifying the shared materials, e.g., types of books brought in.
  - A display table can be used to sort the materials brought for sharing.

Open Space Sorting

Small group activities outside and in the gym lend themselves to sorting children as a means of organization and management. Take advantage of these opportunities by having the children sort themselves according to a given criterion and then label their groups. For example, **We are the squad that picked the large balls. We are the blue team. We are the group with numbers.**

People Sort

- Loops of colored yarn

Place large circles of yarn in 2 (or more) different colors on the floor. Say, **Look at what everyone is wearing today. Do you see something that is the same about some children's clothing?** As a child identifies a feature, say, **All the children who are wearing short sleeves stand in the red circle.** Ask, **What is the same about all the children in the red circle?** Direct their attention to the other children and say, **Is there anything the same about the length of their sleeves?** As a child responds, direct the children with long sleeves to the green circle. Ask, **What is the same about these children? Is there anyone left?** Continue to sort the children if necessary. Then say, **We sorted you by the length of your sleeves. If you were wearing short sleeves, sit down. If you were wearing long sleeves, sit down.** Ask, **How else could we sort you by what you are wearing?** Repeat People Sort many times throughout the course of the year.

People Sort

Find Them All

- Collections of materials (buttons, lids, coupons, keys, shells, etc.)

Present similar collections of materials to pairs of children. Have the children examine the materials. Say, **Tell me about the buttons.** As a child identifies a feature (round), say, **Let's look at all the round buttons.** Ask the children to find all the round buttons in their collection. Ask, **What is the same about all the buttons in your group?** Continue, **Look back at your collection of buttons. Are there any other shapes? Let's find all the square buttons and put them in a group.** Once the children have grouped and described the square buttons, ask them to sort and describe the rest of the buttons according to shape. Have the children put the collection back together and repeat this activity. Find Them All should be played with different materials as well.

Suitcase Sorting

- A container (suitcase, briefcase, trick-or-treat bag, mug, bowl, shopping bag, drawer, etc.)

Present a container to focus the discussion, and pose a situation for the children to consider. For example, **If we packed this suitcase to go to the beach, what might we put in it? If this was your suitcase and you could pack 1 favorite thing, what would it be?** You could list and sort the children's suggestions.

What If ...?

Pose different situations that direct the children's attention to specific attributes. For example:

- **What if we could only eat yellow foods; what could we eat?**
- **What if we could only play with plastic toys; what could we play with?**
- **What if we could only draw things that were square; what could we draw?**

Once the children have generated many ideas for a set, have them restate the criterion. For example, you could continue, **What could we call the set we listed?**

Stop!

- A collection of sorting materials (puzzle pieces)

Display and begin to sort puzzle pieces and identify your sorting criterion. For example, **I'm going to sort these by the number of bumps.** As you place the items, say, **I'm going to put the 1-bump pieces here, the 2-bump pieces here, and the 3-bump pieces here.** Ask the children to watch you carefully as you place the puzzle pieces because you are going to try and trick them by placing 1 piece in a set where it doesn't belong. Have the children quietly chant, **Sort, sort, sort all the things.** When you place the item incorrectly, have them say, **Stop!** Discuss why the item doesn't belong and in which set it should be placed.

Some children will enjoy assuming the role of the sorter while the others chant.

Find It

- A collection of sorting materials

Display materials and silently sort out a set of items, e.g., broken shells. Include 1 item that does not fit your sorting criterion. Sing:

Find it, find it, find it.
Find it, find it, find it.
Find the one that just doesn't fit!

Have the children identify the misplaced object and explain why it doesn't belong in the sorting group. Some children may enjoy creating the set with a misplaced item for the others to examine.

We Could

- A collection of sorting materials
- A hoop or a mat for sorting

Present a collection, e.g., soaps, to a small group of children for them to sort and re-sort. Ask, **How could we sort the soaps?** Decide on a sorting rule: **We could sort the soaps as to whether they are wrapped or unwrapped.** Have the children take turns picking a soap from the collection and placing it in the appropriately labelled sorting area.

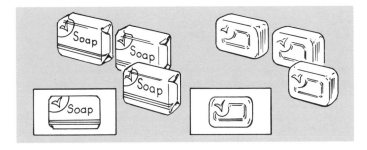

You might ask:

- **How did we sort the soaps?**
- **Why do these soaps belong together?**
- **What did we name this set? And this one?**
- **Where would I place this soap?**
- **What other way could we sort the soaps?**

We Could should be repeated many times with many different collections over the course of the year.

What's My Rule?

- A collection of sorting materials

Display the collection and begin to isolate a set. Once a reasonable number of items have been placed in the set, ask, **What's my rule for sorting?** If no one guesses correctly, place about 3 more items in the set before you ask them to guess again.

Once the sorting criterion has been identified, have the children name the group, e.g., a set of round things.

After many experiences, play What's My Rule? by sorting a collection into 2 or more groups.

Mystery Set

- Objects that have a common attribute, wooden (e.g., block, pencil, stick, geometric solid, etc.)
- Objects that do not have the common attribute

Display a set of wooden objects and a set of objects that are not wooden. Spread out about 4 objects, some wooden and some not, beside the 2 displayed sets. As you point to the set of wooden objects, say, **This is my mystery set. There is something the same about all these things.** Then point to the other set and say, **None of these things belongs in my mystery set.** As the children identify objects for the mystery set, ask, **Why does the mallet belong in the mystery set?** As you point to the items not selected, ask, **Why are these not part of our mystery set?**

Mystery Set

Patterning

Children should be given the opportunity to experience visual, auditory, and kinesthetic patterns. Many and varied patterning experiences should be offered in a group situation to expose children to different patterns and to different ways of reading the same pattern.

Act out the Pattern

Tell the children that they may join your pattern when they feel ready. Begin to act out a pattern, e.g., clap, clap, snap; clap, clap, snap; clap, clap, snap; and maintain the repetition and the rhythm as children join in.

Children should be exposed to many different patterns (ab, abb, abc, aab, aabc, etc.) as well as to different actions to represent the same pattern (clap, snap; snap, nod; tap, rub; brush, slide; etc.) Children will enjoy suggesting the actions for the pattern.

Later you can begin to say the pattern as it is being acted out by naming the actions: **Tap, brush, brush; tap, brush, brush ....** You might also say nonsense words for each action: **Zum, ziggle, zong.**

Move to the Pattern

Identify actions with the children to use in a pattern. Begin to demonstrate the movement pattern, e.g., stamp left, stamp right, arms up high; stamp left, stamp right, arms up high; stamp left, stamp right, arms up high. Continue the repetition as children join in.

Play Move to the Pattern often, providing different patterns (abb, abcc, ab, aab, etc.) as well as different movements to represent the same pattern. Eventually children could say the pattern as they move. Encourage children to say the same pattern in different ways.

Conduct the Pattern

Divide the children into 2 or 3 groups. Identify a different sound for each group to make: animal, machine, instrument, or vehicle. These sounds could be used in addition to clapping and snapping types of sounds.

Conduct the groups by pointing to each one when it is to make its sound. Ask the children to describe the pattern, e.g., **Quack, baa, baa; quack, baa, baa;** or **duck, sheep, sheep.** Some children will enjoy being the conductor as well.

Circle Patterns

• Interlocking cubes (2 or 3 colors) or other small objects

Provide the children with interlocking cubes which they are to place in their laps. Tell them that you are going to chant a color pattern for them to make in their circle. Begin to chant, **Yellow, blue, white; yellow, blue, white; yellow, blue, white.** Encourage the children to join in. Gently tap the children on the head and have them place the appropriate color cube on the floor in front of them. Once the cubes are in place, continue to chant the pattern as you point to each cube. Encourage the children to read the pattern other ways, e.g., **Sun, sky, cloud; sun, sky, cloud;** or give an action or sound to each color, e.g., hum, clap, snap.

Repeat this activity frequently, including different attributes (size, shape, or texture) as well.

If there is an uneven number of children in the circle, you should join the group after the tapping is complete so that the pattern continues around the circle.

Act out my Patterns

As children develop patterns at the centers or in their theme work, have them share these during Circle Activities. Encourage children to describe the pattern in different ways. From time to time children might enjoy translating a pattern into sounds or actions. For example, an abb pattern represented by print making with potatoes at the Art Center could be read as, **Whistle, shh, shh; whistle, shh, shh; whistle, shh, shh; ... or stride, hop, hop; stride, hop, hop; stride, hop, hop; ....**

Read the Pattern

• A pattern made from concrete objects

Present a pattern with at least 3 repetitions to the children. Begin to chant the pattern as you point to each element, e.g., **Blue, blue, red; blue, blue, red; blue, blue, red.** Invite the children to join in with you. Ask, **If we wanted to make our pattern longer, what would we put next? And next?** Add to the pattern as you resume chanting. Ask, **Can we read our pattern another way?** Read the pattern as suggested or present an example if necessary, e.g., **Triangle, triangle, square; triangle, triangle, square; triangle, triangle, square.** Continue to read the same pattern in many different ways.

Daily Patterns

- Patterning materials (consumable materials, pictures, or figures from current themes or topics of interest)

Present a pattern with at least 3 repetitions, and ask the children to read the pattern with you. For example, **What will we say for this picture? And this one? And this one? Read the pattern with me: egg, chick, hen; egg, chick, hen; egg, chick, hen.** Each day read the pattern and extend it by asking, **What comes next?** You may wish to use a class list to ensure that each child has a chance to add to the daily pattern.

People Patterns

Ask a group of volunteers to line up in front of the other children to create people patterns. You may wish to focus on 2 or 3 positions. For example, **How can we show "up" with our bodies? How can we show "down" with our bodies?** Once the 2 positions have been determined, guide the volunteers in creating an up, down, down pattern. Invite the other children to describe and possibly extend the pattern. Encourage the children to suggest other patterns that can be created using the 2 positions.

On other days, create new positions, e.g., high, low; straight, bent; wide, narrow.

Pattern Watch

Have the children identify patterns in their environment. Focus their observations for the discusssion, e.g., their clothing, the classroom, the school halls, their homes.

Display Patterns

Take advantage of display boards or calendars to create patterns for the children to discuss and describe. For example:

People Patterns

Seriation

The Seriation Circle Activities that you select should provide the children with many opportunities to order and compare objects by a variety of different attributes, e.g., size, texture, preference, color, features. Through these activities, you will have an opportunity to model and encourage the use of comparative language.

Which Is?

- 3 or more objects to compare their mass, size, height, texture, sound, or color tone

Present 2 objects that emphasize your current focus. For example, if your focus is mass, you might display a large, light item and a small, heavy item. Ask, **Which do you think is heavier?** Invite the children to state their opinion, then ask a volunteer to hold an object in each hand. Ask, **Which is heavier? Which is lighter?** Replace 1 of the objects and repeat the procedure.

Scavenger Hunt

- A light object (crayon)

Provide the children with a crayon to use as a reference for finding another object based on the criterion you give them. For example, **Find something that is heavier than your crayon.** In turn, have the children identify what they found and compare the mass of the 2 objects, e.g., **I found a book that was heavier than my crayon. The book is heavy. The crayon is light.** You may wish to display some of the children's discoveries.

On another day, repeat the same procedure, but have the children use the same crayon and find something that is lighter.

Compare the 2

- A collection of 6 similar items that vary in size, texture, sound, mass, height, or color tone

Have a small group of children sit in a circle around the collection, and pass 2 of the items, e.g., bowls, around the circle. Have the children describe and compare the bowls by the identified attribute (size). For example, a child might say, **This bowl is big and this bowl is small.** Ask, **Which bowl is bigger? Which one is smaller?** Substitute 1 of the bowls for 1 of a different size and repeat the procedure. Continue to pass around various combinations so that the children can see that the same bowl can be larger in one comparison and smaller in another.

Repeat the activity featuring different collections which emphasize various attributes. Ensure that you include the mass, capacity, and sound of the containers in these comparisons.

This End or That End

- A collection of similar items (balls, blocks, toys, bottles, etc.) that vary by 1 attribute, e.g., size, mass, texture, or shade

Have a small group of children sit in a straight line in front of the collection of items, e.g., bottles. Choose 2 bottles and ask the children to compare them using a selected attribute. For example, **Tell me about the height of this bottle. And this one.** Direct the children's attention to the collection and continue, **Can we find a bottle that is taller than this one?** Once a volunteer has selected a bottle, ask, **Where do you think we will place it to show it is taller, this end or that end?**

Continue, **Look at the height of the bottles. We went from the tallest to the shortest.** Repeat many times, using different items, showing various combinations of tallest to shortest as well as shortest to tallest. Ensure that the children have many experiences comparing 2 items and then adding a third to either end to create a sequence. A variety of different attributes should be examined and described.

Search and Find

- A reference object (block)

Provide a small group of children with a block, which acts as a reference. Ask the group to search around the room and find 2 objects, one that is larger than the block and one that is smaller. Have the children bring their objects back and sit in a straight line. They then arrange their objects in a row in front of them with the block in the middle. In turn, have the children identify what they found that was larger and smaller than their block. For example, **I found a box that was larger than my block and another block that was smaller.** Ask, **How did you arrange your objects? Do they go from largest to smallest or smallest to largest?**

Where Do You Fit?

Once a small group of children is sitting in a straight row, ask 3 volunteers to step forward and face the others. Ask, **Who is the shortest? The tallest?** Once the children have responded, say to the 3 children, **I'd like you to stand so that you are arranged from shortest to tallest.** Have a fourth child come forward who is either taller or shorter than all the others, and ask, **Where do you fit? Who is the tallest now? Is Maria still the shortest?** Repeat the same procedure many times. Where Do You Fit? can be played and developed over time. For example:

- Have 3 children arrange themselves and describe their order. Then have them reverse their order.

Where Do You Fit?

- Have 3 children order themselves, and have a volunteer select 2 other children who can fit on either end of the order.
- Have 4 children arrange themselves from shortest to tallest or tallest to shortest.

One for Each End

- A collection of similar objects (paper towel rolls) that vary by size, texture, sound, mass, height, or color tone

Present the collection and place 2 of the items, e.g., a tall paper towel roll and a short paper towel roll in front of a small group sitting in a straight line. Say, **Tell me about the height of this cardboard tube. And this one.** Have the children examine the other tubes and select one to place on either end of the tubes displayed. For example, **Look at these tubes. Which one is taller than this tube? Where will you place it in the order? Which tube is shorter than this tube? Where will we place it? Look at the 4 tubes. We've placed them from tallest to shortest.**

Remove the 4 tubes. Ask a volunteer to select 2 tubes and place them side by side. Say, **Tell me about the height of this tube. And that one.** Direct the children's attention to the other 2 tubes and say, **Find one for each end of this order.** Once a volunteer has placed a tube at either end, ask, **How have we arranged the tubes, from tallest to shortest or shortest to tallest?**

Repeat this activity over an extended period of time using different materials to compare height. Ensure that a variety of materials are used to represent different attributes.

How Did I Order Them?

- A collection of items (pencils)
- Ordering mat (Line Master 28)

Present a collection of pencils to a small group of children sitting in a straight line. Select 3 (or more) pencils and place them in an order, e.g., shortest to longest. (If ordering by length, ensure that they are lined up along a base line.) You may wish to use an ordering mat. Ask, **How have I ordered the pencils?** Guide and encourage children in their responses. Once the order has been described, order the pencils in a different way, e.g., dull to sharp.

Repeat How Did I Order Them? many times throughout the year, using a wealth of different materials and focussing on different attributes.

How Did We Order Ourselves?

Guide or observe a small group of children as they decide on a method and sequence for ordering themselves. Once the children have had time to decide on their presentation, invite them to stand in order in front of another group of children. Have them ask, **How did we order ourselves?** Children might consider length of hair, shades of hair coloring, or height.

How Did I Order Them?

Where Does It Go?

Have a small group of children order a set of items by a given or chosen attribute. For example, they might order 4 lids by the size of their ridges: from biggest to smallest. Once the children have described the order, present a fifth lid. Ask, **Where would we place this lid in our order?** Have a volunteer place it and ask, **Why does it fit there?** Repeat, using different materials and attributes.

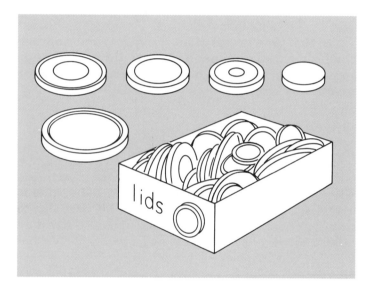

Who Used?

Use everyday experiences to draw attention to natural seriation experiences. For example, when children are in the Art Center, you might ask, **Who used the darkest shade of blue? The lightest? Who used the biggest piece of paper? The smallest? Let's display the work from biggest to smallest today. Would you hang the pictures up please?** Or, when the children are in the Dramatic Play Center, you might ask, **Who used the largest pot for cooking? The smallest? Would you please put those pots away on the shelf from largest to smallest.**

Number: Counting

Counting is a satisfying achievement and will assist a child in acquiring an understanding of number. However, a child's ability to recite a sequence of numbers does not necessarily mean that there is an understanding of number. Counting experiences can be interspersed and repeated throughout your program but should not be a focus for developing understanding.

Warm-ups

Have the children count aloud to a designated number over and over again to establish the counting sequence as they do action warm-ups. For example, the children can count **1, 2; 1, 2; 1, 2** as they perform 2-step actions, e.g., up, down; hop, kick; or stride jump, legs together.

Children can count **1, 2, 3; 1, 2, 3; 1, 2, 3** as they perform 3-step actions, e.g., bend to the left, stand up tall, bend to the right; hop, kick left, kick right; or jump, stride jump, bend.

Children can count **1, 2, 3, 4; 1, 2, 3, 4; 1, 2, 3, 4** as they perform 4-step actions, e.g., jump forward, back, left, right; or hands up high, held out wide, resting on hips, held down low.

Invite the children to suggest the warm-ups and the counting sequence.

Warm-up and Change

Have the children count aloud to a designated number over and over again. Repeat a set action but change it when the last number in the sequence is said. For example, if the children are counting aloud to 5, they could hop, hop, hop, hop, straddle or kick, kick, kick, kick, clap.

Let's Work Out

Have the children count aloud as they repeat an action a designated number of times. For example, if the children are counting aloud to 8, they could clap 8 times, jump on the spot 8 times, or pat their head 8 times.

Clap to the Music

- A classroom instrument

Select a counting sequence to emphasize on a classroom instrument, e.g., drum, triangle, xylophone, piano, maraca. Have the children count and clap softly as you play 4 soft beats: **1, 2, 3, 4.** As you play the fifth beat louder, the children clap and say **5** louder than before. Repeat, **1, 2, 3, 4,** *5* ; **1, 2, 3, 4,** *5* ; **1, 2, 3, 4,** *5* , . . .

Let's Work Out

Show the Beat

- A classroom instrument

Using a classroom instrument, sound out rhythm patterns for the children to perform actions to and count. For example, while counting **1, 2; 1, 2, 3; 1, 2; 1, 2, 3;** the children could do these actions, **clap, clap; pat, pat, pat; clap, clap; pat, pat, pat.**

Say It Out Loud

- A classroom instrument

Identify a counting sequence, e.g., to 7. As you tap or shake an instrument, have the children mouth the counting of beats, say the final number out loud, and clap their hands, e.g., **- - - - - - 7; - - - - - - 7.**

Starting Numbers

Identify a starting number, e.g., 5. Have the children mouth and clap the counting sequence until they reach the starting number. The children then count aloud and perform a silent action until they've reached an appropriate end point.

Clap It Instead

Identify a counting sequence, e.g., to 10. Have the children count the sequence aloud. Each time the sequence is repeated, a clap replaces one more number, until the entire sequence is being clapped out. For example: **1, 2, 3, 4, 5, 6, 7, 8, 9, 10; clap, 2, 3, 4, 5, 6, 7, 8, 9, 10; clap, clap, 3, 4, 5, ...** To continue the counting activity, the process can be reversed so that a number replaces one clap each time, until the entire number sequence is being said aloud.

Forward and Back

Have the children count to a designated number, e.g., 4, and then count back from that number. Ask the children to suggest an action to perform as they count forward and back.

BLAST OFF!

Display a model or picture of a rocket ship to initiate counting back from a designated number, e.g., **6, 5, 4, 3, 2, 1, BLAST OFF!**

Count This Way and That

Identify a counting sequence, e.g., to 5. Have 5 children crouch down and, in turn, stand and say the next number in the sequence, e.g., **1, 2, 3, 4, 5.** The fifth child then begins the counting of the sequence backwards and crouches down again. Each child, in turn, does the same until they are all crouching down again: **5, 4, 3, 2, 1.**

Open Space Counting

Use opportunities that arise in outdoor or gym activities to incorporate counting. For example, **How many giant steps do you think it will take to get from the school wall to the fence? Let's find out. Count while you step. What number did you get to today?**

Treasure Hunt Counting

In a large space or outdoors, guide the children on a treasure hunt. For example, **Walk straight ahead 51 baby steps. Face the tree. Take 12 hops.**

Counting Walks

Identify objects for a pair of children or the class to count before they begin their counting walk. For example, children could count the number of houses, street signs, fire hydrants, parked cars, or mailboxes in a designated area.

Count How Many

Have the children put their legs out in front of them. Ask, **How many feet do you think are in our circle?** Have the children count aloud to find out. Repeat at different times using different features, e.g., hands or fingers.

Counting Container

- A clear container
- Small collections of like objects

Place the objects in the container, and ask the children to estimate how many objects they think might be in there. Empty the container and have the children count aloud as you move each object aside.

Number: Numeral Recognition

Numeral recognition does not indicate understanding of number nor should it become a focus in planning number experiences. Exposing children to numerals from time to time will assist them later in connecting a visual model of the symbol to their actions and descriptions. Select from these activities and intersperse them throughout your program.

Show Your Number

- Numeral cards (Line Masters 11 to 13): 1 per child and a demonstration set

Give each child a numeral card which they are to look at while concealing it from the group. Begin to chant a familiar counting rhyme. As a number is mentioned, e.g., **1,** hold up a sample numeral 1. The children who have the appropriate numeral also hold up their cards.

Number Stepping

- Large paper or plastic numerals

Scatter and tape the numerals to the floor (no more than half a metre [yard] apart). The children direct a volunteer to place body parts on different numerals. For example, **Put your foot on 3. Put your hand on 5.**

Number Actions

- Numeral cards (Line Masters 11 to 13): 1 per child and a demonstration set

You may have the children pick up a numeral card as they come to the circle or distribute the cards once everyone has settled. Have the children place the card face up in front of them. Identify a number and, if necessary, hold up a sample of the numeral (5). Give an instruction, e.g., **Number 5s dance on the spot.** The children holding a numeral 5 follow the instruction. Continue by identifying a new number and a new instruction.

Number Necklaces

- Number necklaces (large cardboard numeral cards)

Have the children wear the number necklaces for the day, and use these numbers to initiate a variety of activities. For example, the numbers can be used to give directions:

- **Everyone wearing a 6, sit at this table.**
- **Find a partner who is wearing the same number as you are.**
- **All children wearing a 3 may go with Mr. Klassen.**

Select a group of children to stand in front of the others. Ask questions such as:

- **Who is wearing number 2?**
- **Shake hands with someone wearing number 4.**

The number necklaces can be used to initiate interaction between the children. For example:

- **Find someone who is wearing the same number as you are, and tell that person your favorite game.**
- **Find someone else who is wearing the same number, and tell that person the name of your number and how old you are.**

For those children needing further guidance, you might consider holding up a model of the number.

Number Necklaces

Number Path

- Large numeral cards

Create a number line on the floor or the playground with chalk or large numeral cards. Ask volunteers to follow directions. For example:

- **Stand on 5. Move back to 3. More forward to 6.**
- **Stand on 2. Move to 7. Did you move forward or backward?**
- **Stand on 4. Move forward 1 step. What number are you standing on?**

Print a sequence on the chalk board, e.g., 3, 5, 9. Have a volunteer follow that path as the others say the numbers aloud.

Number Land

- Large numeral cards

In the gym or any large area, post large numeral cards. Give the children directions to follow based on the numerals posted. For example:

- **All children wearing red, skip to 5.**
- **All children walk in slow motion to number 9.**

My Own Numbers

Telephone numbers, street addresses, ages, and other personal numbers can be used as a source of numeral recognition. Have children identify and share these numbers.

Telephone Numbers

- A large demonstration telephone dial or number pad
- A list of children's telephone numbers
- A model telephone

Ask a child to select a telephone number and say it aloud as he or she points to each numeral on the telephone dial. Have the children chant, **Ring! ring! ring!** The child whose telephone number was selected and dialed picks up the telephone and responds accordingly. This child then takes a turn selecting and pointing out a different telephone number on the demonstration dial.

Body Numbers

- Demonstration numeral cards

In the gym or in another large space, have the children use their bodies to form a given numeral. For example, hold up a numeral card and ask, **What number is this? Make your body look like a 7.** From time to time, children can work with 1 or 2 other children to create a numeral.

Number Concentration

- 5 pairs of matching picture cards from Line Masters 33 or 34
- A large display board labelled with numerals 1 to 10

Post the 5 pairs of pictures face down as shown. Children take turns trying to locate a matching pair. 2 numerals are identified, e.g., 4 and 10. A volunteer turns over the picture cards above those numerals. If the pictures match, the pair is removed from the display. The game continues until all the picture cards are removed. Once the pictures are shuffled and posted again, the game can be continued.

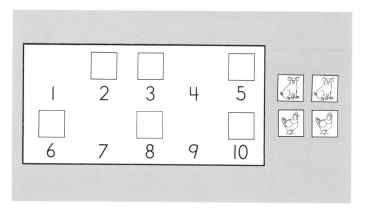

Everyday Numbers

- Numeral cards

Use numerals to label classroom items such as crayon containers, pencil cans, and tables. These labels can be used to facilitate classroom organization. For example:

- The children can select a numeral card on Monday to identify which table they will sit at for the week. The members of that table use the supplies, such as crayons or pencils, that are labelled with the corresponding numeral.
- Shelves can be labelled with a number line or maps of the objects to designate the sequence and placement of materials.

Mystery Numbers

- Numeral cards (Line Masters 11 to 13)
- A demonstration set of numerals

Place a numeral card face down in front of each child. Tell the children not to look at their cards. Demonstrate how the children are to pass the cards by sliding them along the floor to the next child. Establish a signal for passing, e.g., **Pass, pass, pass, pass, . . . stop!** After you have given the signal to stop, tell the children to look secretly at the card they are holding. Begin to chant:

Mystery number, mystery number,
What could it be?
I'll hold it up high,
So you can all see.

Hold up a numeral card, e.g., 7, and continue:

Around the circle all 7s will fly.
Fly 7s. Fly!

The children turn over their cards, and the ones who have the mystery number stand up and fly around the outside of the circle before returning to their spots. The game continues with a new mystery number.

Number Hunt

- Numerals printed on strips of paper or adding machine tape

Give each pair of children a sequence of numerals, e.g., 0 to 5, on a strip of paper. While children are on a walk outdoors, have them look for each numeral. The children should mark the numerals off as they are spotted to help them keep track. Discuss the results of their hunt back in the classroom. You may wish to use questions such as these:

- **Where did you find some of your numbers?**
- **Which numbers did you find?**
- **Which numbers couldn't you find today?**
- **Which was the hardest number to find? Why do you think that?**

Turn Them Over

- 2 sets of numeral cards (Line Masters 11 to 13)
- Demonstration numeral cards

Place pairs of numeral cards face down in random order. Present a demonstration numeral, e.g., 4. Ask, **What number will we look for in this game?** Have children take turns turning over 2 cards. The 2 numerals are identified aloud. If they are not a pair of 4s, they are turned back over and the next child takes a turn. The game ends when a pair of 4s is found. A new numeral can be selected and the game resumed.

Mystery Numbers

Number: More/Less/Same

Experiences in which children compare the quantity of 2 sets of objects are important for developing an understanding of number. Therefore, comparing activities should be a focus when planning number experiences. As you work with the children on comparing activities, you will learn about their understanding of number. Two common methods children have of proving that a set has more, less, or the same as another are as follows:

- to match the objects from one set to the other using one-to-one correspondence
- to count and make a comparison using number

It is through experience, discussion, and time that the understanding develops. Being able to prove an answer demonstrates understanding of number, which is your ultimate goal.

Passing Them Out

Use everyday experiences to have children compare quantity. For example, before you have pencils, papers, or snacks distributed to the children, you might ask, **Do you think we have enough pencils for each child? Do you think there might be too many and we'll have some left over, or do you think that we won't have enough pencils and there will be some children without one?** Distribute the material, discuss the results, and then state, **We had more pencils than children. There are some pencils left over.**

Are There Enough?

Set up 3 (or more) chairs and ask 1 to 5 volunteers to take a seat. Say, **We need a chair for each child. Do we have enough chairs?** Have the children verbalize the correspondence as you point to each child on a chair. For example, **1 child on a chair, 1 child on a chair, 1 child on a chair. Every child has a chair so we have the same number of chairs as children. There are enough chairs.**

Repeat many times using the same procedure but changing the number of items and varying the equivalency. Also, repeat by changing the materials, again offering situations that reveal the same number, more, and less.

Put Them Together

- Collections of equivalent and non-equivalent sets of materials that go together (spoons and cups, straws and glasses, eggs [cotton balls] and egg cartons, envelopes and cards, lids and containers, etc.)

Presenting a collection of spoons and cups, ask, **Do you think there are the same number of spoons as cups?** Have the children put the 2 sets together and discuss the results. You might ask, **Which set has more? Less?** Or, **Are there more spoons than cups? Are there less cups than spoons? Are there the same number of cups and spoons?** You might continue, **There are more spoons than cups. Are there a lot more or just a few more spoons than cups?** For some children, you might ask, **How many more (less) spoons are there than cups?** Repeat, using new collections of materials.

In the Box

- 2 boxes
- Collections of small objects (coins, counters, pebbles, buttons, bread tags, etc.)

Present the boxes and a collection of coins. Alternate between boxes as you drop 1 coin into one box and 1 into the other. When you have finished, ask, **Are there the same number of coins in each box? How do you know? How could we check?** Repeat the activity showing equivalent and non-equivalent distribution of items between the 2 boxes.

*After engaging in this activity several times, you may notice more children are able to suggest matching as a means of checking. Continue to use the opportunity to extend the activity for those children who have a greater understanding of numbers by asking, **Is there another way we can check?** Asking this question from time to time offers a challenge for some children and models another way of approaching the same task.*

More or Less Towers

- Interlocking cubes

Have the children sit with a partner, and provide each child with the same number of interlocking cubes. Say, **Make a tower with some of your cubes.** The children secretly snap their cubes into a tower. Have the pairs of children compare their towers to determine who used more or less or if they used the same number of cubes. Ask, **Who has more cubes in their tower? Who has less? Who has the same number? What did you do to find out?**

For those children who counted, you may wish to provide a further challenge by asking, **How many cubes did you use? How many did your partner use? How many more did Sue have than Jason? How do you know?**

Packing a Lunch Bag

- Paper bags
- Small objects (counters)

Present a set of lunch bags and engage the children's interest by telling them that they are going to be packing lunch bags. Ask, **How many people are we packing lunch for?** Select a corresponding number of bags. **What would you like to put in their lunch bags?** Once a suggestion has been given (sandwich), have a volunteer place a counter in each bag while saying, **Each person will need a sandwich.** Repeat a similar procedure several times. Once the bags are packed, ask, **Do all the bags hold the same number of items?** You might want to have the children confirm that each bag holds the same amount by emptying several of them and matching the counters.

This activity can be adapted to suit many different situations by tapping the children's imagination and changing the materials.

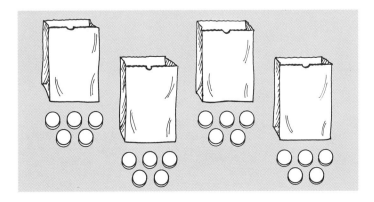

Pack the Picnic Basket

- Blanket or large sheet of paper
- Collections for setting a table (cutlery, dishes, glasses, napkins, straws, etc.)

Place the blanket in the middle of the circle, and set the scene with the children. For example, **Some people are having a picnic today. How many people will there be?** Invite 5 children to sit by the blanket. Engage the other children's interest by telling them that they are going to pack an imaginary picnic basket. Say, **If we have 5 people, we will need a plate for each person.** Have a volunteer set out the appropriate number of plates. Continue the same procedure for other items. You then might ask:

- **Are there the same number of plates as forks? How do you know?**
- **Are there the same number of napkins as glasses? How do you know?**
- **Tell me about the number of glasses and straws.**

If We Have

Present practical situations for the children to demonstrate or act out so that they are creating equivalent sets. For example:

- **If we have 5 visitors, how many chairs do we need?**
- **If we have 3 baskets, how many balls do we need?**
- **If we have 4 people in our group, how many skipping ropes will we need to get?**

Dot Cards

- Dot cards (Line Masters 8 to 10)
- Counters

Provide each child with a dot card and a set of counters. Have the children create an identified set. For example, **Make a set that is the same as your dot card.** Once the sets have been created, you might ask, **How do you know your set is the same as the dot card?** Demonstrate how the children are to pass their dot cards to the next child by sliding them along the floor. Repeat the same procedure, asking the children to make a set of cards with the same number, more, or less than their dot cards.

Restaurant Servings

- Paper plates or mats
- Counters
- Demonstration menu drawn on the chalk board or in a large booklet

Provide pairs of children with 2 plates and a set of small counters. Have a volunteer identify an item from the menu, e.g., eggs. Have a child in each pair serve herself or himself some eggs by placing counters on a plate. Have the other child serve herself or himself an appropriate serving of eggs. For example, you might say, **Serve yourself more eggs than your partner has. How do you know you have more?** Repeat the procedure. Have the children change roles.

Act It Out

- 1 story board per child (any of Line Masters 15 to 20)
- Small objects

Provide each child with a story board and small objects to represent story characters. Have the children use the objects to act out a story. Each story should have a situation where the children make a set equal to (or a set with more or less than) the one they have already created.

For example, **There were some children playing in the meadow.** (Children place a set of objects on the story board.) Continue, **It was so warm outside that other children decided to play outside too. There were as many children playing by the tree as there were playing in the field.** (Children place an equivalent set on or by their story board.) After volunteers have retold the story in their own words, continue, **Everyone had fun, but at 5 o'clock it was time to go home.** (Children clear their story boards.)

Match Yourselves Up

Present a variety of different situations in which the children in 2 groups match themselves up to determine if the sets are equivalent (or identify which set has more or less). For example:

- **Do you think there are the same number of children wearing short sleeves as long sleeves?**
- **Do you think there are as many children wearing running shoes as other types of shoes?**
- **Do you think there are as many children who have read *Chicken Soup with Rice* as have not?**

Encourage the children to estimate if the groups have the same number before they line up the 2 groups. After the matching is complete, you can guide the children's interpretation of the matching experience by asking, **Are there as many children wearing a patterned top as there are children wearing a plain top? How can you tell?**

Counter Toss

- A set of 2-sided counters
- A cup

Place a set of 2-sided counters in a cup. Toss them onto a space in clear view of the children and ask, **Do you think that there are more red or yellow counters? How can we make sure?** Repeat the procedure several times, and ask, **Which has shown up more, red or yellow? What do you think will happen when I toss the counters this time? Why do you think that?**

Counter Toss

Number: Sets to 10

The experiences children have with number through use of concrete materials are critical for developing an understanding of number. These experiences should be an important focus in planning your program. To promote understanding of a number, it is suggested that you introduce a new number in the context of the previous number through the notion of 1 more. You may wish to introduce, explore, and reinforce number to 5 before exposing the children to number to 10 through Circle and Math Center Activities.

It is intended that favorite activities be repeated over and over again. Changing the material and using a different number will help to maintain interest. After some of the initial activities have been introduced, you might consider displaying a model of the numeral. The numeral offers another way of labelling the sets children create and corresponds with their familiar verbal descriptions. This modelling is an important stage in moving children towards work with numerals and symbols and needs to be addressed before children are asked to interpret numerals.

Stories

- 1 story board per child (any of Line Masters 15 to 20)
- Counters

Tell stories that require the children to create sets, add 1 more, or remove 1 using their story boards. For example, **There was 1 bird sitting on the tree.** The children place 1 counter on their story board. Continue the story: **Another bird flew to the tree and landed.** The children place 1 more counter on the story board. Guide the children in saying, **1 and 1 more is 2. 1, 2.** You may wish to continue to add 1 more counter each time or remove 1 counter. When the story is over, say, **There was a loud noise and all the birds flew away.** The children clear their boards. A new story is told.

What Will We Need?

- Counting boards (cookie or candy dividers, egg cartons, muffin tins, etc.) or a 2 by 5 grid (Line Master 14)
- Counters

Provide the children with counting boards and the same number of counters, e.g., 5. Engage their interest by pretending they are going on a trip. Ask them to suggest where they might go, e.g., to the beach. Ask, **What will we need to take with us?** As a volunteer suggests an item, initiate a counting situation. For example, **Stephen says we will need bathing suits.** Print 4 on the chalk board and say, **We'll need 4 bathing suits for our trip to the beach.** Point to your counting board and say, **I haven't any bathing suits.** Place a counter on the board and say, **And 1. I have 1 bathing suit.** Place another counter on the board and continue, **1 and 1 more is 2.** Ask the children to count with you to check: **1, 2.** Ask, **Do I have my 4 bathing suits yet?** After the children respond, add another counter and say, **2 and 1 more is 3.** Count and ask, **1, 2, 3. Do I have enough bathing suits yet?** Add 1 more and say, **3 and 1 more is 4. 1, 2, 3, 4. How many bathing suits do I have?**

Have the children pack their own bathing suits in response to your **And 1 more** statements. Once 4 has been made and counted, clear the board and ask the children to suggest what else they will need to take with them, e.g., 2 toys. Repeat the procedure.

Numbers in the Gym

In the gym or any open area, give instructions that require children to work with numbers. For example:

- **Move on 3 body parts. Move on 1 body part.**
- **In groups of 4, make yourselves into a boat.**
- **Make a circle of 6 children.**

Stories

Under Cover

- A container (yogurt or margarine tub, shoe box, large piece of folded paper, etc.)
- Small counters

Display a container and a set of counters. Provide the children with the same number of counters, e.g., 5. Set the stage with the children by identifying what the counters and container might be. For example, the counters could be people and the container a bus stop shelter.

Take a counter, place it in front of you, and ask, **How many people are waiting for the bus?** After the children respond **1**, slide the counter under the container. Say, **It started to rain and this person ran into the bus shelter. How many people are in the bus shelter? Show me with your counters.** As the children place 1 counter in front of them, ask them to identify how many. You may wish to model the numeral 1 at this point. Then slide another counter under your container and say, **1 and 1 more. How many people do you think are standing in the bus shelter?** After the children have predicted, ask them to add 1 more to their collection. Then ask again, **How many people do you think are standing in the bus shelter?** Once the children have responded, lift the container and have them count to check: **1, 2.** Print a model of the numeral 2 on the chalk board if you wish. Cover the set and continue to add objects in a similar procedure until the desired number has been reached.

Same or Different?

- A set of objects

Display a set of objects (an overhead works well as do large configuration cards) and ask, **How many do you see?** (5) Turn off the overhead and display another set in a different arrangement beside the original display. Turn the overhead on and say, **Are they the same or different? How do you know?** Have the children check.

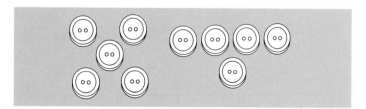

Repeat several times, maintaining the original set, rearranging the original set, or changing the quantity of the original set.

Show It

- Counting boards (cookie or candy dividers, egg cartons, muffin tins, etc.) or a 2 by 5 grid (Line Master 14)
- Counters

Provide the children with counting boards and the same number of counters, e.g., 5. Display or print a numeral, e.g., 4, and say, **Show 4 on your board.** Have some children volunteer to describe how many they have and possibly how they arranged the counters on the board. For example, **I have 4. 3 here and then I put 1 over here.** Say, **Take 1 of the counters off your board and place it somewhere else on the board. Are there still the same number of counters on your board? How many do you have now?**

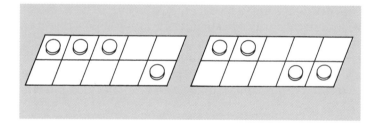

Repeat so that the children arrange, rearrange, and describe a set several different ways.

Rolling and Showing

- Counting boards (cookie or candy dividers, egg cartons, muffin tins, etc.) or a 2 by 5 grid (Line Master 14)
- Counters
- Cube numbered 1 to 6

Provide the children with counting boards and the same number of counters, e.g., 5. Display the cube and ask a volunteer to roll it and call out the number shown for the others to show on their boards.

Make It Just Like Mine

- Counting boards (cookie or candy dividers, egg cartons, muffin tins, etc.) or a 2 by 5 grid (Line Master 14)
- Small counters

Provide the children with a counting board and a set of small counters. On a large display area, arrange a set of counters. Have the children create a similar set on their boards. Ask, **How many counters are on my board?** (5) **How many counters do you have on your board?** Repeat by concealing your set and rearranging it or presenting a new quantity.

Look and Say

- A container or sheet of paper
- A set of objects

On a large display area, conceal the set of objects, e.g., 3, under the container. Display the set briefly, and ask, **How many did you see? Let's look again and check.**

Repeat using different arrangements of the same set as well as other quantities (up to 5). Over time, numerals can be applied to this activity by recording a number sequence on the chalk board. Show the set for 1 or 2 seconds. Then pass your finger under the numerals. When you reach the numeral that corresponds to the set shown, the children say the number aloud.

Tell Us About It

- Work mat divided into 2 sections
- Counters

Provide the children with a work mat divided into 2 sections and a set of counters. Display or print a numeral, e.g., 3. Say, **Show me 3 things on your mat.** Ask, **How many things are on your mat? How many on this side? And this side? Tell us about it.**

You might continue, **Does anyone else have 2 on one side and 1 on the other?** Or, **Did anyone show 3 another way? Tell us about it.**

Look and Say

Roll, Add, Take Away

- Counting board (cookie or candy dividers, egg cartons, muffin tins, etc.) or a 2 by 5 grid (Line Master 14)
- Counters
- Number cube

Provide the children with a counting board and a set of counters. Roll a number cube and say, **Show 3.** Roll again. **3. Add 3 more to your board. How many do you have now?** Roll again. **5. Take 5 away from your board. How many do you have now?** Continue the procedure, having children add or remove sets.

This method allows you the freedom to observe the strategies children use to form their sets and to check that their sets are correct. For example, a child rolls 3 and says, Show 3. The others display 3 counters on their boards and count to check: 1, 2, 3. The number cube is rolled again and a new set is formed on the board, e.g., 5. From time to time, you might like to have some children describe their strategies for creating the new set on their boards. You might observe a child adding 2 more or clearing the board and counting to 5.

Tap a Set

- Dot or numeral cards (Line Masters 8 to 13)

Provide each child with either a numeral card or dot card, or ask them to pick up a card on their way to the circle. Tap a number of children lightly on the shoulder and ask them to stand at the front of the room. Say, **Show me how many children I tapped.** The children who have the corresponding numeral or dot card hold it up in the air. Ask, **How many children?** Have the children return to their spot in the circle and repeat the procedure.

What Did I Do?

- Large display board
- A set of objects

On a large display board or an overhead projector, present a set of objects and say, **How many are there? Let's check: 1, 2, 3, 4.** Conceal your actions or have the children close their eyes as you take away or add to the set. Continue, **I had 4. Do I have more or less than I had before? How many do I have now?** To challenge some children, you might like to ask, **How many do you think I took away?** Repeat the procedure several times.

Number: Ordinals to 5

An understanding of ordinals to 5 is best developed over time and through the use and labelling of natural situations as they occur in the classroom.

Where Is It?

- 5 cups labelled with the worlds "first" to "fifth"
- 1 small object

Display the 5 labelled cups, and have the children close their eyes as you hide the object under one of the cups. Then say, **I've hidden Malcolm's action figure, Joe, under one of the cups. Where is it?** As you point to each cup, say, **Is it under the first, second, third, fourth, or fifth cup?** Have the children state their guess by identifying the ordinal position of the cup. Invite volunteers to lift the cups to check. Repeat the process by asking a volunteer to hide an object under a cup.

Which One Is It?

- 5 stuffed animals

Display the 5 stuffed animals (or have 5 children sit in front of the other children). Say, **I'm thinking about one of these stuffed animals.** As you point to one, say, **Is it the first, second, third, fourth, or fifth one? Which one do you think I am thinking of?** Change the position of the stuffed animals and repeat the same procedure.

It Happens Every Day

Take advantage of everyday situations to model the ordinal language and have children identify the corresponding position. For example, **Would the second person in the line please hold the door open? I'd like the fourth book. Who's standing in the fifth position at the drinking fountain?**

Geometry: Geometric Solids

Children need many opportunities to manipulate, explore, and talk about a variety of different 3-dimensional objects. The Block Center is an ideal setting for children to explore, make discoveries, and gain further experience.

Shape Match

- Pairs of different objects that share a similar shape

Display the pairs of objects randomly. Have the children find the objects with matching shapes and describe why they are a pair. You may wish to ask, **What else would match your pair? Why?**

Find Its Partner

- Pairs of objects with distinctive shapes
- Feeling box or bag

Collect the pairs of objects, display one of each pair, and place the others in a feeling box or bag. Have the children, in turn, touch and describe an object in the box and find its partner. To check, the child pulls the object from the box and matches it to the identified object. The object is then returned to the box. After the children have had many experiences, select objects that are less distinctive in shape.

What Is It?

- Objects with distinctive shapes
- Feeling box or bag

Place the objects in the box or bag. Have the children, in turn, touch and describe an object. The others try to identify the object based on the descriptive clues given. When the child feeling the object thinks someone has guessed the object, it is then pulled from the box and displayed. Later, place geometric solids in the box.

Match It

- Pairs of common objects with distinctive shapes
- Feeling box or bag

Place the pairs of objects in the box or bag. Have the children, in turn, touch the objects to find a matching pair. The child displays the objects and describes the shape.

After the children have had many experiences, select items that have a less distinctive shape and that are less common or familiar. Later, the children can find 3 items that match.

Roll or Slide

- A board
- A variety of real-world objects and/or commercial geometric solids

Set up an inclined plane by propping up one end of a board with a stack of books. Hold up a geometric solid and ask, **Do you think this will roll or slide down the slope?** After the children have offered their predictions, ask a volunteer to check. Sort the solids into 2 groups (rolls or slides) to show the results.

Solid Sort

- Geometric solids
- Real-world objects

Present a collection of real-world objects and commercial solids. Have the children sort and re-sort the solids. See Sorting, pages 44 to 47, for suggestions on different sorting experiences and procedures.

Solid Walk

- Geometric solids

Focus the children's observations on a selected solid before taking a walk in the school, neighborhood, or playground. Encourage the children to observe and identify real-world objects that have the same shape as the selected solid.

What Could This Be?

- Geometric solids
- A pointer, ruler, or wand

Present a geometric solid, e.g., a sphere. Say, **This is shaped like a ball. If you could tap this with the magic wand and turn it into something else with the same shape, what could it be?** Encourage volunteers to suggest various real-world objects that have the same shape.

Find the Same Shape

- Pairs of different objects that have similar shapes (a ball and an orange, a pencil and a straw, etc.)
- Feeling box or bag

Place the pairs of objects in the box or bag. In turn, have the children find and describe the objects that have the same shape. After the children have had many experiences, increase the number of items that have the same shape.

Body Geometry

In a large space or the gym, have the children create body shapes in response to a direction. For example:

- **Shape your body so that it rolls.**
- **Shape your body so that a ball would roll down it.**
- **Form a triangle with your body. A square. A circle. A rectangle.**
- **Shape your body so that someone can pass under it.**

Body Geometry

Geometry: Geometric Figures

It is important that children have many opportunities to manipulate geometric figures and discuss their actions, observations, and discoveries. Ensure that the children's group experiences with geometric figures are complemented by free exploration and further activity at the centers.

Figure Sort

- A variety of paper and commercial geometric figures (Pattern Blocks [Line Masters 21 to 26], Attribute Blocks, Relationshapes, etc.)

Have the children sort the figures. Ask, **What is the same about these figures? What do we call these figures?**

Patterning with Figures

- A variety of geometric figures (commercial or paper [Line Master 27])

Present the different patterns for the children to identify and describe. Encourage the children to describe the patterns in different ways.

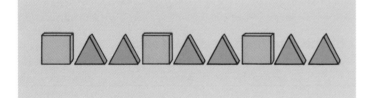

- **Square, triangle, triangle ...**
- **Orange, green, green ...**
- **4 sides, 3 sides, 3 sides ...**
- **Window, roof, roof ...**

Memory

- A variety of geometric figures (commercial or paper [Line Master 27])

Present the geometric figures for the children to identify and describe. Then display 4 (or more), and ask the children to look carefully. They then close their eyes while you remove 1 figure from the display. Ask, **Which figure is missing?**

Gradually increase the level of difficulty by presenting more figures on the display and/or removing more than 1 figure.

Shadow Shapes

Have the children create shadows in response to a direction while outside on a sunny day. For example:

- **Make a circle. A square. A rectangle. A triangle.**
- **Make a shadow that is curved.**
- **Make a shadow above the shadow of your head.**
- **Stand behind someone who is standing straight. Flap your arms. What do you see?**

Magic Figures

- Geometric figures (Line Master 27)

Present a figure, e.g., a circle. Ask, **What shape is this?** Engage the children's interest by telling them that this is a magic circle. It can turn into anything they name, but it must keep the same shape. Ask, **What could the circle become?** Encourage the children to generate many possibilities.

Figure Walk

- 1 geometric figure per child (Line Master 27)

Provide each child with the figure of the day on which to focus. Go on a walk of the neighborhood, school, or playground to observe and identify examples of the selected figures.

String Figures

- Geometric figures (Line Master 27)
- A piece of string for each pair of children

Present a geometric figure, e.g., a circle, and have pairs of children work with the string to arrange it into the shape of the given figure. Ask, **What figure did you make?**

Draw a Figure

- Geometric figures (Line Master 27)

Have the children sit in pairs. One child in each pair should sit with her or his back to you. Present a figure. Ask the children with their backs to you not to peek. They will be given a clue by their partner. Ask the other child in each pair to trace the figure on her or his partner's back. Ask, **What do you think the figure is?** After they have made their guesses have the children turn around to view the figure presented.

Repeat the procedure using a new figure. Ensure that the children change roles.

String Figures

- A variety of geometric figures
- String or yarn

Present a variety of figures along with the string. Say, **Use your string to make a circle.** You may wish to have a child pick a circle from the collection to act as a model for the group or allow individuals to select a circle to act as a personal model. Encourage children to identify and describe their figures.

Repeat using different directions. For example, **Make a long, thin rectangle. Make a triangle with the point at the bottom.**

Pick a Figure

- A large number of geometric figures (Line Master 27)
- A large floor-sized graphing mat
- A container (yogurt or margarine tub, box, etc.)

Have the children select a paper figure from a container before they sit in a semicircle around a graphing mat. Ask, **Which figure do you think was picked the most?** After the children have predicted, have them create a graph to find out. Guide the children in placing their figures in the appropriate column on the graph. Ask, **Which figure was picked the most? How do you know?**

My Figure

- 1 geometric figure per child (Line Master 27)

Provide each child with a circle, triangle, square, or rectangle at the beginning of the day. This will identify their figure for the day. Provide activities and instructions which allow the children to find others with similar figures and identify them. For example:

- **The circles can get their snacks now.**
- **Find a partner who has the same figure as you.**
- **Let's line up in a pattern: circle, rectangle, square, triangle; circle, rectangle, square, triangle; circle, rectangle, square, triangle.**
- **How many circles are here today? Please stand so we can count you.**

Repeat this activity several times so that the children have an opportunity to identify the different figures.

String Figures

Graphing

Children apply their sorting and correspondence skills when interpreting a graph. It is recommended that most of your graphing experiences take place in a group situation with topics and questions that are directly related to the ideas and experiences of the children. Initially you will need to guide children carefully in the procedures for establishing and creating a graph. You may also wish to restrict your graphs to 2 columns until the children are comfortable interpreting the results of the graph.

People Graphs

• A large graphing mat

The children, themselves, can form graphs based on an unlimited number of questions that can be asked. For example:

- **Are there more children with brown hair than blond hair?**
- **Are there more children wearing stripes or no stripes?**
- **Are there less children with a picture on their clothing than there are without pictures?**
- **Do less children walk or get a drive to school?**
- **Do more children prefer animal or people stories?**
- **Do more children put their right foot or left foot into the circle?**
- **Do more children use their left eye or right eye to look through the telescope?**

Shoe Graphs

Guide the children who did not form the graph in a discussion of their observations and interpretations.

Shoe Graphs

• A large graphing mat

Have the children sit in a semicircle facing a large graphing mat. Ask the children to take off one of their shoes and look at it carefully. Ask, **What can you tell me about your shoe?** From this discussion, define a graphing purpose. For example, you might ask, **Do you think there are more children with running shoes or more children without running shoes?** After the children have responded, guide each group, in turn, in placing their shoes on the mat in the appropriate column and space.

Any of these questions may be used to guide the children's observations and interpretations of the graph:

- **What is the same about all the shoes in this column? And this column?**
- **Point to the column that has more.**
- **Point to the column that has less. Are there more running shoes than other shoes?**

Some children may be able to respond to these challenges:

- **How many more running shoes are there?**
- **How many other shoes do we need so that there are the same number in each column?**
- **How many shoes are on our graph?**

Repeat the activity often using a variety of criteria, e.g., features, size, left/right, color, or material.

Flip It

- A large graphing mat and graphing labels
- A name card for each child
- 1 coin, 2-sided counter, or bottle cap per child

Gather the children around the graphing mat. Give each child her or his own name card. Distribute a coin, a 2-sided counter, or a bottle cap to each child.

Tell the children they are each going to gently flip their object onto their name card. Ask the children to predict which side they think will appear more (less). For example, **Do you think we'll see more yellows or more reds?** Have the children place the 2-sided counter in their hands and gently open them above their name card. Construct a graph with the children to show the results. Discuss their observations by asking:

- **Which color appeared more? How do you know?**
- **Which color appeared less? How do you know?**
- **Are there more yellow or red counters?**

You may wish to keep a record on another graph to show which appeared more. You may wish to repeat this activity many times.

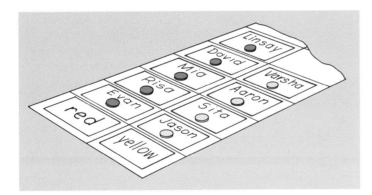

Pick It!

- 2 colored cubes per child
- A bag
- A graphing mat and graphing labels

Place cubes of 2 (or more) colors in a bag. Have each child pick a cube from the bag before coming to the circle or have the bag passed around the circle. The children place their cube in front of them. Ask, **Do you think there are more green cubes or white cubes?** After the children have predicted, create a graph to find out. Guide the children in placing their cubes in the appropriate column on the graph. Have the children create a concrete bar graph by linking the cubes of a similar color together. Have the children interpret the graph.

Center Graphs

- A large graphing mat and graphing labels
- Center labels (Line Master 3)

There are several questions you can ask related to the children's work at their centers. For example:

- **Which center would you like opened next?**
- **Which center is your favorite?**
- **Which center did you go to today?**

Children can use the center labels to record their responses to create a pictograph. These center labels can also be used to label the columns on a floor graph if a people graph is being created.

Graphing Your Sorting Groups

After the children have sorted themselves, objects, or pictures, you might like to initiate a graph by asking, **Which group do you think has more (less)? Let's graph the sets to find out.**

Name Graphs

- A large graphing mat
- Name cards

Have the children sit in a semicircle facing a large graphing mat. Give each child her or his name card to act as their response to a question. For example, **Which song would you like to hear?** Guide the children in placing their name cards in the appropriate column. Ask any of the these questions:

- **Which column has more (less, most, least)?**
- **What does it mean when one column has more than the other?**
- **Are the columns the same?**
- **Which song will we hear?**
- **What does this graph tell us?**

Repeat this activity often using a variety of different questions.

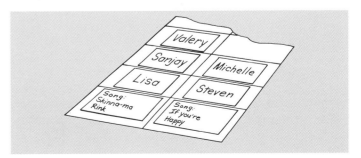

Measurement: Time

Time is a very abstract idea and one which is not quickly understood. References to time should be made in context on a day-to-day basis. The following activities offer suggestions for focussing the children's attention on time and its vocabulary.

What Do You Do?

Present an event in the children's day, e.g., lunch, and ask them to identify events they would do before or after it. You may wish to discuss these events and/or list them on a chart. Alternatively, after the discussion has taken place, some children might like to draw a picture of their event and post it on a display.

Before and After

Have the children watch you carefully as you perform 3 (or more) different actions in succession. For example, you might clap, put a book down, and then jump. Ask,

- **What did I do before I put the book down?**
- **What did I do after I clapped?**
- **What did I do after I put the book down?**
- **What were 2 things I did before I jumped?**

Some children will enjoy performing the actions for the others.

When Would You?

Pose different situations for the children to consider and discuss. For example:

- **When would you have lunch, before or after dinner?**
- **When do you see a picture, before or after you've turned on the TV?**
- **When do you see the moon, before or after the sun sets?**
- **When do you say hello, before or after the phone rings?**

Show Us What You Do

Identify an event in the children's day, e.g., snack time. Ask volunteers to act out an event that might occur before or after. Before the child performs, have her or him specify whether the event is one that happens before or after.

Let's Plan

Use practical events in the classroom to stimulate a discussion of before and after events. For example:

- **It is almost recess. What will we have to do before we go outside?**
- **What will we have to do after we get back from the market?**

Short Time/Long Time

- A picture collection

Present the collection or have the children cut out pictures of actions or events from magazines to bring to the circle. The children identify and sort the pictures by whether the actions or events take a long time or a short time to complete.

How Long Do We Have to Wait?

Identify events and have the children specify and discuss whether they will have to wait a long time or a short time for the event to take place, e.g., recess, Christmas, summer, Monday, night, gym, or Meagan's birthday in June.

You may wish to use pictures to illustrate the events.

Will We Finish Before or After?

- A non-standard timer

Use a non-standard timer such as a sand clock or egg timer as a reference for starting various classroom activities. You might ask, **Do you think we will finish our song before or after the timer? Let's find out.** You may wish to keep an ongoing record of the classroom events you tested.

Use the Classroom Clock

Take advantage of opportunities to refer to the classroom clock. For example:

- **It's 10:00. Time to get ready for our snack.**
- **It's 2:00. What is going to happen now?**
- **We need to stop our activities at 10:30. The classroom clock will look like this** (model the time on another clock) **at 10:30.**
- **We have about 10 minutes to wait until it's 12:00. What can we do while we wait for lunch?**

Measurement: Temperature

Children learn best about temperature through practical situations and in a day-to-day context. It is these opportunities that should become the focus of your discussion. You might also consider the following activities.

Hot or Cold?

Describe times, events, places, and objects that are hot or cold. Have the children respond by pretending they are hot or cold. For example, **You take a sip of a chocolate drink that has just been poured from a pot on the stove. Is it hot or cold?**

What Should You Wear?

Present different times, events, or places that reflect different temperatures, e.g., running a race or walking on a beach in winter. Have the children specify whether they would wear heavy or light clothing and why.

Clothes

Have the children identify the clothes they wear when it is hot and when it is cold. You may wish to keep a record of their responses.

Measurement: Length

Children should have had many experiences comparing and seriating objects by different attributes before they are asked to consider length. The use of a base line helps children to understand that direct comparisons of length are only valid when made from a common point. Encourage children to estimate before they actually compare or measure.

The Same Length

- Lengths of paper strips, string, wool, ribbon, or straws (some the same, some different)
- A base line (Line Master 28, string, or paper)

Present a small collection, e.g., straws cut to various lengths. Include a pair that are the same length.

Tell the children to look carefully at the straws. Ask, **Can you see 2 straws that you think might be the same length?** Encourage predictions. Ask, **How can we check to find out if these 2 are the same length?** Accept all reasonable responses and try them out. Once the 2 have been found, add new straws to the collection. Ask, **Are there any straws in this collection that you think are the same length as these 2?** This activity can be made more complex by increasing the number of materials in the collection gradually, mixing different types of materials, or having less distinctive differences in length.

The Same Length

What Do You Think?

- Objects of similar and different lengths

Present 2 objects on a display area in clear view of all children. Position the objects so that they are parallel but not aligned. Ask, **Do you think these 2 straws are the same length? How could we find out?** Accept and test the children's suggestions. Once the comparison has been made, remove one of the items and add a new one. Continue by asking, **Do you think these 2 straws are the same length? How can we find out? Is there another way we can check to be sure that they are the same length?**

Snap and Measure

- Interlocking cubes

Have the children take a handful of cubes and snap them together. Ask each child to display her or his train of cubes. Say, **Look at your neighbor's cubes. Are they the same length? How can you quickly check to make sure?** Discuss the children's observations and discoveries. You might continue, **Look around the circle. Do you see any cube trains that might be the same length? How can we quickly check to make sure?**

Are They the Same?

- 2 pieces of string

Display the 2 pieces of string in 2 different positions as illustrated.

Ask, **Do you think that these are the same length?** Continue by asking, **How can we check?** Once the comparative lengths have been tested, reposition the same pieces of string or present 2 new ones and repeat the procedure.

Base Line

- A common reference object for each child (popsicle stick, straw, stir stick, etc.)
- A base line for each child (paper or Line Master 28)
- A collection of objects

You may wish to have each child pick up a reference object, e.g., a straw, from a designated container and another object from a different container before coming to the circle. Distribute a piece of paper (or Line Master 28) to each child. Have the children run their finger along the straight line made by the bottom of the paper. Tell them that this can be used as a starting line for comparing lengths of different objects. Have the children place their reference object on their starting line. Tell the children that they are going to compare their other object to this straw. Say, **Place your other object on the starting line too. Check to see if it is longer or shorter.** Ask, **Who has something that is longer than the straw? How do you know that it is longer?** Guide these children in placing their object in a common set. Repeat a similar procedure for objects that are shorter and those that are the same length as the straw.

String Comparison

- Strings cut to various lengths (1 per child)
- A base line for each child (paper or Line Master 28)

Provide each child with a piece of string and a base line, if desired. Guide the children in working in pairs. Ask, **Look at the 2 pieces of string. Which one do you think is longer (shorter)?** Have the children compare the lengths of their string. Ask, **Whose string was longer? Whose string was shorter? Did anyone have a string the same length as her or his partner's?** Guide the children in passing their string to the person on their right. Repeat the procedure.

Which Is Longer?

- A large collection of objects
- A base line for each child (paper or Line Master 28)

Have each child select 2 objects for comparing length. Guide the children in placing their objects on the base line. Ask, **Which one is longer? Show me by placing your finger on the longer object. Which one is shorter? Put your finger on the shorter object.** Have the children remove the 2 objects from their sheet of paper, and guide them in passing one of their objects to their right. Repeat the procedure.

Measurement: Money

The following activities suggest some experiences to promote the identification of coins. Encourage the children to share personal experiences they have had with money so that the activities are given a context and a purpose.

Tell Me About It

- A collection of pennies, nickels, and dimes

Present a coin for the children to observe. Pass it around the circle and invite the children to tell something they observe about the coin. Assist the children when necessary by asking questions such as:

- **What shape is it?**
- **What color is it?**
- **What do you see on it?**
- **Would anything happen to the coin if you dropped it on a hard floor?**
- **Close your eyes and feel it. How does it feel?**

Repeat a similar procedure for the other coins on other occasions.

Surprise Packages

- Several surprise bags that contain an item priced at 1¢, 5¢, or 10¢
- 1 penny, nickel, and dime per child (Line Master 29)

Present the surprise packages, and provide each child with a penny, nickel, and dime. Ask a volunteer to select a surprise package, reveal the contents, and identify the cost, e.g., **It's an eraser. It costs 5¢.** In response, the children present the appropriate coin.

Pass the Coins

- 1 penny, nickel, or dime per child (Line Master 29)

Ask the children to lay the appropriate coins on the floor in response to your comment, **I wonder who has pennies.** After the children have presented the coins, you might like to ask, **How many pennies are there?** Once the children have retrieved their coins, have the nickels and dimes identified in the same manner. Show the children the procedures you want them to follow in passing their coins around the circle. On one cue, the children pass the coins; on your next cue, they stop and look at their coin. Repeat the procedure for identifying the coins. For example, **I wonder who has dimes.**

Coin Collections

- A container of pennies, nickels, and dimes or Line Master 29
- A 3-column graphing mat

Ask the children to select a coin from the container before they gather around a 3-column graphing mat.

Have the children present their coins and ask, **Do you think there are more pennies, more nickels, or more dimes?** Guide the children in placing the coins on the graphing mat in the appropriate section and column. Engage the children in a discussion related to the completed graph. Ask questions such as these:

- **What did we want to find out?**
- **What does the graph tell us? How do you know that?**

Coin Sort

- A collection of pennies, nickels, and dimes or Line Master 29
- 3 piggy banks (boxes with slot or paper mats)

Present a collection of coins, and have the children sort the coins into pennies, nickels, and dimes. Ask the children to label each group.

Stop at the Bank

- Envelopes
- A collection of pennies, nickels, and dimes or Line Master 29
- A bank (box or cut milk carton)

Prepare wallets (envelopes) from the collection of coins, and place them in a bank. Ask the children to pick a wallet and come to the circle. Have the children empty their wallets and sort their coins. Encourage the children to describe their collections by asking questions such as:

- **What types of coins were in your wallet?**
- **Do you have more pennies or more dimes?**
- **How many pennies do you have?**
- **Which would you rather have, 5 pennies or 5 dimes? Why?**

After the discussion, have the children return the coins to the wallets. As they leave the circle, ask them to return the wallets to the bank. This activity can be repeated many times using the same set of wallets.

Activity Centers

Activity centers form the core of any good early childhood program. In this unit, you will find many suggestions for implementing mathematical activities at those centers typically found in early childhood classrooms: Mathematics, Sand, Block, Art, Dramatic Play, Water, and Science. Included for each center is an introduction that describes:

- the mathematical potential of the center
- vocabulary to be modelled and encouraged
- materials suggested for use in the center
- practical suggestions for arranging and maintaining the center

The children should be given many opportunities to freely explore the materials at the centers. Through this self-initiated activity, they will quite naturally discover interesting mathematical relationships, pose new questions, and be motivated to initiate a new activity. When the children are exploring at the centers, the careful observer will undoubtedly see and hear mathematical activity and discussion. Examples of the types of activity that might occur spontaneously are photographed and described each time a new collection of materials is added to a center.

Often by asking a question or posing a problem, you can extend the mathematics inherent in the child's self-initiated activity. Suggestions are included for questions or nudges that might be used to extend an activity. You can select the one that is most appropriate to the child's interest, ability, and development. Examples of the different ways you might extend a child's activity are described after the first presentation of Free Exploration in each center. It is important to remember that at times the best response to a particular child's activity may be to silently observe rather than attempt to direct the child into an extension of the activity.

While the children are involved in Free Exploration at a center, you are free to engage small groups of children in an activity, observe and evaluate, or talk with individuals or small groups about their activity. These discussions provide an excellent opportunity to model the language necessary for the children to express the concept they are exploring. Only through hearing and using language in the context of real situations will the children develop the ability to express their new learning accurately.

After the children have explored and played with the materials extensively, you might present one of the many suggested activities for the children to pursue. The selection will depend on the activities that have been observed, the children's interest, and the mathematical concepts to be focussed on. Activities for the various mathematical strands are identified for each center. Certain activity centers are particularly conducive to the development of specific mathematical concepts. For example, children can discover a great deal about the concept of capacity at the Sand or Water Center, while patterning can be investigated more readily at the Math or Art Center.

Classroom space and materials should be considered before you decide which centers to operate and where and when to operate them. It is not necessary to have all the centers operating at the same time. Many teachers rotate the sand and water table. Some teachers close the Dramatic Play Center occasionally to accomodate a larger area for the Block Center. Often teachers place activities at the Math Center in containers, such as shoe boxes, so that they become portable; the child can then find the appropriate space to pursue the activity. Many suggestions for material storage, tracking of children's activities and evaluation are included on pages 20 to 28.

The Math Center

Mathematics at the Math Center

The Math Center provides an ideal setting for reinforcing many mathematical concepts. Some children will spontaneously transfer ideas and experiences from the Circle Activities to their play and exploration at this center. Other children will respond to the gentle nudge of a suggestive question or comment and pursue an investigation or extend an idea. The Math Center houses selected activities and materials designed to reinforce specific concepts and skills.

Three sets of activities are organized around materials: those that can be used with collected materials (Collection A), those that can be used with commercial materials (Collection B), and those that use prepared materials (Collection C). Many activities suggested for the collected materials can be used with some of the commercial materials and vice versa. You might have children explore freely some of the collected and commercial materials at the same time, allowing a combination of materials to be used in subsequent activities.

The activities you select or adapt will be a result of your observations and your curriculum objectives. The choice of materials will depend on what is available, as well as the versatility and potential of the materials to demonstrate and reinforce mathematical ideas. You may wish to refer to the following list to locate activities for specific objectives.

- Observation Skills, pages 92, 97
- Sorting, pages 84, 92, 97
- Patterning, pages 84, 92, 97
- Seriation, pages 85, 93, 98
- Number: Numeral Printing, page 98
- Number: More/Less/Same, pages 85-86, 93, 98
- Number: Sets to 10, pages 86-88, 93-95, 99
- Geometry: Geometric Solids, page 89
- Geometry: Geometric Figures, page 95
- Graphing, page 88
- Measurement: Linear, pages 89, 95
- Measurement: Mass, pages 89, 95
- Problem Solving, page 89

Instructions and procedures should be familiar to facilitate independence and to maximize the value of the experience. Therefore, it is recommended that these suggestions be considered before establishing an activity at the Math Center.

- Introduce ideas and procedures during the Circle Activities or introduce the activities and procedures to small groups of children.
- Ensure that the children have had enough prior experience with the skills and concepts through group activities to be successful in their independent activities.
- Plan activities which can be used over a long period of time or which can be repeated.
- Change the materials of a given activity to maintain interest and to present the same idea in a different context.
- Place favorite mathematical games, puzzles, and activities from home and school at the Math Center.
- Allow for free exploration of materials before presenting a specific task or activity.
- Provide a range of materials so that the children can find a comfortable level and work successfully at a given task. For example, providing both numeral and dot cards allows different levels of interpretation for labelling sets; or providing pattern cards with patterning materials allows children to work on any of these skills:
  - copying the pattern
  - extending the pattern
  - creating their own pattern

Vocabulary

- As many as, Equal, Less, Least, Match, More, Most
- Member, Set, Sort
- Pattern
- One, Two, Three, ... Ten
- Number
- Same, Different
- Longer, Longest; Shorter, Shortest; Taller, Tallest; Heavier, Heaviest; Lighter, Lightest; Loudest, Softest; Roughest, Smoothest; Lightest, Darkest

Suggested Materials

Collection A

- A variety of collected materials

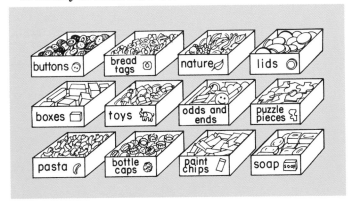

- A variety of sorting mats

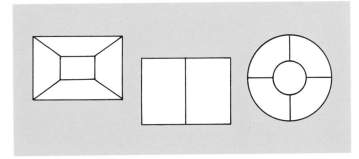

- A variety of pattern cards to accompany the collected materials

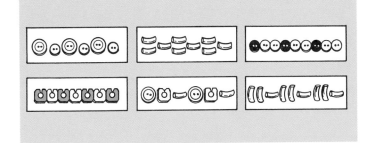

- Counting mats and boards (egg cartons, bedding plant holders, ice cube trays, etc.)
- Paper and paper plates divided in half
- Containers (boxes, fruit baskets, cut milk cartons, envelopes, etc.)
- Graphing mats
- Number cards (Line Masters 6 to 13)
- A 2 by 5 grid (Line Master 14)

Collection B

- A variety of commercial materials (counters, 2-sided counters, Attribute Blocks or Relationshapes, Pattern Blocks, interlocking cubes, geoboards, peg boards, balance scale, geometric models, beads, stamps and ink pads, etc.)
- Pattern Block puzzle cards

 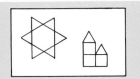

- Pattern cards to accompany materials

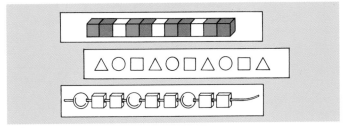

- Number strips

- Dot cards (Line Masters 8 to 10)
- Numeral cards (Line Masters 11 to 13)
- A 2 by 5 grid (Line Master 14)
- Interlocking cubes (Line Master 31)
- Story board characters (Line Masters 33 and 34)
- Story boards (any of Line Masters 15 to 20)

Collection C

- A variety of prepared materials for printing (sand tray, tracing paper, Plasticine, markers, small flashlight, finger paints, etc.)
- Large numerals painted on cardboard and covered with plastic
- Large numerals cut from textured paper or cloth and mounted on cardboard
- A collection of similar and different containers for sorting
- Velcro cardboard strips (prepared by gluing Velcro to strips of cardboard)

- Collections of small objects for use with the Velcro strips (prepared by securing small pieces of Velcro to small objects, e.g., pompoms, buttons, bottle caps, etc.)
- Theme-related cutout figures or pictures that reveal a graduated sequence
- A variety of different pattern strips

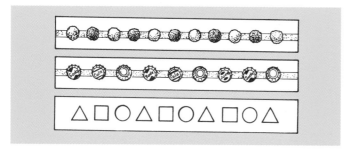

- Banks for coin collections (made from boxes or cups)
- Sets of ordering containers that reveal a graduated sequence of sound, mass, capacity, and color:
  - Sound containers are filled with different materials to reveal a graduated sequence of loudness when shaken.
  - Capacity containers are filled with rice, sand, or colored water to show a graduated sequence of fullness (1 to 2 cm difference).
  - Mass containers are filled with different amounts of a similar substance, such as rice or sand, or with objects that reveal obvious distinctions in mass.
  - Color containers are filled with water tinted with food coloring to reveal different shades of colors.
- Sets of sound, mass, capacity, and color containers prepared as follows:
  - a collection with 1 matching pair
  - a collection with all matching pairs
- Children's name cards
- Penny or counting boards

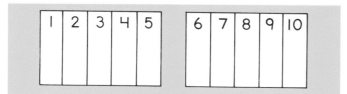

- A variety of game boards (see page 99)
- Sets of dot cards (Line Masters 8 to 10)
- Sets of numeral cards (Line Masters 11 to 13)
- Story boards (any of Line Masters 15 to 20)
- Story board characters (Line Masters 33 and 34)
- Coins (Line Master 29)

Setting up the Math Center

The Math Center can be a permanent or portable center depending on the space available and the desired organization. If you plan to establish a permanent Math Center, you will need a spacious area for children to work in and ample room to store and display materials. If a portable Math Center is desired, put those materials in current use in sturdy labelled containers or bins and place them on a shelf or tabletop or even under a table. The storage area should contain the same labels as the bins for easy clean-up. The children take a bin of materials to a general work area to complete their task.

If you are operating several different centers simultaneously, e.g., Dramatic Play, Art, and Blocks, you may wish to feature one type of activity at the Math Center, e.g., sorting. You could also have a mixture of activities from different strands that have been introduced in the circle, e.g., Sorting, Patterning, Number, Observation Skills, and Geometry. Select an appropriate number of materials for current use, and consider how many children will be visiting the center at one time. Allow for variety in materials.

It is recommended that you do not put all materials out at once. Materials that are not being used can be placed in labelled bags or boxes and stored in a cupboard, under the Math Center table, on a shelf, or in a school supply and storage room.

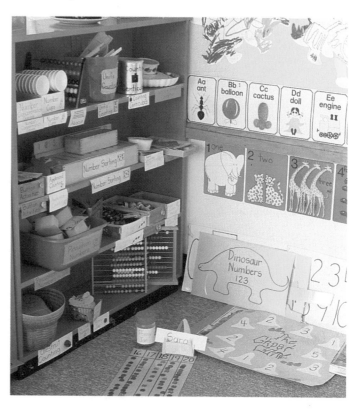

Recording at the Math Center

These photographs show some ways children can make a record of selected discoveries while working at the Math Center.

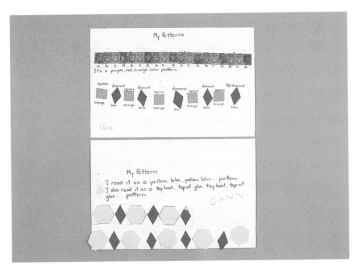

Children can record their work by:
- gluing the object to stiff paper
- tracing the objects to make mystery maps
- drawing the arrangements
- gluing paper cutouts or gummed shapes to represent the objects
- using templates to create the object
- using a line master of pattern cards to color in a pattern

Labels can be added to the child's record by gluing numeral sentence cards to the recording or by your printing on the words or numerals.

Entries in the child's math scrapbook provide a record for you as well as the child.

Children can create a display of their work to share with others. At times, this display could be used to initiate further activity.

Cooperative graphs, chart records, and lists can be made.

Free Exploration with Collection A

Children should have frequent and ongoing opportunities to freely explore the bins of collected materials placed at the Math Center. Provide time for uninterrupted play. You may wish to circulate among the children, silently observing their actions and listening to their comments. On the occasions when you would like to engage a child in discussion, consider the discussion related to Free Exploration, page 12.

Suggested Materials: Collection A

- Bins of collected materials (buttons, bread tags, nature items, lids, boxes, toys, odds and ends, puzzle pieces, jewellery, pasta, bottle caps, paint chips, soaps, etc.)

Observations

Stewart is building a train with the straws selected from the odds and ends bin. The straws have been linked together like a real train. Stewart has spontaneously isolated a set of straws from a collection.

Sanjay has made a design with the buttons from the button bin. When asked to tell about her design, Sanjay said she made a big circle with lots of little circles. She is making a recording of her work to take home.

Elton, Yvonne, and Lotus are playing with the cars from the toy bin. The children are using comparative language in their play: **faster, slower, too fast, too slow.** They are driving the cars to the city that they worked on cooperatively.

Melissa spontaneously sorted the bread tags by color. She has noticed that they have numbers on them and has enlisted her friend Kevin to share this discovery. They are now reading the numbers on the blue bread tags.

Asma has appeared to pick a random selection of paint chips. When her teacher asked her to tell about what she was doing, Asma responded that these were colors she liked. The teacher noted that Asma has been able to isolate a set from a collection and identify her sorting rule. Further discussion revealed that Asma is able to name all of the colors in her collection.

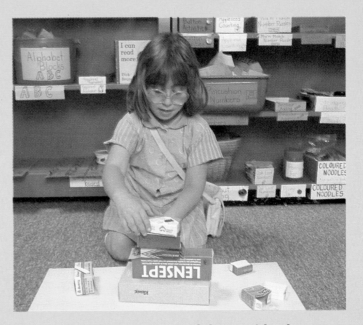

Shaindy is building a tower with boxes. After her tower fell over, she decided to change the position of the boxes so that the largest ones were on the bottom. All the boxes have now been placed on their largest face to provide greater stability. Shaindy is learning some important properties of 3-dimensional objects as she plays. She is very proud of her tower.

Extending Free Exploration

Free exploration is a time when children discover relationships, concepts, and properties. It is also a time you gather information about the children's interests, learning styles, knowledge, and attitudes. This profile of the child, in conjunction with program objectives, affects the planning of each learning experience. It is this knowledge of child and program that will allow you to observe and recognize an opportunity to use a child's natural play as a starting point to initiate a learning experience aimed at a specific program objective. The decision as to how and when to engage a child in discussion or further activity rests with you.

Stewart's train building could act as a starting point for developing several mathematical ideas. You might present one of the following activities to him during free exploration to see if he is interested in pursuing the investigation.

Number: More/Less/Same

- Stewart could pursue a counting or one-to-one correspondence activity if he wished to find out whether he used more (less) blue straws in his train than white straws.

- You might ask Stewart to estimate how many straws he thinks he has used in his train and then ask him to count and find out. You might also wish to ask, **How many more straws do you think you will need before you reach the table?**

Measurement: Linear

- Suggest making another straw train the same length (or longer or shorter). If Stewart is ready for a greater challenge, he could make another train the same length but use different materials, e.g., stir sticks, popsicle sticks. You might ask,

  - **What is the same about your 2 trains?**
  - **What is different?**
  - **Did it take more straws to build a train that length or did it take more stir sticks? How do you know that?**
  - **Can you find something in the room that is as long as your train?**

- Ask, **How many straws tall you are, Stewart? Would you like to find out? After you lie down, maybe Jules will count the straws for you.**

Sorting

Ask, **Are the straws you used different in any way?** If Stewart identifies a difference, e.g., some are blue and some are white, suggest that he sort the cars (straws) by color when he puts the train away.

Problem Solving

If you want Stewart to explore other possible ways to make a train, you might ask, **What other things could you use to make a train? What else?**

Activities with Collection A

Patterning

- Include different pattern cards with at least 3 repetitions in the bins of materials, or begin different patterns with the bin materials and display them at the Math Center.

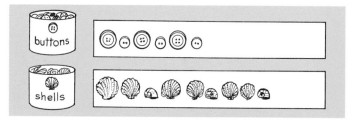

Children can select a card or display to copy. You might ask:

- **How could you read this pattern?**
- **What is another way to read the pattern? And another way?**
- **What would you put next in this pattern? And after that?**

After the children have had many opportunities to copy a variety of patterns, have them use the cards and display to extend the pattern. Say, **Show me more of this pattern.**

Some children will begin to make their own patterns which you may wish to investigate further. Some may be able to create their own patterns but become confused when asked to extend a given pattern. When recording your observations, you may wish to indicate the patterning skill (creating) and the pattern type (ab, ab, ab).

- Children can create their own patterns using the materials from the bins. Some children may wish to record their patterns by drawing, tracing, or gluing, and/or you could print the child's description. Some of these recordings could be placed with the materials for others to copy and/or extend. Continue to encourage the children to describe their patterns in many different ways.

*A child may place 3 or 4 materials in a line and ask you to look at the pattern and listen to the description: **Acorn, chestnut, chestnut, chestnut.** This child does not yet understand that a pattern is not just items laid out and labelled, but a repeated sequence. To guide children towards this understanding, recognize the work and then ask the child to make the pattern as long as the rug, table, or the child's arm. Return to observe how the child responded to your challenge and comment on how long the pattern became and how it repeats so nicely that you can guess what would come next.*

Sorting

Provide a variety of sorting mats so that the children can sort and re-sort the materials from the bins.

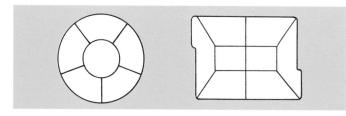

If you are observing certain children and wish to find out more about their thinking, you might ask any of these questions:

- **What is the same about the things in this set?**
- **How did you sort the buttons?**
- **What is the same about these buttons? And these?**
- **What could you name this set?**
- **In which set would you put this button?**
- **Why does (doesn't) it belong here?**
- **Are there any more buttons that could go in this set?**
- **What is another way to sort the buttons? Would you show me?**
- **Do you think you have more big buttons than small buttons? Will you count or match them to find out? Show me.**

Some children may include an item that does not appear to belong in the set they have created, e.g., a black button in a set of red buttons. If the child names the set as a set of red buttons and cannot identify which button does not belong, reduce the number of objects. That is, present 3 red buttons and 1 black button and then ask the child, **Which does not belong in a set of red buttons?**

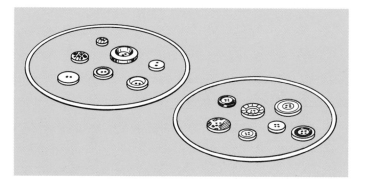

Seriation

- A variety of the collected materials can be used to show a graduated sequence of an attribute. Prepare and present collections of 3 or more objects that emphasize various attributes, and have the children order them. There are many different attributes that could be presented. For example:

  - texture: roughest–smoothest
  - size: smallest–largest
  - preference: best–worst
  - width: narrowest–widest
  - mass: heaviest–lightest
  - color: brightest–dullest or lightest–darkest
  - height: tallest–shortest
  - smell: strongest–faintest
  - number: least–most

  When appropriate, have the children describe the order of their arrangement, e.g., **Light, lighter, lightest** or **Dark, darker, darkest.**

  Many children will use their own language to label the order they created. You may wish to:

  - *accept this and continue to model and reinforce the correct language through circle activities*
  - *ask if they can describe it another way*
  - *model the correct language at that point*

- Children can select 3 or more items from the bins of materials and place them in an order. For example, a child may take 4 shells and order them from smallest to largest. You might wish to say, **Tell me about the materials you chose. How have you ordered them?** Children who cannot verbalize an order will benefit from hearing you model the appropriate language.

Number: More/Less/Same

- Place sets of picture cards, dot cards, and numeral cards (Line Masters 6 to 13) with the bins of materials. Have the children select cards and create a corresponding set with the materials. Repeat this activity at a later time, having the children create a set with more (less).

  By including a variety of different cards representing different numbers, you are opening up the activity so that children can find their own level and work successfully with the task.

- Place work mats divided into 2 sections at the Math Center. Have each child create a set on one side of the mat. The child then creates an equivalent set on the other side or presents the mat to a partner to complete. Repeat this activity at a later time and have the children create a set with less (more) on the other side.

  Some children use numbers to help them create the equivalent set while others will match using one-to-one correspondence. Note the child's approach; it offers some indication of the level of understanding. For children who have the idea of more, less, or the same established, begin to offer experiences that focus on identifying how many more or less one number is than another.

- Place sets of materials from the bins into cloth or paper bags and have the children select and feel the contents of a bag. Based on this observation, the child creates an equivalent set (or a greater or less set). The contents of the bag are then emptied and the sets compared. The original items are returned to the bag before a new bag is selected. Children will enjoy creating these set bags.

- In bins or bags, place sets of objects that go together, e.g., buttons and paint shirts, birthday candles and candle holders, straws and cups, plastic spoons and cups, small salt packages and small pepper packages, lids and jars, soda pop cans and straws, nuts and bolts, clothespins and cloth samples, or muffin tins and muffin papers. Have the children determine if there are the same number in each set. You may wish to provide labels with the sets of material.

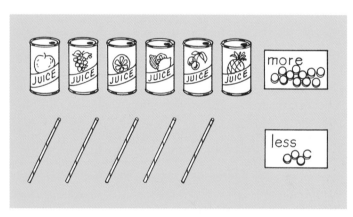

- Place 2 sets of materials in clear labelled containers and display them at the Math Center. Have the children identify which container they think has more (less). Then have them find out. You will notice that some children will count while others will match the objects.

Change the materials and number of items frequently to maintain interest and to challenge the children.

Number: Sets to 10

- Children can be assigned or may select a numeral or dot card (Line Masters 8 to 13) to identify which number they are working on, e.g., 3. The children count out 3 objects from the selected bin of materials and arrange them on a work mat or table. They continue to make as many different arrangements of 3 objects as they can. When appropriate, you might ask a child any of these questions to gain further insight into her or his thinking:

  - **What number are you working with?**
  - **How many are in this set? And this one?**
  - **Tell me about this arrangement of 3. And this one.**
  - **If I spread this arrangement out, how many are there now?**

- Place counting boards, e.g., egg cartons, 2 by 5 grids (Line Master 14), or bedding plant holders in selected bins of small collected materials. Give or have the children select a dot and/or numeral card (Line Masters 8 to 13) to identify which number they are working on, e.g., 7. Have them count out a set of 7 and arrange it on a counting board. They then continue to arrange 7 as many different ways as they can using a different counting board for each arrangement. Encourage the children to describe their arrangements. You might ask:

  - **Is there the same number in this egg carton as this one? How do you know that?**
  - Take an item from the child's arrangement, place it in a different position, and ask, **Are there still the same number? Why do you think that?**

Children who are not conserving number may think that the arrangement of the objects affects the quantity. These children should then spend more time creating sets in a variety of arrangements. Do not rush these children or try to teach conservation of number. They will reach that level of development with further experiences and time.

- Prepare the Math Center for making and recording a variety of sets. Place glue, tongue depressors, lids, and cardboard with selected bins of consumable collected materials.

  Give or have the children select a number card (Line Masters 6 to 13) or sample set to identify which number they should be creating, e.g., 4. The children count out 4 objects and arrange and glue them on a recording surface. Another layer of glue should then be placed over the objects.

  Some children may have had enough experiences connecting symbols to quantity and possess the physical dexterity to be able to print their own numerals for the sets they create. You may wish to suggest this to these children.

  Keep some of these set cards and sticks for use in future activities. By maintaining a set making center, children are reinforcing number concepts as well as generating classroom materials.

- Place number cards (Line Masters 6 to 13) and sets made by the children in a container of collected materials. Give or have the children select a card to identify the number they are to work on, e.g., 5. Have them sort and create sets that mean 5. Encourage the children to describe the sets they select and create.
- Place the set cards and sticks made by the children in a container with a variety of collected materials and number cards (Line Masters 6 to 13). Place a large strip of paper, e.g., mural paper, wallpaper, or waxed paper, sectioned and labelled with numerals or configurations for 0 to 5 or 6 to 10 in the container as well. Have the children select and arrange the materials onto the appropriate section of the paper strip.

- Place work mats divided into 2 sections , e.g., paper or plates with a line drawn down the middle, at the Math Center. Children are given or select a number card (Line Masters 6 to 13) that identifies which number they are working on, e.g., 4. The children count out 4 items from the bin and place them on their work mat. They continue to make arrangements of 4. You might ask:

  - **How many things are on each of your plates?**
  - **On this plate of 4, how many things are on this side? (1)**
  - **How many are on this side? (3)**
  - **How many things are on your plate? (4)**
  - **Do you have another plate of 4 where you put 1 on one side and 3 on another?**
  - **If I move this one to the other side, how many things are on your plate?**

  Children will respond to the last question differently. Some children may count the objects because they do not realize the quantity has remained constant. Other children will know the quantity has remained the same and will respond without hesitating.

- Place containers (boxes, fruit baskets, cut milk cartons, envelopes, etc.) labelled with dots, numerals, and/or a combination of both at the Math Center. Children can use the materials in the bins to fill the containers with the appropriate number of objects.

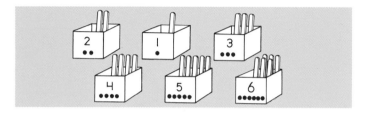

You are asking children to associate a numeral with a quantity by having them create appropriate sets for each numeral presented. Children must have had many prior experiences in which symbols were used to label what they created. Since this is an independent activity, it is important that children are able to work successfully with the numerals that are presented. Therefore, provide many containers that represent different ranges of numbers, e.g., 1 to 3, 1 to 5, 1 to 8, 1 to 10, 5 to 10. In this way, many children can work side by side at their own level of understanding.

- Have the children create story boards or use the story boards provided (Line Masters 15 to 20) with selected bins of materials.

Give or have children select a number card (Line Masters 6 to 13) to identify which number they are to work on. A child takes several, e.g., 5 to 8, story boards and creates the appropriate set on each one.

This activity allows children to use their imaginations and develop their language skills while reinforcing number concepts. Encourage the children to describe to you the scenes they create on their story boards.

- Place collections of materials with numerals printed on them, e.g., packages, birthday cards, wrappers, bottle caps, or playing cards, in a container. Provide small objects for counting. Have the children select a numbered item, e.g., a V8 can, and create a set of 8 to correspond with the numeral.

Graphing

The children receive or select a dot or numeral card (Line Masters 8 to 13), e.g., 8. They place 8 bottle caps or bread tags in a cup and empty it onto a work area. The objects are sorted and arranged on a graphing mat to show if they landed print side up or down. You might ask any of these questions as you guide the children in interpreting the graph:

- **How many did you place in the cup?**
- **Which bottle caps did you place in this column? And this one?**
- **Which column has more? Less?**
- **Are there the same number in each column?**
- **If you did this again, do you think there would be more print side up or print side down? Why?**

Geometry: Geometric Solids

Make mystery maps to accompany the odds and ends, nature, jewellery, puzzle piece, box, or toy bins. Place different items on a large sheet of stiff paper and trace them to make a map of the object. The children match the object to the outline. Some children will enjoy making mystery maps to add to the Math Center.

Measurement: Linear

- The children select a piece of string and a set of objects from a bin of materials. Have the children identify which items are longer than their piece of string. You might ask:

  - **Which things did you discover that were longer than the string?**
  - **How did you make sure the pencil was longer?**
  - **Do you see anything else in this collection that might be longer?**

Repeat this activity many times:

- using different reference lengths
- having children identify items that are shorter than the string
- having children identify items that are the same length as the string

It is recommended that this activity be introduced after children have had many group experiences comparing length.

- Children who are ready for a challenge can select a piece of string and compare its length to a set of objects. Discoveries can be displayed by placing the objects into groups: longer, shorter, or the same length as the string.

  - **Which things are longer than the string? Shorter? The same length?**
  - **Can you find something else in the bins that you think might be longer than (shorter than or the same length as) the string?**
  - **Did you pick out more (less) things that were longer or more (less) things that were shorter? How could you make sure that there are more (less) here than here?**

Repeat many times using different reference lengths.

Measurement: Mass

The same procedure described in Measurement: Linear can be used to sort objects by mass. Place a reference object at the Math Center, e.g., a block. Children compare the mass of various objects from the bin with the reference object and sort them accordingly: heavier than the block, lighter than the block, or about the same mass as the block.

Problem Solving

You might present this measurement challenge for some children to investigate. Place an object at the Math Center, e.g., a shoe, glove, or mallet. Display sets of standard length objects, e.g., bottle caps, paper clips, or bread tags. One of the sets equals the length of the displayed object. Have the children predict which set of materials, when laid end to end, will match the length of the object. Then have them find out.

Free Exploration with Collection B

Children will need frequent opportunities to explore these materials; each one has unique attributes and features. Provide the children with opportunities to talk about what they can do with the different materials. This is valuable time for incidental learning and fun. Watch for opportunities to extend the children's activity during free exploration.

Suggested Materials: Collection B

- Bins of commercial materials (counters, 2-sided counters, Attribute Blocks, Pattern Blocks, geoboards, peg boards, interlocking cubes, geometric models, beads, stamps and ink pads, balance scale, etc.).

Observations

Salma is playing with the geoboard. She has followed the safety routines for carrying and handling geoboards very carefully. Salma is investigating properties of shapes as she moves the elastic bands about to make a design.

Toli and Karim have combined the geometric solids with blocks from the Block Center. They are selecting all the solids that stack to build their structures.

Allison is making a design with the Pattern Blocks. When asked to tell about her design, Allison said she had made a yellow and green flower. As she works with the blocks, she is discovering relationships among them.

Charlene and Harpreet have piled up the interlocking cubes to load onto the vehicles headed for their construction site. They have discussed which vehicle holds more cubes.

Stephen placed several interlocking cubes on one side of the balance scale and then watched the balance pan tilt down. As he places some on the other side, he comments, **Look how this side has gone down.** Stephen is exploring mass and the workings of a balance scale as he plays with the materials.

Joey is making pictures with the counters. When asked by his teacher, he could identify that he has used more blue counters than any other color. She confirmed his response by counting.

Activities with Collection B

Observation Skills

Use interlocking cubes, peg boards, color cubes, or Pattern Blocks to make designs and simple patterns. Display these models at the Math Center, and have the children reproduce the same design. Later make design cards on stiff paper by gluing down paper cutouts (Line Masters 21 to 26) or gummed figures of the Pattern Blocks or interlocking cubes. Place these design cards with the appropriate bin of materials, and have the children reproduce the design. Design cards can also be made on dot paper (Line Master 32) and placed with the geoboards.

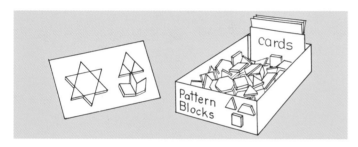

Sorting

- Children can sort the Attribute Blocks in many different ways, e.g., by color, shape, size, or thickness.
- Have the children sort a set of beads and make a necklace. Encourage them to describe their sorting rule, e.g., **I made a necklace with red beads.**
- Collections of coins can be sorted in different ways, e.g., by color, value, type, pictures, dates, or size.
- Children can use a peg board as a sorting mat for sorting pegs by color.

Patterning

- Pattern cards can be cut from Line Master 30 or made from Line Master 31. These cards, or others you prepare, can be placed with appropriate materials.

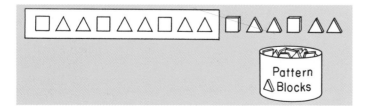

Have the children copy and/or extend the pattern represented. They will enjoy creating their own patterns as well. If some children make a record of their pattern, they might like to add it to the collection of pattern cards.

Encourage children to describe their pattern in many different ways. A child may focus on color and describe a pattern as: **Black, white, white; black, white, white; black, white, white,** etc. Another child may focus on shape and describe the same pattern as **Big, smaller, smaller; big, smaller, smaller; big, smaller, smaller,** etc.

- Children can create their own pattern using many of the different collections of materials, e.g., interlocking cubes, stamps and ink pads, Pattern Blocks, peg boards, geoboards, or counters. Continue to encourage the children to describe their patterns in a variety of ways.

You may wish to place some of the patterns created by the children with the collections of corresponding materials. These patterns can be copied or extended by others.

Many children, in the initial stages of creating their own patterns, will form ab patterns with the different materials. To help children broaden their experiences, continue to expose them to more complex patterns in the Circle Activities. When children are working independently, you could suggest that a child make a pattern using 3 colors of the cubes or with 2 orange blocks touching.

Seriation

Randomly place a series of interlocking cube towers of varying heights at the Math Center. Children reproduce these towers and order them by height. Encourage the children to describe their order, i.e., tallest to shortest or shortest to tallest.

Number: More/Less/Same

- Place sets of interlocking cubes cut from Line Master 31 with collections of loose cubes. Have the children snap cubes together to make sets equivalent to the pictured trains.

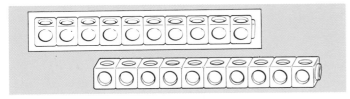

This same procedure can be repeated having the children create sets with more than the pictured set as well as less than the pictured set.

Many children will have greater difficulty with the concept of less than they do with the concept of more. This is understandable when we think that we are asking children to recognize what is not present in the set rather than what is there. Ensure that children have many group experiences as well as independent activities that address the concept of less.

- Place stamps, stickers, pictures cut from Line Masters 33 and 34, crayons, and scissors in a bin with pieces of stiff paper. Have the children cut a piece of paper to form 2 pieces of a puzzle. Over time, the children can use the materials to create a variety of puzzles depending on the focus you provide, e.g., more, less, matching equivalent sets, matching sets to numerals.

    Other children can also use these puzzles at the Math Center to reinforce different concepts.

Number: Sets to 10

- Children may receive or select a dot or numeral card (Line Masters 8 to 13) to identify which number they are investigating, e.g., 4. The children can use a variety of commercial materials to show the number arranged in different ways. Encourage each child to describe her or his arrangements.

Children will use their own language to describe their set of cubes. This description may not include number. You may wish to model the description using the number, accept the child's response, or ask how many cubes he or she used.

- Provide hole-punched numeral cards (Line Master 35), string, and beads in a bin. Give or have the child select cards to identify the sets of beads that he or she will string.

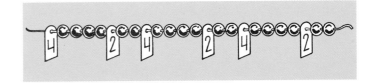

- Sort the interlocking cubes, counters, pegs, and Pattern Blocks by color, and store each type of item separately by color. Children may receive or select independently a numeral and/or dot card (Line Masters 8 to 13), e.g., 3, to identify which number they will work on. The child takes 2 colors of one item and makes combinations of 3. You might ask a child working with interlocking cubes:

    - **How many cars are in each of your trains?**
    - **How many yellow cars are in this 3-train?**
    - **How many green cars are in your trains? How many cars are in your train?**
    - **Do you have another train that has 2 and 1?**

- Place numeral cards (Line Masters 11 to 13) with the geoboards. Have the children select a card (4) and arrange the geoboard bands so that they touch 4 pegs.

    On another occasion, the same materials can be used with a different number.

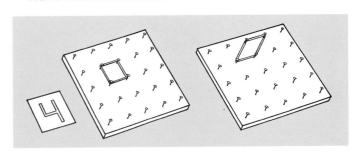

- Place several small, clear containers and numeral cards (Line Masters 11 to 13) with the collection of cubes. The children select a container and estimate how many cubes they think will fit in it. The container is filled, the cubes counted, and a numeral card selected to label the number of cubes in the container.

- Prepare Line Master 24 as shown. Place copies of the line master with a bin of cubes or counters.

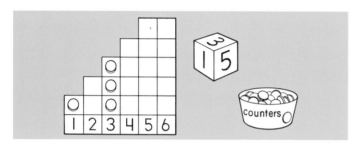

The children roll a number cube and create an appropriate set on the mat. The activity continues until each set has been made.

- Print the numerals 1 to 6 on strips of paper or adding machine tape. Place these strips with collections of counters or cubes and a cube numbered 1 to 6. Have the children roll the number cube and create a corresponding set in the appropriate section of the number strip. The activity continues until each section has a set.

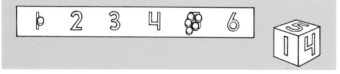

- Place a collection of dot cards or numeral cards (Line Masters 8 to 10 or 11 to 13) with a collection of counters and a number cube. Two or more children select 5 numeral cards and place the cards in front of them. In turn, each child rolls the number cube. If the child has the corresponding card, he or she places the appropriate number of counters on the card. The activity continues until each child's cards have been covered.

- Place number cubes or numeral cards (Line Masters 11 to 13) and a variety of colored and textured paper, to act as story boards, with the bins of counters and cubes. The children imagine the paper to be a particular setting, e.g., black – night or space; green – meadow or playground; blue – water or sky; sandpaper – beach or sandbox. The objects are then identified as creatures or characters that would be found in that setting.

  The children roll the number cube or select a numeral card and create a story board scene with the appropriate set. For each number, a new story is created. Encourage the children to describe the scenes they create.

- Place number cubes and 2 by 5 grids (Line Master 14) with the interlocking cubes. Have the children roll a number cube, snap together an equivalent set of interlocking cubes, and place the set in a section of the grid. The activity continues until a set has been placed in each section of the grid.

  You might ask any of these questions to gain further insight into a child's thinking:

  - **How many are in this set? In this one?**
  - **Is there a set that has the same number as this one? Why do you think that?**
  - **Which sets have more (less) than this one?**

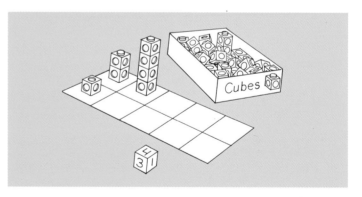

- Children are given or select a dot and/or numeral card (Line Masters 8 to 13) to identify how many objects they are working with, e.g., 4. The children can use 2-sided counters, cubes, or counters of 2 colors. Sets containing the designated number of counters are displayed. Encourage the children to describe the sets. You might ask any of these questions to gain further insight into a child's thinking:

  - **How many counters do you have in this set? In this set?**
  - **In this set of 4, how many are yellow? How many are red?**
  - **Are there the same number in the 2 sets? How do you know?**

- To challenge some children, give or have them select a dot and/or numeral card (Line Masters 8 to 13) to identify how many 2-sided counters to select, e.g., 5. The children place the 5 counters in a cup and spill them onto the table or work area. Using a red and yellow crayon, a record can be made on strips of dot paper (Line Master 32) to show how the 5 counters landed. Encourage the children to describe the arrangements. For example, **My 5 counters showed 3 red and 2 yellow.** You might ask any of these questions to gain further insight into a child's thinking:

  - **Do you have another arrangement of 5 that shows 3 red and 2 yellow?**
  - **How often did 3 red and 2 yellow show up?**
  - **Could you have 5 red and 0 yellow?**

Geometry: Geometric Figures

- Make Pattern Block puzzle cards by tracing some of the blocks, gluing figures cut from Line Masters 21 to 26, or securing Pattern Block stickers onto a piece of stiff paper. Place these puzzle cards with the Pattern Blocks, and have the children cover the puzzle with the block pieces.

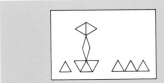

When some children complete 2 puzzle cards, you may want to have them compare which card required more (less, the same number of) blocks to complete.

Some children might enjoy making Pattern Block puzzle cards to add to the collection.

- Children can make designs with the Attribute Blocks. Ask them to identify the figures that they used.

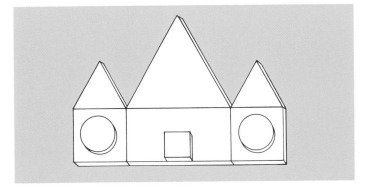

- Place sorting mats with the Attribute Blocks. Have the children sort the blocks by shape.

Measurement: Linear

Display a model, e.g., a robot, built from interlocking cubes at the Math Center. Over time, children could use this model to complete different tasks. For example, the children could:

- build a robot that is the same height
- build a taller or shorter robot
- build 2 robots, one shorter and one taller than the model
- build 2 robots so that the model is the shortest (or tallest)
- build a model of their own using the same number of cubes (or 1 more [less] cube)

This activity can also be completed with Pattern Blocks. Display a design and have the children use it as a model to complete any of these tasks:

- Make it bigger.
- Make 2 more designs so that the model is the smallest.
- Use the same blocks and make a new design.
- Copy the design and add to it.

Measurement: Mass

Place an object, e.g., a shoe, block, or toy, in one pan of a balance scale. Display several other objects, one of which has the same mass as the object in the balance pan. Have the children identify which item they think will balance the shoe. A record of their discovery can be made by drawing or tracing.

Change the items and repeat the procedure. Later a collection of about 4 to 6 items can be displayed on the table beside the balance. The children find the 2 objects of equal mass.

Free Exploration with Collection C

Children should have many opportunities to play with these materials in their own way before the materials are used in a specific learning task.

Suggested Materials: Collection C

- Bins of prepared materials (story boards and characters; sound, mass, capacity, and color containers; materials for printing; Velcro strips and collections of small items with a piece of Velcro attached; game boards; theme-related figures or pictures; banks; coins; etc.)

Observations

John is working with the story boards, acting out a story of his own. He is so intent on what he is doing that he is unaware that he now has an audience.

Jamie has decided to explore the sound containers today. He has taken them over to the rhythm band area where he and Steven are making up their own music. He offered the following directions: **You make yours go louder and I'll make mine go softer.**

Brita is exploring the containers of colored water. She appeared to have placed the water jars randomly. However, Brita's teacher overheard her telling Kathy that the 4 containers she put together all had some glue on them from the labels and that they were still a bit sticky if Kathy would like to feel.

Activities with Collection C

Observation Skills

- Present a set of sound, mass, color, or capacity containers. Prepare 2 identical containers, and have the children compare all the containers to identify the 2 that are the same.
- Present a collection of sound, mass, color, or capacity containers in which all the containers have a twin. Have the children compare and match the similar containers.
- Present sets of pictures or characters cut from Line Masters 33 and 34. Have the children locate and match pairs of pictures that are the same.

Sorting

- Present a collection of small objects, and have the children sort and secure them to the Velcro cardboard strips. Encourage the children to describe how they sorted the objects.

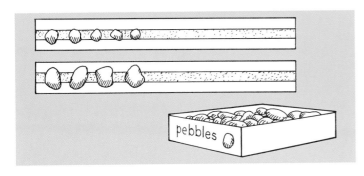

- Present collections of story characters cut from Line Masters 33 or 34 in 3 or more colors. Have the children sort the pictures according to a given or a selected criterion. Encourage them to identify their rule for sorting.

If you find that some children are not ready to sort independently, you might suggest a criterion for the child to work with. For example, **Please make a set of blue pictures.** *Make it part of your agenda to return to this child and talk about the results of the activity.*

- Present collections of sound, color, mass, or capacity containers which present different attributes for sorting, e.g., loud and soft; heavy and light; full and not full. Have the children compare and sort a collection. Encourage them to identify their sorting rule.

Patterning

- Use a variety of materials to prepare and display patterns of at least 3 repetitions. Place the patterns with collections of similar materials, and have the children either copy or extend these given patterns. Encourage the children to describe the patterns that they create.

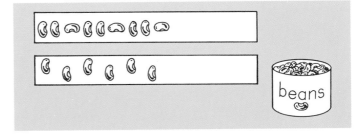

Often, when children read their patterns aloud, they are able to identify inconsistencies in them. This rhythmic, auditory input is a helpful tool, whether children are just learning to recognize patterns or are interpreting and analysing patterns.

- Create a pattern on a Velcro strip, and have the children copy or extend it. Later the children can use the Velcro strip and materials to create their own patterns.
- Present sets of character pictures cut from Line Masters 33 and 34 or theme-related figures or pictures. Children can use the pictures to:
  - copy given patterns that accompany the picture collection
  - extend given patterns
  - create their own pattern

Seriation

- Present sets of ordering containers that reveal a graduated sequence of sound, mass, capacity, or color. Have the children select a set of containers and place them in order. When appropriate, encourage the children to describe the order.
- Present sets of small objects that reveal a graduated sequence, e.g., size, color, or length, and a strip of Velcro. Have the children order the objects on the Velcro strip and describe the order.
- Theme-related figures or pictures can be cut out and prepared to represent a graduated sequence. Present sets of figures for the children to order. Encourage them to describe the order that they create.

Number: Numeral Printing

- Children may practice printing numerals by using a water soluble marker to trace over large plastic-covered numeral cards.
- Children may form numerals out of Plasticine, string, wool, or ribbon and arrange them on large plastic-covered numeral cards.
- A small flashlight can be used to trace the lines of the numerals printed on large cards.
- Provide models of the numerals, and have children form them with a variety of different materials. For example:

  - a wet paint brush on a chalk board
  - chalk on a chalk board
  - magic markers on large sheets of paper
  - finger printing in trays of sand or salt
  - paint or crayons on large sheets of paper
  - finger painting on large sheets of paper

- You may wish to have children gain further practice in writing numerals by having them make oatmeal, sawdust, salt, or sand numeral cards. Have them place glue on the mat first and sprinkle the substance over the glued areas. You may wish to provide printed models for some children to trace and cover over with the chosen material.

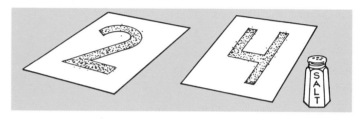

- Textured numerals can be cut from sandpaper, corrugated cardboard, or cloth and glued to a card. Have the children trace these numerals with their fingers.

Numeral printing is a printing exercise rather than a mathematical skill. It is important to recognize that some children may be able to recognize numerals and associate these symbols with a quantity but do not possess the physical dexterity to form the numerals themselves. These activities offer printing practice only. It is strongly recommended that as children gain skill in printing, they be encouraged to print their own numerals as a record for sets they create.

Number: More/Less/Same

Prepare a set of banks and place them with a collection of coins. Have the children place the same number of each coin in each bank.

You might ask:

- **What type of coins did you put in each bank?**
- **How did you make sure that you put the same number of pennies and dimes in each bank?**
- **Let's match the coins from these 2 banks and make sure.**

Number: Sets to 10

- Prepare sets of 5 or 6 story boards (Line Masters 15 to 20) and story characters (Line Masters 33 and 34), and place them in envelopes or file folders. Give or have the children select a numeral card to identify which number they will be creating, e.g., 6. The children lay out the set of story boards in a large work space. Encourage them to make up a story for each board by placing 6 characters on each one.

- Children can select several (5 to 8) dot and/or numeral cards (Line Masters 8 to 13) and Velcro strips. They secure sets of small objects to the strips to represent each numeral card selected.

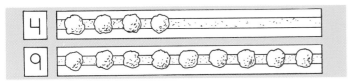

- Provide a counting board with a collection of pennies. Have the children create sets of pennies to correspond with the numerals at the top of the board.

- Banks can be prepared, labelled, and placed with collections of pennies. The children fill the banks with the appropriate number of pennies.

- A store display can be prepared with priced objects or pictures. Provide labelled wallets or envelopes of pennies. The children match the collection of pennies in the wallets to the prices of the store items.

- Game boards can be prepared and used to reinforce number to 10 in a variety of ways.

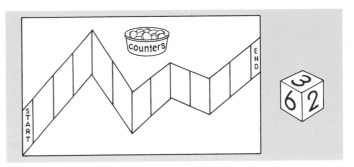

Numerals are placed in each section. When a child's marker lands in a square, a set is created to correspond to the printed numeral.

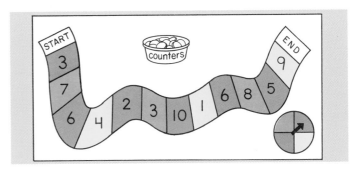

A number cube can be rolled to identify how many spaces to move. Before the move is made, a corresponding set is made.

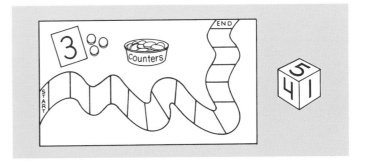

A number cube is rolled to identify the number of spaces to move. Before the marker is moved ahead, a numeral card is turned over and the corresponding set is made.

The Sand Center

Mathematics at the Sand Center

The Sand Center provides many informal opportunities for children to explore a variety of mathematical concepts. Through their play, children will have an opportunity to explore the texture and characteristics of sand, as well as to manipulate and experiment with a variety of different containers and tools. Comparisons of size, shape, capacity, and mass will naturally evolve if you provide appropriate materials and encourage experimentation. Take advantage of the children's natural interest in working at the Sand Center to reinforce counting and number skills by asking them to use number to describe and compare estimates, actions, and products.

The very nature of sand and the materials at this center creates a focus on estimation and measurement. Since the Circle Activities do not address capacity, much of the teaching, discussion, and investigation pertaining to capacity will take place at the Sand and Water Centers.

Some activities can be initiated by the gentle nudge of a suggestive question or comment. The purpose and complexity of other activities may require more explanation and direction. You may wish to consider these management suggestions:

- Gather the children around the sand table when you wish to present instructions or discuss estimations, predictions, observations, or strategies for a large group activity.
- For some activities, you will wish to present the instructions or problem to a small group. Plan a follow-up with these children after their investigation.
- Present a task to one child to pursue. Plan a follow-up with the individual as part of your agenda.

Be selective when using the suggested questions which accompany many of the Sand Center Activities. They are intended to serve as a resource and demonstrate the potential of the activity or material, as well as assist you in observing the children. Too much questioning can interrupt a child's thinking and observations and therefore distract from the learning that is taking place.

On the other hand, careful questioning may unlock a child's thinking and provide you with greater insight about her or his level of development.

Many of the activities described in this section should be repeated several times throughout the year with containers of different sizes and shapes. They can also be repeated using other types of sand and related materials such as rice, gravel, corn, or puffed rice to promote further comparison, estimation, and discussion.

Many of the same experiences and ideas can be tested at the Water Center as well. It is through this repeated exploration and observation that children will discover many mathematical concepts and skills.

More activities are presented than you will be able to use, and they represent only a sampling of the many possibilities at this center. The activities you select or adapt will be a result of your observations, your curriculum objectives, the materials available to you, and the children themselves. The decision to remove, add, or change the materials should be made with an eye to maintaining a high level of interest and learning. You can use the following list to find activities for specific strands.

Vocabulary

- Fast, Faster; Slow, Slower; Wide, Wider; Narrow, Narrower
- Shape, Round, Curved, Straight, Mold
- Around, Between, In, On top, Out, Through, Under
- Big, Bigger, Biggest; Small, Smaller, Smallest; Tall, Taller, Tallest; Highest; Lowest
- Full, Empty; More than, Less than; Most, Least

Suggested Materials

Collection A

- Dry sand and variety of containers of different shapes and sizes (pails, bowls, plastic food tubs, cleaned milk and cream cartons, boxes, plastic bottles, plastic cups, jugs, measuring cups, yogurt cups, etc.)

Collection B

- Wet sand and variety of containers, as suggested in Collection A, and a variety of molds of different sizes (plastic beach molds, jelly or cake molds, cookie cutters, muffin tins, various containers, lids, etc.)

Collection C

- A variety of sifting items (funnels, salt and pepper shakers, watering cans, strainers, colanders, screens, containers with holes punctured in sides and/or bottom, etc.)

Collection D

- A variety of containers, as suggested in Collection A, and a variety of digging tools of different shapes and sizes (shovels, spoons, ladles, spades, scoops, etc.)
- A variety of small toys (cars, trucks, planes, animals, trees, mirrors, people, buildings, etc.)
- Dot cards and numeral cards (Line Masters 8 to 13)

Setting up the Sand Center

A spacious area should be set aside for the Sand Center so that the children can move about freely. If a commercial sand table is not available, a small wading pool, wash tub, plastic dish bin, baby's bathtub, or other durable container can be used instead. Place a sheet of plastic under the tub or table and secure it with carpet or masking tape.

If possible, place the Sand Center near the Water Center because water will often be added to the sand. As well, many similar experiences and materials are shared by these centers. You may wish to close the Sand Center from time to time. A lid can cover the table and transform it into a display area or a new center. You may wish to establish one area for a Sand and Water Center and alternate the operation of the centers. If you store all the Sand Center materials in this area, identify and label which materials the children are to select at a given time. You may wish to use a green "go" sticker to highlight the current container of materials or to make traced maps of the current materials on a storage shelf. Materials should be brushed off and sorted into their appropriate containers or matched to their map outline.

You may wish to establish a rule that no water can be added to the sand. Post a sign to remind the children when this rule is in effect. You may consider some of these additional suggestions when establishing a sand center:

- Spray the sand with a mist of water to keep the dust down.
- Place a bucket of water by the sand table to rinse materials and hands.
- Place a broom and dust pan at the center for daily clean-up.
- Place a garbage pail by the Sand Center for disposing of spilled sand.
- Limit the number of children working at the Sand Center at any one time.

Free Exploration with Collection A

Children should have an opportunity to engage in uninterrupted play at the Sand Center. Add small toys and models to the collection of containers from time to time to offer a new dimension to the children's play. Allow the children sufficient time to explore the containers and the properties and texture of both wet and dry sand before engaging them in a specific activity.

Much of the time spent at the Sand Center will be for free exploration. You can, however, facilitate learning and the development of concepts by:

- establishing and reinforcing consistent routines
- providing specific materials and periodically changing them
- encouraging and supporting the child in her or his pursuits
- observing and selecting appropriate opportunities for interaction and/or extension of activity

While the children are engaged in free exploration, you may wish to observe them silently.

Suggested Materials: Collection A

- Dry sand and a variety of containers of different shapes and sizes (pails, bowls, plastic food tubs, cleaned milk and cream cartons, jugs, boxes, plastic bottles, plastic cups, measuring cups, yogurt cups, etc.)

Observations

Shaindy has repeatedly been scooping up the sand and letting it sift through her hands. She is reporting to Jaime that her hill is getting bigger each time she adds sand.

Ron is piling up the sand and patting it to make rounded sand mounds. He is telling James that he is going to try to make them bigger. The 2 boys are working beside each other in the same type of activity, but each is pursuing it independently. Each boy has his own goals and a task in mind but is willing to discuss his activity and direction.

Tori and Reena have been digging holes while playing in the sand. They have selected several different containers for scooping and digging. Tori has used her hands to pat the sides of the holes and to carve some small tunnels. She has shown persistence and patience despite caving walls.

Michael is pouring the contents of one container into another. His teacher overheard him comment that the container was just about full and that he only needed to scoop up a bit more sand and pour it into the container. Michael is discovering the relationship between these 2 containers.

While playing in the dry sand, Nancy filled some of the containers with sand. She levelled some of the tops with her hand and added a bit more sand to others to make certain they were full. Nancy is showing an awareness of full, an important concept to foster and clarify before comparisons of capacity can be made.

Extending Free Exploration

Free exploration is both a time for the children to discover relationships and a time for you to reinforce routines and gather information about the children's interests, learning styles, knowledge, and attitudes. This information about the child, in conjunction with program objectives, affects the planning of each learning experience. It is this knowledge of child and program that will allow you to observe and recognize an opportunity to use a child's natural play as a starting point to initiate a learning experience aimed at a specific objective. The decision as to how and when to engage a child in discussion or further activity rests with you.

Ron's rounded mounds of sand could act as a starting point for developing several mathematical ideas. You might present one of the following activities to him during free exploration to see if he is interested in pursuing the investigation.

Observation Skills

- If you wish to engage Ron in a discussion about what he observed, you might ask any of these questions:

  - **What does the sand feel like?**
  - **How did you make your hills?**
  - **What did you notice about the sand when you were making your hills?**
  - **How did you make this hill so rounded on the top?**
  - **I wonder how you could make it pointed on the top.**

- You could also ask, **What changes do you think you would see in the morning if you left your hills out overnight? Would you like to leave them out and see what happens?**

Measurement: Linear

- You might use Ron's comment to James as a starting point by asking, **How high do you think you can make your hill? Would you like to mark that on this straw and see if you can build your hill that high?**
- You might show a toy car and say, **Suppose this car had to drive over your hills. Which hill would take it the longest to go up and over? Why do you think that? If this car had to drive all the way around each hill, which one would take the shortest time? Why?**
- You might ask Ron to consider the size and shape of one of his hills in relation to other objects. If so, ask, **I wonder what special thing might be the right size to bury in this hill. What do you see in the classroom that would be about the same height as your hill?**
- You might have Ron build 2 more hills and ask, **Which hill is the shortest? Which hill is the tallest?**

Problem Solving

- Ron could identify possible ways of making a hill. Ask, **What other ways could you make a hill? Would you show me?**
- Use information the child gives you about the hills and small objects to create and act out situations. For example, if Ron has described the sand mounds as the hills he toboggans down in winter, you could use popsicle sticks and say, **There were 2 children at the top of this hill waiting for their turn. Each child had a toboggan. How many toboggans do you think there were? Why? Show me with these materials. Or, There were 3 children at the top of the hill ready to toboggan down. There were more than 3 children at the bottom. Show me with these popsicle sticks how many children might be at the bottom of the hill.**

Number: Estimating

You might ask, **How many of these popsicle sticks do you think it would take to build a fence around your hill? Would you like to build a fence and find out? Or, How many of these pebbles do you think it would take to build a path around your hill? Let's count and find out.**

Activities with Collection A

Measurement: Capacity

- In a circle, you might identify 1 container, e.g., a blue tub, as the standard. Ask, **Which of these containers do you think holds more sand than the blue tub?** You might have a volunteer go to the Sand Center and test a prediction while you continue the discussion. When the volunteer reports back, you might ask, **How can you tell that the orange cup holds more than the blue tub?** Inform the children that when they visit the Sand Center, you would like them to sort the containers they think might hold the same amount as the blue tub. Then have them check their predictions. You might ask any of these questions:

  - **Which containers held the same amount of sand as the blue tub?**
  - **Which containers did not hold the same amount as the blue tub?**

  You may wish to direct the children towards organizing their discoveries in either of these ways:

  - by sorting the containers as they complete the task
  - by placing the containers on a graph labelled with pictures

- Display a mystery mound (a pile of sand on a display board placed across the sand table or in a plastic tray or dish) formed by 1 of 2 (or more) labelled containers. Invite the children to the display and ask, **Which container do you think I used to make this pile of sand?**

  Predictions can be recorded in several ways. For example, a graph could be made by having the children place their name cards in columns labelled with the containers, or the children could place their name cards in the actual container.

You might ask a volunteer to test the predictions. Any of these questions could be asked to initiate discussion:

  - **How can we find out which one made this pile?**
  - **Which container did not make this pile of sand? Why do you think that?**
  - **Do you think the other container holds more or less sand? How can we find out?**

Some children will enjoy creating mystery mounds for their classmates to investigate. Change the containers and present the same task again. Later you may wish to include another container.

- Present 3 containers: 1 large container and 2 smaller ones that are equal in capacity. Have the children investigate this situation: **Pour a pretend snack into containers for you and a friend. Make sure you have the same amount.**

  You may wish to ask any of these questions to encourage discussion:

  - **What kind of snack are you serving?**
  - **Who are you sharing it with?**
  - **How did you make sure that you both have the same amount?**
  - **Could you pour the 2 containers of (cereal) into this bowl? Why do you think that?**
  - **Does the larger bowl hold as much as the 2 other containers?**

- Have the children select 2 containers. Whenever possible, ask them to predict which one holds more (or less). Then have them test their prediction.

  If you want to find out more about a child's thinking as he or she approaches this task, you can ask any of these questions:

  - **Which container did you think would hold more?**
  - **Which container did hold more? Less? How did you find out?**
  - **If you pour the sand back, will it fit?**

- **What is the same about these containers? What is different?**
- **I wonder if there is another way that you could show that this holds more.**

Change the containers and present the same task again many times. You could also invite the children to bring in containers from home that they would like to add to the Sand Center.

The children will approach this task in different ways. It is important to recognize that a child's approach to a problem provides further information about her or his level of thinking. Talk about the child's strategy if you wish, but do not attempt to teach a better or more efficient way of completing the activity.

- Present a small collection of different-shaped containers that each holds the same amount, as well as 1 container that holds more (less) than the others.

  Have the children identify which container holds more (or less) than the others. You may wish to silently observe some children as they pursue this task, or you may wish to find out more about some children's thinking by asking any of these questions:

  - **Which container held more? Why?**
  - **What did you find out?**
  - **How did you find out?**
  - **Did you try others first? Which ones? Why did you think that one might hold more?**

Repeat this activity several times. Increasing the size of the collection will make the task more challenging. Alternatively, you could present containers of different capacity and include a pair of equal capacity. Children identify which containers hold the same amount.

- Present a container, e.g., a shampoo bottle, to act as a standard. Have the children select a few containers and identify whether they think each one will hold more than, less than, or the same amount as the shampoo bottle. Ask the children to test their predictions.

You might ask any of these questions:

- **What is the same (different) about the containers?**
- **How many containers do you have that hold less than this bottle? Can you find another one?**
- **Which containers hold more than (less than, the same amount as) this shampoo bottle? How do you know?**
- **Does the milkshake cup hold more than the bottle? Does the bottle hold less than the milkshake cup? What could you do to make sure?**
- **Would you want a bottle or milkshake cup filled with your favorite drink? Why?**
- **What do you notice about all the containers that hold less than the bottle? Is there anything the same about them? Anything different?**

Repeat this activity many times throughout the year, occasionally changing the standard container as well as the selection of containers.

Children need many experiences comparing the capacity of containers of different sizes and shapes. Many young children are influenced by the height and think that a tall, thin container holds more than a wide, shallow one. Through many experiences comparing capacity, children begin to develop conservation of capacity.

Measurement: Mass

- Provide a balance scale at the Sand Center along with the containers, and have the children fill a pair of containers with sand. Ask, **Which one feels heavier? Lighter? Are they the same?** Have them empty the contents into the pans of the scale to find out.

  You may wish to look on supportively as the children pursue the task, or find out more about the thinking behind their actions by asking any of these questions:

  - **Which one did you think was heavier? Lighter? Did you think they were the same?**
  - **What did you find out?**
  - **How did you go about discovering that?**
  - **What happened to the pans when you put the sand on them?**
  - **Can you make the scale balance? How?**

- Have the children identify which container they think is heavier, a tubful of dry sand or a tubful of wet sand. Then have them test their predictions.

  Repeat the activity comparing different materials such as rice, cereal, sawdust, or gravel to either wet or dry sand. You may wish to model some statements for the children to help them develop an understanding of how the balance scale works. For example, **I see that the tubful of wet sand made this end of the balance scale go down. It must be heavier than the dry sand.** You might also wish to ask questions to initiate discussion.

  - **What is happening to the balance scale?**
  - **Which is heavier? Lighter? How do you know?**
  - **Can you make the 2 tubs balance the scales? How?**

When the children repeat the same experiences many times, they will make certain generalizations based on the repeated outcome of their actions. Keeping a record of their discoveries and discussing them help the children to form these generalizations.

Measurement: Linear

- The same containers can be used for other investigations. For example, you might ask some children to pour out dry sand to make a curvy road and a straight road or a wide road and a narrow road. Some children may be interested in measuring the length of the roads with string to determine which is shorter (longer) or wider (narrower). You might also ask, **Can you use the same container of sand to make a longer road? A shorter road? A wider road? A narrow path? Would you like to show me?**

- Have the children make 3 hills and ask, **Which of your hills do you think is the highest? How could you check?**

Free Exploration with Collection B

Allow the children time to explore and use the materials in different ways. Encourage them to talk freely amongst or to themselves. This time provides a secure and accepting setting for children to pursue their own goals as they investigate and experiment with materials, ideas, techniques, and strategies. Continue to watch for opportunities to extend the children's activity and learning.

Suggested Materials: Collection B

- Wet sand and variety of containers, as suggested in Collection A, and a variety of molds of different sizes (plastic beach molds, jelly or cake molds, cookie cutters, muffin tins, various containers, lids, etc.)

Observations

Daniel has levelled the sand and is drawing various roadways with his hands rather than using any of the materials. Melody offers her toy cars and trucks so that they can play at the scene that Daniel has created. They create an elaborate story of a fire at the milk plant. The trucks have to travel to the next town to get enough milk to deliver to the people and stores while the plant is being rebuilt. The children are combining their imaginations and knowledge of a recent community event in this drama.

Jaime has made 3 mounds of sand by filling the lid, the tub, and the cup with wet sand and unmolding them onto a levelled area of the sand table. He is pretending the mounds are pies that he will serve to his toy friends which he brought to school today. He plans to serve the biggest mound to the biggest toy.

Dwayne has selected 3 containers of varying size, ordered them from largest to smallest, and built a tower. Details are being added around the tower which he pretends is a castle.

Activities with Collection B

Sorting

Children can create sets of sand pies that are similar in some way, e.g., shape: round, square, rectangular; size: large, small; or features: designs or no designs.

Patterning

- Begin a pattern at the sand table using molds, imprints, or figures drawn in very wet sand. Have the children copy and/or extend the pattern. Some children will enjoy making their own sand patterns. Encourage them to describe the pattern in different ways.

- Place sets of pattern cards at the Sand Center, and have the children copy a pattern from a card. Ask them to extend the pattern if they like.

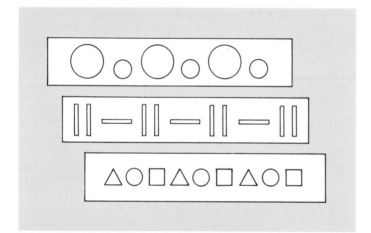

If you would like to engage a child in discussion, you might ask any of these questions:

- **What did you use to make the pattern?**
- **Read me the pattern. Can you describe it another way?**
- **What would come next? Next?**

To provide a further challenge, other materials, such as toys, figures, or blocks, can be placed at the Sand Center to facilitate a variety of different patterns.

The Sand Center offers an ideal setting to address many skills and concepts primarily using a kinesthetic approach. If you have children who work best at the sand table, take advantage of this interest to suggest and present mathematical tasks.

Measurement: Capacity

Invite the children to group around the sand table, and present 3 different sized characters, puppets, or dolls. Have the children discuss and select 3 containers that they think would make a pie which would be the right size for each character.

When the children go to the Sand Center, have them select 3 containers and create a large, a medium, and a small pie for the 3 characters. It is important to plan a follow-up time with these children. You may wish to supportively observe their procedures or end product, or you may want to initiate a discussion. If you want to initiate discussion with some children, you could ask any of these questions:

- **Why did you give this pie to Papa Bear? Mama Bear? Baby Bear?**
- **Which pie do you think needed the most sand? The least? Why?**
- **How many animals are there? Are there enough pies so that each animal can have one? How do you know?**

You may want to separate the containers and say, **I wonder which container you used to make this size pie. Would you show me?**

- Over time, you might have the children select containers to create pies for the following:

  - a pie that will fill the paper plate
  - the smallest possible pie
  - the thickest pie
  - the thinnest pie
  - the pie that would feed the most people
  - round pies (square pies, rectangular pies)

- Invite a small group of children to stand around the sand table, and present a collection of small objects, e.g., yogurt cups. Have the children discuss and identify how many different pies they think they can make that could be stored under an identified container, e.g., cake holder.

  When you follow up on this investigation, you might ask, **How many pies did you make that fit under the cake holder?**

  Change the container and repeat the task.

Measurement: Linear

You might have the children unmold a container of wet sand and ask them to build a tower that is higher (and/or lower) than the molded sand. Encourage the children to describe what they did and how they went about it.

You may wish to challenge some children to find out the height of each of their towers. Ask them to measure the towers using string, straw, or other non-standard measures, e.g., linking cubes or paper clips.

Geometry: Geometric Solids

- Set up a display at the sand table, and ask the children to match the molds that were used to make the various mounded shapes or imprints. Children may enjoy making the mystery shapes in the sand for others to investigate. If you would like to engage a child in discussion you might ask:

  - **Which mold did you think fit? Did it?**
  - **How many other molds did you try first?**

- To create a display at the sand table, you might use a child's model or construct a model made from several containers. Suggest to the children that they sort which containers were used to create the display.

Free Exploration with Collection C

Children should have an opportunity to explore these materials using dry and wet sand as well as other materials, e.g., rice, oatmeal, salt, or flour, to observe the physical properties of the various substances.

By working with a wide selection of materials, the children will naturally engage in many experiences that will allow them to observe and compare occurrences and relationships. They will be able to use this knowledge to make future inferences and predictions.

Observe silently and interact selectively. Watch for opportunities to extend a child's activity during free exploration.

Suggested Materials: Collection C

- A variety of sifting items (funnels, salt and pepper shakers, watering cans, strainers, colanders, screens, containers with holes punctured in sides and/or bottom, etc.)

Observations

Alyse has been filling the various funnels and emptying them into the clear containers. When asked to tell about what she is doing, she is able to describe her purpose and the sequence of her activity.

After filling their funnels with sand, Sarah and Michael watched and felt it as it flowed through the holes. They filled the funnels again and controlled the flow of sand by covering the holes.

Roni and Brandon are working together to watch the effects of the sand sifting through the different containers. Both children are excited about their discoveries. They are verbalizing their observations and predictions.

Activities with Collection C

Number: Sets to 10

You might wish to set up the sand table for a treasure hunt by burying different sets of materials in the sand. The materials could be enclosed in small boxes or bags. Post a numeral card(s) to describe the number of treasures that the children should be searching for, e.g., 4. If a treasure is found that has more or less than 4, it is buried again and the search continues.

Some children will enjoy creating and burying the treasures for the treasure hunt.

Measurement: Time

- Present identical containers that have a different number of holes punctured in their sides and/or bottom. Have the children select 2 (or more) containers. Ask them to tell which one(s) they think will empty faster (and/or slower) than an egg timer or sand clock.

  If you wish, a record of the children's predictions can be made in several different ways. For example, a label card can be placed by each container or a graph can be used to record the children's predictions.

Then have the children determine which container empties faster. You may wish to ask some children questions to pursue their thinking further. For example:

- **Which container did you think would empty faster? Slower?**

- **Which container did empty faster? Slower? Why do you think that happened?**
- **How did you find out?**
- **Were there any containers that emptied at the same time as the egg timer? Which ones?**
- **What do you notice is the same about the way the sand has piled up in the timer and on the sand table?**

- Funnels or containers with holes placed in clear containers can be used to create sand clocks. Some children may enjoy exploring duration of time by emptying a standard measure of sand, e.g., a cupful of sand, into the funnel while another child performs a task, e.g., filling as many Dixie cups of sand as possible or building the highest hill. Encourage the children to repeat the task at least twice for comparison before switching roles.

Measurement: Capacity

Present a collection of funnels, and have the children tell which funnel they think holds the most (least). You might want to have some children plan their own investigation, or you might suggest that they fill each funnel by holding a finger over the hole before emptying the contents into identical clear plastic glasses or containers to test their prediction.

Free Exploration with Collection D

Children should be given uninterrupted time to play with the toys in the wet and dry sand. This time will give them a chance to utilize their models and drawings made at other centers in dramatic and social play.

Suggested Materials: Collection D

- A variety of small toys (cars, trucks, planes, animals, trees, mirrors, people, buildings, etc.), a variety of digging tools of different shapes and sizes (shovels, spoons, ladles, spades, scoops, etc.), and a variety of containers as suggested in Collection A

Observations

The children have been talking about dinosaurs this week. Steven, Jason, Alex, and Craig have created a setting for the different dinosaur models. As they play with the models, they are representing the knowledge that they have been acquiring during the dinosaur unit of study.

Soula is filling 1 of the containers using shovelfuls of sand. She was not keeping track of how many shovelfuls she had used. Her teacher had commented in passing, **How many shovelfuls do you suppose it takes to fill that pail?** Soula did not respond then but came up to her teacher later in the day to tell her how many were needed.

Anna has selected to play with the cars. She is telling her teacher a story about her own family.

Activities with Collection D

Seriation

Have the children create a parade of animals, vehicles, or toys. Ask them to select members or present 3 (or more) objects that can be ordered, e.g., tallest to shortest, least wheels to most wheels, or lightest color to darkest color.

Number: Sets to 10

- Post a dot card or numeral card (Line Masters 8 to 13), e.g., 5, at the Sand Center along with the collection of toys and figures. Suggest that the children create a number land for the numeral presented by arranging everything in sets of 5.

- Place a collection of dot cards and numeral cards (Line Masters 8 to 13) at the Sand Center along with a collection of toys and figures. Suggest that the children are to create Numberville by arranging the toys in sets and using the cards as signs to label them.

- You may wish to post a task card at the Sand Center, inviting the children to create a scene that includes specific features. For example:

> Sand Center
> Use
> 1 car
> 3 trees
> 5 people

- You could use scenes that the children create to assess their concept of number. For example, **Line up the 5 people.** Ask, **How many people are there?** Change the arrangement of the people. Ask, **How many people are there?** Repeat. **Are there more people or cars in your scene? How do you know?**

  The children will respond differently to these questions. Some will count each time the set is rearranged, an indication that the child is not conserving number. Conservation of number is a product of development and experience. Provide this child with more opportunities to arrange and describe number.

- You may wish to use the scenes the children create and the descriptions they present to develop story problems. For example, if the children had created a driveway for the toy cars, you might ask, **If there is 1 car in the driveway and 2 more cars arrive, how many cars are there altogether? Show me.**

Measurement: Capacity

- Invite the children to identify how many spoonfuls they think it will take to fill the blue pail. Have them find out.

  They can repeat the activity using cupfuls or ladlefuls. Later you might change the container to be filled. Some children might enjoy keeping a record of their discoveries. You can assist them in their record keeping. You might like to challenge some children by asking:

  - **I wonder if it would take more shovelfuls to fill this other container?**
  - **Do you think it would take more ladlefuls than cupfuls to fill the container? Why?**

- Present 2 different containers and small cups. Have the children tell which container they think holds more cups of sand. Encourage the children to find out.

  To help a child keep track, a new cup can be used each time a cup of sand is added to the container. Each cup should be placed aside after it is used. You may wish to discuss the results of the activity with some children. For example:

  - **Which container held more cups of sand? How do you know that?**
  - **Do you know how many cups it took to fill this container? And this one?**

  Present the same task using other containers.

- Present 3 containers with different volumes and shapes, e.g., bowls, glasses, and spoons, along with 3 teddy bears of different sizes. Have the children pretend that the sand is cereal, and have them match the containers to the bears. **Papa likes the most. Baby likes the least.**

  If you would like to find out more about a child's thinking, you could initiate discussion with questions such as:

  - **Tell me about the size of each bear.**
  - **Tell me about the size of each bowl. Glass. Spoon.**
  - **Why did you match this bowl to this bear?**

The Block Center

Mathematics at the Block Center

Both the Large Block Center and the Small Block Center are natural settings for exploring 3-dimensional geometry. As the children handle and arrange the various blocks, they become aware of similarities and differences in their shape, size, and physical properties. This manipulation also assists in the development of spatial representations and relationships. Children should be given time to explore the properties of the blocks, in conjunction with real-world solids and structures, in order to have the opportunity to see the relevance of the geometric nature of the blocks and their relationship to the world around them.

Handling, building, arranging, and playing with blocks provide experiences that foster discussion, comparative language, and creative role playing. You can act as a resource for children by responding to their questions, modelling appropriate language, and commenting on specific mathematical features of their work.

As the children approach their work at the Block Center, problem-solving strategies will be in effect as they plan, execute, and assess the results of the structure they visualized or intended.

Children should have many opportunities to engage in free exploration at the Block Center. When you decide to pose a challenge or question for children to investigate at the Block Center, you can use this list to identify activities for specific strands.

- Observation Skills, page 122
- Sorting, page 122
- Patterning, page 122
- Seriation, page 122
- Number: More/Less/Same, page 123
- Number: Sets to 10, page 123
- Geometry: Geometric Solids, page 124
- Measurement: Linear, pages 124-125
- Measurement: Area, page 125
- Problem Solving, page 125

Vocabulary

- In, Out, On, Off, Over, Under, Through
- Roll, Slide, Stack
- Top, Middle, Bottom, Left, Right
- Build, Model, Pile
- High, Low, Higher, Lower
- Ramp
- Tall, Taller, Tallest; Short, Shorter, Shortest; Long, Longer, Longest
- Add to, Take away
- Same, Different
- Large, Larger, Largest; Small, Smaller, Smallest

Suggested Materials

Collection A

- Large blocks of various sizes and shapes (There are many different blocks available commercially.)
- Small blocks and construction toys (There are many commercial sets from which to select.)
- Support materials for building and dramatic play (small toys and props, old machines or parts, signs and labels, cushions and blankets, etc.)
- Real-world solids (large and small boxes, balls, cone hats, plastic and cardboard cylinders, etc.)

Setting up the Block Center

You might consider establishing 2 Block Center areas in your classroom: one for the small blocks and one for the large blocks. Alternatively, you may wish to have an area that combines both large and small blocks. The small block or construction center can be portable if the materials are stored in labelled baskets or bins. The large block center, by its very nature, is a permanent center.

A large area, away from quieter classroom activities, should be considered for the large block center and storage area. You might like to keep in mind these points when planning its location.

- Carpet helps to reduce noise level.
- A corner or space under shelves helps to provide a safe and compact area for storing blocks.
- Locating the Large Block Center adjacent to the Dramatic Play Center and Small Block Center provides for a greater range of materials and for role playing.
- Defining the children's building space with a taped or chalked boundary will provide an element of safety for children not involved at the Block Center.

When selecting materials, ensure that there are enough blocks to facilitate cooperation and to create structures large enough to be satisfying to the individuals involved. Different support materials, toys, and props should be made available from time to time to expand interests and dramatic play.

The storage of materials can provide a learning experience if blocks are organized by size and shape. This will offer further opportunity for sorting, ordering, and matching and guide the cleanup and storage of materials. Some ways of achieving this are:

- posting pictorial representations of the blocks to indicate where they are to be stored
- presenting maps of the blocks to indicate their placement
- giving oral instructions from time to time to indicate a method of ordering or sorting the blocks. For example, **Place all the large blocks under the shelf.**

Clear, consistent routines are essential for the success, safety, and enjoyment at this center. Consider:

- an acceptable noise level for sharing, talking, and role playing
- safety factors in respect to climbing or how high a structure may be
- how many children may work with the blocks at one time. You might make a set number of clothespins available and have the children pin a clothespin to themselves when they are at the center.

You might consider developing a photo album or a photo display of the children as they perform different tasks and actions or represent different situations at the Block Center. You might decide to print a description of the child's activity and language to accompany each photograph. Displaying these photos in the classroom gives the children a sense of pride and communicates to visitors some of the activity, learning, and thinking that is taking place.

Occasionally you might like to incorporate the Block Center into a current theme by transforming it into a specific setting, such as a castle, a farm, or a space station.

Free Exploration with Collection A

Allow the children time to engage in spontaneous self-initiated activity in both the large and small block areas. Interchange between these 2 areas should be encouraged. Children will develop an awareness of the properties of the blocks and their relationships as they build in many different areas and directions. This time also allows children to represent their knowledge and exhibit their vocabulary and creative thinking through representational and dramatic play. Ensure that the children have access to support materials and the Dramatic Play Center.

Suggested Materials: Collection A

- Large blocks, small blocks, support materials (small toys, cardboard boxes, cushions, blankets, dress-up clothes, road signs, etc.), and real-world solids (boxes, balls, cone hats, plastic and cardboard cylinders, etc.)

Observations

Michael and Joey have worked cooperatively to create a bridge and road with the large blocks. Michael showed leadership and direction in the planning and organization of their structure. Joey was attentive and very involved in the process.

Matthew built a truck and Misha built a person with the small building blocks. They have brought them over to the large block area to build a home and a garage. A great deal of experimenting has occurred to build structures that are appropriate sizes.

Angel and Shaura are creating a symmetrical structure by adding blocks to each side of their structure. The girls are using numbers to guide them in their search for what they need. They are also using positional vocabulary such as "on", "over", "under", "on top of", etc. as they discuss the placement of the blocks.

Zachary constructed a store using the large blocks. He added signs and made coupons and sales tickets. His classmates have kept him busy filling their orders. It is interesting to watch which shape of block Zachary selects to fill the orders.

Renee and Lauren are executing their plans for a parking lot. Renee has made signs at the writing center and is adding them to the construction she made with Lauren. While Renee was on her own, she described their structure to her teacher using a wide range of positional terms and comparative language.

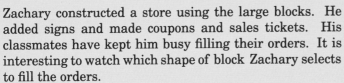

Steven, Adam, and Kathy each have a plan and are working with the blocks independent of one another. Steven stood several blocks on edge and has been running his cars through the spaces. He is now moving the blocks closer together so that he can lay the long blocks on top to create an arch. Adam has been building and rebuilding his tower. Kathy has been rolling balls and cars down the ramp she made adjacent to the stacked blocks.

Extending Free Exploration

Free exploration is not only a time for children to discover relationships, but it is also a time for you to gather information about the children's interests, learning styles, knowledge, and attitudes. This information of the child, in conjunction with program objectives, affects the planning of each learning experience. It is this knowledge of child and program that will allow you to observe and recognize an opportunity to use a child's natural play as a starting point to initiate a learning experience aimed at a specific objective. The decision as to how and when to engage a child in discussion or further activity rests with you.

Michael and Joey's building of the bridge and road could act as a starting point for developing several mathematical ideas. You might present one of the following activities to these boys during free exploration to see if they were interested in pursuing the investigation.

Geometry

- You could use this situation to foster the children's awareness of positional relationships. Provide them with a small object and direct its placement as follows:

  - **Place the car under (on) your bridge.**
  - **Have the car pass under (over) the bridge.**
  - **Tell me a route to the house so that I can drive the car in the proper direction.**

- To have the boys identify similarity in shape or size of the blocks, hold up a block and ask, **Did you use any blocks that are the same shape as this? Which ones?**

Number: Estimating

You might engage the boys in a discussion about their structure and include any of these questions:

- **How many blocks do you think you used for the road? For the bridge?**
- **Do you think you used more blocks for the bridge or more blocks for the road? How could you find out? Show me.**

Measurement

To promote comparative language, you might ask, **How high is your bridge? What else is about the same height as your bridge? What would be longer than (shorter than or the same length as) your bridge?**

Sorting

You might suggest to the boys that they sort the blocks into groups before they put them away.

Activities with Collection A

Observation Skills

- To challenge some children, you may wish to ask them to create a structure or model that is the same as another child's or one that has been placed on display.
- While children are working, you may wish to have them compare existing structures or reflect on a structure they built yesterday. You might like to use any of these questions as a guide when engaging a child in discussion:
  - **Do you put the blocks together the same way when you build a tower and a house?**
  - **How are these built the same? Differently?**
- A simple structure made by a child or a group of children can be used for an extended observation activity. For example, the morning class could leave a structure for the afternoon class to admire and discuss. These children change the structure in 1 way and leave it for the morning class. The morning class admires the structure, identifies the change, and then changes the structure in 1 way for the afternoon class to examine. This process continues as long as the children are interested.
- Some children will want to share their large and small structures and models with their classmates. From time to time, the children can gather at the Block Center to observe and discuss the displayed structures or models. You may wish to ask the child to describe her or his work, or you may wish to have the other children describe their observations.

Sorting

- You may encounter opportunities to ask the children to isolate a set of blocks that are similar (in size, type, shape, color, or feature) and build a structure, design, or model using that one set of blocks.
- If you would like some children to investigate specific properties of the different blocks, you might have them test a selection of blocks as to whether they roll or don't roll. The blocks can be sorted to display the results of the investigation. Children can also investigate and sort blocks by whether they stack, slide, or both stack and slide.
- By having the children tidy up the blocks and sort them into designated areas or storage bins, you are reinforcing sorting skills and demonstrating the usefulness of sorting to organize and maintain their environment.

Patterning

Some children might enjoy using the blocks to create a variety of patterns. You could suggest that they build a patterned wall, a patterned roadway, or a patterned floor. Encourage them to describe their pattern in different ways.

Seriation

- You might suggest to some children that they create a structure that shows a graduated sequence. For example:
  - **Would you like to build some stairs up to the top of your building so that they go from low to high?**
  - **Can you build a building that orders the blocks from largest to smallest (smallest to largest or longest to shortest)?**
- You might suggest that the children select 3 or more blocks or construct 3 simple structures that show a graduated sequence, e.g., tallest to shortest or widest to narrowest. Encourage children to describe their sequence.

Number: More/Less/Same

- After the children have made many structures, you may wish to watch for opportunities to pose challenges for some children to pursue. For example:

  - **Make something using more (less) big blocks than small blocks.**
  - **Make something using the same number of blue blocks as red blocks.**

- When appropriate, encourage the children to describe structures they make. You might ask any of these questions:

  - **Did you need more (less) big blocks than small blocks to make your castle? Why?**
  - **How many wooden blocks did you use?**
  - **If you were to build another layer on your wall, how many blocks do you think you would need?**

- You might consider displaying a child's model for posing certain challenges. Make sure that there is a reasonable number of blocks in the structure.

  - **Would you please build something with the same number of blocks as this model.**

  - **What kind of model could you build with less (more) blocks?**
  - **Build something with 1 less (more) block than the model.**

You may wish to display several models and challenge a few children further by asking any of these questions:

- **Which model has more (less) blocks?**
- **How many more (less) did you need?**
- **What is different (the same) about your model?**

Number: Sets to 10

You may wish to present some children with a challenge by asking them to work with a specific number of blocks. For example, **What can you build using just 8 blocks?**

If a child has responded enthusiastically, you may wish to extend the activity by suggesting that he or she either make something else with 8 blocks or build as many different things as possible using 8 blocks for each structure.

Geometry: Geometric Solids

- You may wish to present a challenge that asks some children to address and describe positional relationships. You might suggest an idea based on a child's play or current interest. For example:

  - **Build something that the boats can pass under but the cars must travel over.**
  - **Build something that 5 of us could fit inside.**
  - **Build something outside (inside) of this wall.**
  - **Build something you can crawl through (over, under).**
  - **Make a building that is higher (lower) than this table.**
  - **Build something so that these blocks are in front of (behind, on top of, or under) the table.**
  - **Make a building beside the bridge.**

- Display a block or blocks. Ask the children to select blocks with a similar shape and then use them to build a structure.

- You could present a real-life solid(s), e.g., a box, a ball, or a party hat, to correspond with a shape(s) in the block collection. Invite the children to select only the blocks that have the same shape as the real-life models to use when building a structure.

- Set up a ramp at the Block Center using a collection of blocks. Some children will enjoy investigating which blocks roll down the ramp and which will not.

Measurement: Linear

- From time to time, you could present a challenge for some children to investigate. The suggestions represent an unlimited number of possibilities:

  - **Build something that is taller (shorter) than you are.**
  - **Build something that is wider (narrower) than your arms can stretch.**
  - **Build something that is longer than (shorter than, as long as) this piece of string.**

- Encourage the children to compare the structures they make. Then have them identify which structure or model is the longest, the shortest, the highest, the lowest, the widest, or the narrowest.

- Some children might like to measure the height (width, length) of their structure with string. You may wish to use the string to show the order of several structures from tallest to shortest or shortest to tallest.

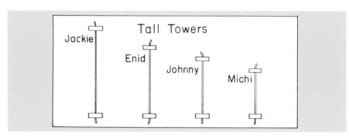

- Some children will enjoy rolling 2 (or more) solids or toys down a ramp and comparing the distance travelled by each one. You may wish to have some children measure this distance with string.

- Some children may be ready to use non-standard units such as cubes, popsicle sticks, or toothpicks to determine the length, width, or height of a structure.

Measurement: Area

- You may wish to define an area by chalking or taping the floor or by using a mat or paper. Ask the children to build a structure with a floor or bottom that covers the defined space.

- Some children might enjoy creating a floor for their structure. Suggest that they use the small blocks and make sure that none of the classroom floor shows.

- You may have the opportunity to present some children with a challenge that requires them to cover an area with blocks. For example, while children are working with the big blocks, they might enjoy following either of these suggestions:

  - Create a raft or boat with the blocks placed tightly together so that no water leaks in.
  - Cover the bottom of a box with blocks for shipping.

Problem Solving

- From time to time, you might like to present a challenge for some children to pursue. Any of these suggestions could act as a catalyst for an activity:

  - **Use only these blocks to build a castle (bridge, spaceship).**
  - **I wonder if you could build something that moves.**
  - **Build something around the dragon so that it can't get out (in).**
  - **Construct a building, a vehicle, or an animal.**
  - **Build something so that this ball can balance on top.**
  - **Build a structure using all of these things** (a set of blocks, a rope, a board, and a hoop).
  - **Show the story we just read, or create a story using the blocks.**
  - **Make the tallest tower you can with the largest (smallest) block on the top (bottom, in the middle).**
  - **Make the tallest (shortest) tower you can using these 6 blocks.**
  - **Make a building that has room for this box to fit into.**
  - **Without using any round blocks, make something that moves.**

- Invite the children to sit around a structure. Ask the children to generate ideas as to what it could be.

- For children who are at a stage where they can work cooperatively to plan and follow through on a group task, consider presenting an open-ended challenge. You might consider suggesting one of these possibilities:

  - **Build something that you would find at a construction site.**
  - **Build a place where people would buy things.**
  - **Build a building where something is made.**
  - **Build something that would help someone move from one place to another.**
  - **Build a building where you would find people and/or animals living.**

The Art Center

Mathematics at the Art Center

The Art Center provides an important focal point for your classroom. It should be a large area that houses a variety of art materials, art work, and interesting objects and pictures. Using these art materials, the children can make a record of mathematical experiences and ideas. The children's spontaneous creations can also be used as a basis for discussion of a variety of mathematical concepts, such as larger and smaller, positional relationships, number, etc. Drawing, painting, and construction materials should be easily accessible so that the children can use them to record activities or experiences and create support material as needed throughout the course of their day's work. As the children observe, explore, and create line, color, and texture, opportunities will arise for sorting, patterning, seriating, and matching.

The children are given an opportunity to work on a 2-dimensional surface when drawing, painting, printing, and pasting. Modelling and assembling offer children the opportunity to handle, construct, and explore the relationship of 3-dimensional materials. Most of the activity at the Art Center will be child-initiated, springing from the art and motivational materials you provide. You may wish to refer to the following list to locate activities for specific strands.

Vocabulary

- Bumpy, Rough, Smooth, Soft
- Circle, Rectangle, Square, Triangle
- Design, Pattern
- Flat, Round
- Light, Lighter; Dark, Darker
- Straight, Curvy

Suggested Materials

Collection A

- Drawing materials (crayons, chalk, felt markers, a variety of papers, e.g., manilla, small booklets, construction paper, etc.)
- Painting materials (paint, finger paint, a variety of brushes and applicators, e.g., cotton swabs, sponges, straws, or toothbrushes, a variety of paper, smocks or old paint shirts, etc.)
- Modelling materials (soft pliable materials, e.g., Plasticine, clay, or salt and flour mixture, modelling tools, e.g., spoons, forks, popsicle sticks, rolling pins, etc.)
- Collage and construction materials (magazines, newspapers, fabric, wallpaper, paper of all kinds, junk box collection, scissors, glue, etc.)
- Print making materials (Plasticine, corks, cookie cutters, sponges, thickened tempera paint, stamp pads, etc.)

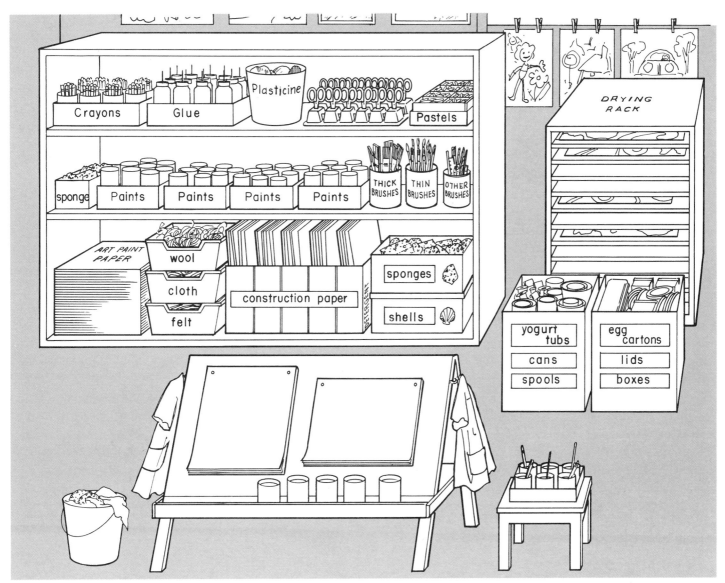

Setting up the Art Center

You will need to designate a large open area for the Art Center so that the children have space to work in and can set their work out to dry and/or to finish later. This area should be large enough to feature and house a variety of art materials for drawing, different types of painting experiences, print making, modelling, assembling, and construction. These materials need to be stored so that the children can easily find and return what they need. A sink, bucket of water, or water trough should be near by for cleaning equipment and the Art Center.

You might like to consider some of the illustrated suggestions in the planning of the Art Center, especially for the storing and arranging of materials.

You will need to consider the routines you wish to establish with the children for:

- the care and handling of different art materials
- the cleaning of art tools and the work area
- the number of children the space will accommodate
- the permanent and the portable materials
- the protection of the children's clothing and the surrounding area
- the procedures for each new art experience

These routines will need to be introduced and consistently reinforced and reviewed.

You will need to consider your program guidelines and the experience and interests of your children when selecting materials and suggesting activities.

Free Exploration with Collection A

Children should be slowly introduced to the routines, purpose, and procedures for the handling and caring of the different sets of art materials (drawing, painting, modelling, collage, construction, and print making). They will need time to explore line, texture, and color; the potential and limitations of various media; and techniques for expressing their feelings and ideas. Repeated exposure to the same type of materials should be offered to allow children time to manipulate and experiment with the materials and discover new methods and techniques. By providing stimulating experiences and a supportive atmosphere, the children will be able to express their creative ideas and their awareness of what they have learned.

Suggested Materials: Collection A

- Drawing and painting tools and paper, print making materials, collage and construction materials, and modelling materials

Observations

Katie loves to do art work and talk about her work. Her teacher saw this cut and paste picture as an opportunity to talk about shapes.

Sarah has carefully selected the junk materials that were the right size and shape for her truck. She has shown initiative in obtaining and adding color and additional material for detail. Sarah included number and shape in the description of her truck when sharing it with David and then later the rest of the class.

Christy's class has recently returned from a trip to the apple orchard. Several of the apples they brought back were cut in different ways and added to the stamp collection. Christy has been experimenting with these shapes. Derek has carved an apple shape in the flattened end of his Plasticine printer and is stamping a pattern onto his page.

Jarett has been very conscientious about following the general routines and the procedures described by his teacher for mixing and experimenting with color. Jarett's teacher commented on his use of light and dark colors in his painting. Jarett was able to identify the colors and compare them using the language "light", "lighter", "dark", and "darker".

Melissa is using the rolling pin to flatten the Plasticine. Novlett is now imprinting several objects found at the table into it. The children are pleased to talk about their work and share the results of their experimentation.

Extending Free Exploration

Free exploration is not only a time for children to work independently experimenting with materials and expressing ideas, but it is also a time for you to gather information about children's interests, learning styles, knowledge, skills, and attitudes. This information about the child, in conjunction with program objectives, affects the planning of each learning experience. It is this knowledge of child and program that will allow you to observe and recognize an opportunity to use a child's art work as a starting point to initiate a learning experience aimed at a specific objective. The decision as to how and when to engage a child in discussion or further activity rests with you.

Sarah's truck building could act as a starting point for developing several mathematical ideas. You might present one of the following possible questions or activities to her during free exploration to see if she is interested in pursuing the investigation.

Problem Solving

You might use the information Sarah presents about her truck to create story situations for her to consider. For example:

- **How many wheels does your truck have? If you had another truck, how many wheels would you have? How could you find out?**
- **How many boxes did you use? How many rolls? How many pieces of junk did you take from the junk box?**

Geometry

- You might consider presenting a solid to Sarah and asking her to identify similar shapes within her truck.
- You might ask Sarah if she would like to build other structures to accompany her truck. For example:
  - **What would you use to make a garage big enough to hold your truck?**
  - **Can you build a bridge tall enough for your truck to pass under?**
  - **Can you build another truck using only these materials?**
  - **Can you build another truck that could carry a larger load?**
- You might consider asking Sarah to describe the shapes in her truck. To extend the experience further, you could ask, **What else have you seen that has the same shape as your truck's wheel?**

Activities with Collection A

Observation Skills

Present a variety of interesting objects and pictures at the Art Center for the children to examine. Some children will enjoy representing these items with the art materials provided.

Sorting

- Children can create collages by sorting different types of paper or fabric that focus on a specific criterion, e.g., color, texture, size, shape, feature, or type. To create a texture collage, provide a collection of textured papers, e.g., sandpaper, wallpaper samples, corrugated paper, waxed paper, vinyl, glossy magazine pages, and small pre-cut fabric pieces. Have the children cut the paper and sort the pieces by texture. Encourage them to arrange and rearrange the pieces on paper before they use glue.

- A field trip, current theme, or topic of interest can become the focus of a class or small group mural. Have different children responsible for drawing or painting various aspects of the scene. For example, 4 children might draw people, 3 others might draw animals, 2 might draw trees, 5 might draw buildings, etc. These sets can then be sorted and arranged on a background. Encourage the children to describe and label the sorting groups.

- A collage type of mural can also be created on large paper that is broken up by lines. Each area can house materials that are similar in some way. Provide a wide range of interesting materials for the children to sort and glue. Materials such as rice, sand, sugar, oatmeal, crushed leaves, coffee grounds, sawdust, or torn paper could be glued to create an interesting exploration of color which is rich in texture as well.

- Print making offers an excellent means of representing a sorting criterion. Materials such as sponges, junk material, Plasticine, small collected items, vegetable and fruit sections, lids, checkers, shells, or Styrofoam pieces can be used to represent size, shape, or texture. By having children select 1 color of paint or ink, they can also sort by color.

- Use opportunities as they arise to sort and display the children's art work and models. For example, if a group of children create dinosaurs while working with the Plasticine, modelling clay, and junk material, you could have them sort their work by a variety of different criteria such as type of dinosaur, materials used, meat- or plant-eating, habitat (land, air, or water), etc. You might like to create labels for these sorting groups to add to the display.

Patterning

- Print making lends itself nicely to patterning. Materials such as vegetable and fruit sections, sponges, odds and ends, shells, lids, Styrofoam, Plasticine, or children's hands, feet, and fingers can be used in conjunction with tempera paint thickened with cornstarch or white glue. The children could also use homemade stamp pads (damp paper towel or a piece of disposable diaper soaked in tempera paint). You could start print patterns and place them with the print making materials. The children then use the materials to copy the given pattern, extend it, or create their own pattern. Encourage the children to describe their patterns in a variety of different ways.

- Children can paint patterns using different brushes to create a thick– thin pattern. Lines can be used to create long–short patterns or curved–straight patterns. By making different colored paints available, children can create color patterns as well. Patterning with finger paints will also be enjoyable for some children.

- Some children might enjoy making a patterned frame or border for their favorite piece of art work.

- Pattern imprints can be made in flattened pieces of Plasticine using a variety of carving tools or found objects such as bottle caps, shells, or stir sticks.

- Have the children make simple rubbings of different patterned surfaces such as leaves, screens, corrugated cardboard, the soles of their shoes, brick walls, or imprints on cutlery. Note that the children should be shown how to hold (or tape) a sheet of paper over the surface. Encourage them to experiment by rubbing the surface with the side of a crayon. Invite the children to do many rubbings which can be cut out and used to create a picture or a pattern.

Seriation

- Have the children engage in making books. The children act as illustrators and designers as they express their own personal stories or retell a familiar one through a series of drawings. Provide a variety of different types of paper (cut to the same size) or drawing and coloring materials, scissors, glue, and a stapler in an area decorated with pictures, brochures, menus, logos, etc., to motivate story telling. When necessary, encourage and guide children in the story telling process and the compiling of their storybooks.

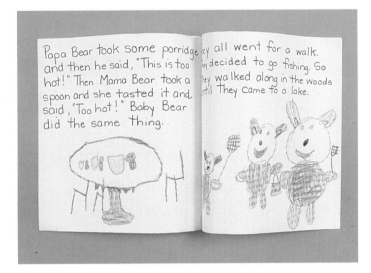

- Provide different widths of painting tools, e.g., brushes, cotton swabs, empty roll-on deodorant dispensers filled with thinned paint. Have the children create designs and patterns that order the line from thickest to thinnest or thinnest to thickest.

Number: Sets to 10

Pose situations involving a particular number for the children to consider while at the Art Center. Some children may be motivated by one of these suggestions:

- **Make a picture about (5).**
- **Make a picture using only (3) colors.**
- **What can you make using (2) big pieces of junk and (4) small pieces?**
- **Make a collage using pictures of things grouped in (2s).**
- **Make a section for our mural "If Everything Came in 3s."**
- **What can you make from the (6) mystery shapes or junk pieces in the Let's Make It bag?**

Geometry: Geometric Solids

- Have the children create junk sculptures using boxes, cylinders, rectangular prisms, and cones. Make support material, such as paint, paper, fabric, and wool scraps, available as well. Encourage the children to identify and discuss similar shapes in their own work and in that of other children.

- Present a variety of empty food boxes. Cut a set of papers that are the same size as some of the faces of the boxes. Have the child select a paper, match it to the appropriate box, draw a new packaging label for the container, and secure it to the package.

- Provide models of different geometric solids and modelling materials such as play dough, Plasticine, clay, or a salt and flour mixture. Some children might enjoy creating the shapes and carving designs on the faces or combining several shapes to make a sculpture. Encourage the children to describe the shapes they make and/or match them to the corresponding model.

- Provide modelling material (Plasticine, clay, play dough, or a salt and flour mixture) divided into portions of similar size and shape. Have the children observe and compare the balls of (Plasticine) to note their similarity. The children take 1 ball and model it into a sculpture. Ask, **Is there the same amount of Plasticine in this rabbit as there is in this ball? Why do you think that?**

Many children think that altering the shape of the Plasticine affects the amount of Plasticine used; they are not yet conserving mass. Do not try to teach this concept as it develops naturally through the passage of time and additional experiences. Provide these children with many opportunities to shape and reshape Plasticine balls.

Geometry: Geometric Figures

- Cut pieces of paper into circles, squares, rectangles, and triangles, and place them with a collection of different types of paper and any small gluable odds and ends of similar shape. Have a child select a paper shape to act as a background and model. Have the children cut out similar figures and select similar shapes to secure to their paper shape.

- Have the children draw 1 (or more) straight and/or curvy lines on a paper. They then use these lines to create a picture or abstract drawing.

- Some children will enjoy tearing paper or cutting and arranging paper to form a circle, square, triangle, or rectangle.

A Triangle

- As the children create drawings and paintings or engage in print making, you may wish to take the opportunity to talk about the geometric figures they have used.

- You might consider placing only circles (squares, rectangles, or triangles) at the Art Center and suggesting that the children make pictures using just that 1 type of geometric figure.

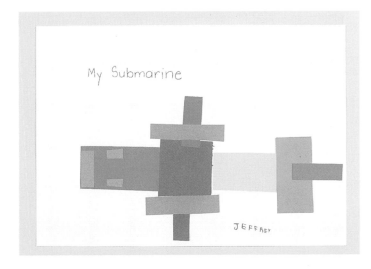
My Submarine
JEFFREY

- You might present a collection of different geometric figures with the art materials. Some children will enjoy using the assorted geometric figures to create pictures. Ask them to tell about the different shapes in their picture.

RACHEL

Measurement: Linear

- Present objects such as straws, sticks, pencils, toy snakes, or rolling pins at the Art Center from time to time. You might consider posing any of these challenges for some children to consider:

  - **Can you make a model that is taller (shorter) than this?**
  - **Can you make something that is longer and/or shorter than this?**
  - **Can you make 3 (or more) things so that this is the shortest (tallest, longest)?**

- When the children are working with the modelling materials, you might want to present a challenge to some of them by asking, **Can you make the play dough as long as this table? Can you make it shorter than this ruler? How did you do it?**

The Dramatic Play Center

Mathematics at the Dramatic Play Center

Much of the children's activity at the Dramatic Play Center will spring from their imagination, imitation, and the materials you present. This dramatic play will often lead to natural mathematical experiences in matching, sorting, and ordering. You may wish to use some of these opportunities to extend or reinforce some children's mathematical language and thinking. Often an appropriate moment will arise for you to offer a suggestion or question that will lead towards a mathematical investigation. Don't hesitate to join in and assume a role at times when the play is wavering.

The setting and materials at the Dramatic Play Center may change from time to time, thereby altering the focus of roles, language, and mathematical experience. There are many different settings that can be simulated in this area. This section features some possible mathematical experiences that could be initiated in 2 of these settings, the house and the store. You can find activities for specific mathematical strands as listed here:

- Sorting, pages 142, 146
- Patterning, pages 142, 146
- Seriation, pages 142, 146
- Number: Numeral Recognition, page 143
- Number: More/Less/Same, page 143
- Number: Sets to 10, pages 144, 146
- Geometry: Geometric Figures, page 144
- Geometry: Geometric Solids, page 146
- Measurement: Capacity, page 144
- Measurement: Area, page 144
- Measurement: Time, page 144
- Measurement: Money, page 147
- Measurement: Mass, page 147

Vocabulary

- Sort, Set, Group, Same, Different
- As many as, More than, Less than
- Next to, On top of, Beside, Under, Over, Inside, Outside
- Buy, Sell, How much, Penny, Nickel, Dime
- Too much, Not enough

Suggested Materials

Collection A

- Equipment for a house center, such as:
  - child-sized furniture
  - sink or tub of water; tea towels and cloths; clothesline; soap; etc.
  - cooking materials: pots, pans, bowls, stove, and cooking utensils
  - table setting: dishes, cups, saucers, glasses, and cutlery
  - dolls, doll clothing, stroller, and bed
  - cleaning materials: dustpan, mop, broom, and bucket
  - telephone, telephone book, and message pad
  - books, newspapers, and magazines
  - mirror
  - clock
  - dress-up clothes (2 to 3 times as big as the children) and jewellery
  - wallpaper books and fabric samples

Collection B

- Equipment for a store, such as:
  - coins
  - shopping bags or carts
  - empty cans, boxes, cartons, and plastic bottles
  - odd jewellery, toys, books, and clothes
  - receipts
  - store flyers, signs, and coupons
  - cash register
  - wallets and purses
  - shopping list pads
  - hats

Setting up the Dramatic Play Center

Since a Dramatic Play Center promotes social interaction and role playing, a large area should be provided for props and furniture and to allow movement. You might consider locating this center out of the general traffic area but close to the Block Center. This twinning of centers allows for a fluid exchange and use of support materials. A writing table located nearby will encourage the printing of signs and labels and drawing of pictures.

Select materials carefully, limiting the quantity and type available. An overabundance of props and costumes can be overwhelming and make tidying up a difficult and uninviting task. Store some materials in labelled boxes or suitcases. Parents and community members may be able to donate props, packaging, clothing, and other support materials to your collection.

Different settings can be established in the Dramatic Play Center. You might consider setting up any or all of these suggested scenes over the course of the year: house, store, post office, different vehicles (bus, airplane, or train), restaurant, bank, fire hall, zoo, hospital, or castle. Different situations can also be presented for consideration, e.g., a party, preparation for dinner, or a holiday.

Routines need to be carefully introduced and consistently reinforced. Having the children maintain a tidy and well organized center allows everyone to work in a secure and safe environment. These procedures also act as a model for the children when approaching similar real life situations or tasks.

Free Exploration with Collection A

Allow the children the time and opportunity to initiate social interaction and creative enactment of real and make-believe experiences and situations. Engaging in this expressive form of play stimulates the children's linguistic, social, and intellectual development. It also presents spontaneous mathematical experiences in the relevant context of the child's world.

Suggested Materials: Collection A

- Home furnishings and setting

Observations

Felicia has washed the doll's clothes. She was careful not to overfill the washtub and to rinse and wring the clothes over the tub. When she was hanging the clothes to dry, she discovered that there were not enough clothespins, so she is taking all the clothes down.

Laura has demonstrated several mathematical skills as she tidied the kitchen cupboard. First she sorted out the lids and jars and matched them to discover that there were 3 extra lids. When her teacher walked by, she expressed her concern that there were more lids than jars. When Laura returned the jars, she ordered them by size on the lower shelf.

Brian was serving food for his party. A guest said he wouldn't come to lunch because he didn't have as many cookies as the other guests. As a result, Brian began to count the cookies as he placed them on each plate. Each person received a cup of juice and 2 cookies.

Laura and Herbie are setting the table for tea. Herbie has asked for 1 more teacup and 2 more knives so that he can finish the place setting for 4 people.

Robert is pretending to make a large pot of rice soup after hearing a story about rice soup. He has made up his own ingredients and proportions and is telling his friend, Andrea, about his recipe.

Jonathan and Devon are pretending that they are moving to a new home. They are discussing which bags are full and how many more bags they need to finish packing the clothes.

Extending Free Exploration

Free exploration is a time for children to discover relationships. It is also a time for you to gather information about the children's interests, learning styles, knowledge, and attitudes. This profile of the child, in conjunction with your objectives, affects the planning of each learning experience. It is this knowledge of child and program that will enable you to observe and recognize an opportunity to use a child's natural play to initiate a learning experience aimed at a specific objective. The decision as to how and when to engage a child in discussion or further activity rests with you.

Felicia's wash day could act as a starting point for developing several mathematical ideas. You might present one of the suggested activities to Felicia during free exploration to see if she is interested in pursuing the investigation.

Seriation

- You might suggest that Felicia order the clothes on the clothesline, e.g., biggest to smallest dress, shortest to longest pants.
- You may wish Felicia to describe the series of steps she went through in washing the clothes. You might ask, **What did you have to do first? What did you do next? And after that?** Felicia might be encouraged to record the activity in a sequence of pictures.

Sorting

You might suggest that Felicia sort a set of clothes that are similar in some way and group them together on the clothesline.

Number: Sets to 10

- You could ask Felicia to tell about her experience using numbers. To initiate such a discussion you could ask:

  - **How many clothespins do you need?**
  - **How many do you have?**
  - **Do you know how many more we will have to get? How could we find out?**

- You might ask Felicia to describe how many of each type of clothing she has to hang up. For example, you could ask:

  - **How many dresses are there to hang up?**
  - **How many socks did you wash?**

Measurement: Time

Since Felicia did not wring out the blue dress, as she did the others, you might want her to compare the time it takes for the blue dress to dry with the time it takes for the red and white striped one. You might ask, **Which dress do you think will dry faster? Why do you think that?** Then have her hang them up and find out.

Measurement: Mass

You might want Felicia to compare a set of wet clothes with a set of dry clothes by asking, **Which do you think are heavier, wet clothes or dry clothes? How could you check?**

Patterning

- You might use this opportunity to have Felicia observe and describe patterns in the doll's clothing. You could direct her attention to the white and red striped dress, and ask:

  - **Is this a pattern in the material?**
  - **Read me the pattern you see in the dress. (White, red; white, red; white, red.)**
  - **Do you see any other clothes that have a pattern?**

- Since Felicia is about to hang up the clothes to dry, you might suggest that she hang them up in a pattern.

Activities with Collection A

Sorting

- Place a variety of empty food packages in shopping bags. Have the children sort the groceries and put them away in the different kitchen cupboards (shelves, bins), the refrigerator, or the freezer.
- If you present a variety of empty food and cleanser packages on the kitchen shelves, you could pose different situations to the children and have them sort the items that they would need. For example:

  - **If you were going to bake a cake, what would you need?**
  - **If you were serving soup and sandwiches for lunch, what would you need?**
  - **If you were having company for tea, what would you serve them?**
  - **Your guests have gone and the baby spilled food all over the floor. What do you need?**

- Place dishes, cutlery, pots, and pans in a dish rack. Have the children sort them and put them away.
- Place a variety of dress-up clothes, jewellery, and accessories in a drawer. Ask the children to sort and pack the things from the drawer because you are moving.
- Place a variety of dress-up clothes in a laundry basket. Have the children sort and re-sort the collection. For example, they could

  - sort the clothes for washing
  - sort the clothes to put away
  - sort for different family members

Patterning

- Prepare pattern cards for setting the table or display a place setting pattern for the children to copy and/or extend, e.g., fork, placemat, knife; fork, placemat, knife; fork, placemat, knife. As the children set the table on their own, draw their attention to patterns they create. Encourage them to describe and extend these patterns.
- Some children may enjoy looking through wallpaper books and fabric samples for patterns. When appropriate, encourage the children to describe the patterns.
- Have the children redecorate the House Center using patterned fabric, wallpaper, or paper. Have them create a variety of different household items with patterns to add to the decor. They might enjoy making any of these items: pattern cups, a pattern quilt, pattern placemats, or a pattern trim for the walls. Encourage the children to add to the collection of pattern decorations.

Seriation

- Pose situations for the children to order themselves as they assume different roles at the center. For example, if a camera is available, have the children pose for a photograph so that they are tallest to shortest, shortest to tallest, or darkest hair to lightest hair.
- When the children are playing in the kitchen, you might suggest that they order food boxes, cans, or bottles on the kitchen shelf. Encourage the children to describe their order, i.e., shortest to tallest, tallest to shortest, or widest to narrowest.

- Dress-up clothes can be ordered in a variety of different ways. You may wish to take advantage of situations as they arise or suggest any of these orderings:

  - washed clothes on the clothesline from quickest drying to slowest drying
  - doll's clothes on a clothesline from largest to smallest
  - shoes on a rack from highest to lowest heel
  - hats on hooks from smallest to largest
  - wigs on hooks from curliest to straightest
  - necklaces on hooks from longest to shortest

- Pictorial sequence cards can be prepared and posted to guide the children as they act out or engage in different roles and situations. For example, the cards might outline:
  - steps for washing dishes
  - steps for washing clothes
  - steps for baking or cooking different items
  - steps to follow in case of fire

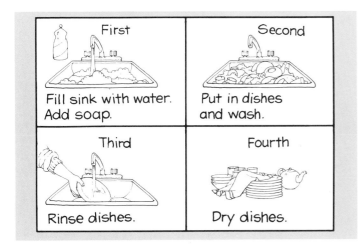

- The House Center offers an ideal setting for cooking activities and the preparation of a daily snack. You may wish to prepare and post a series of production cooking cards (Line Masters 36 to 40) near the appropriate materials and ingredients. A chef's schedule can be developed to identify times and children who are responsible for the food preparation.

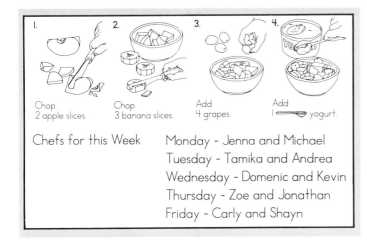

- Present 3 different sized stuffed toys or dolls, e.g., 3 bears, arranged in order of size. Ask the children to select and order a bowl, a glass, a spoon, and/or a chair for the bears. Ask them to describe the order.

Number: Numeral Recognition

Post a telephone directory list by the telephone. You may wish to post local services such as a florist's shop, hairdressing salon, computer store, or movie theater. An emergency directory could also be posted that includes telephone numbers for a police department, a fire department, a poison control center, a doctor, and an ambulance. If you think it is appropriate, you may wish to post a list of children's first names and their phone numbers or a class phone book by the telephone each day.

Number: More/Less/Same

- As the children work with 2 sets of objects, use the opportunity to ask:
  - **Do you think there are the same number of hats as dolls?**
  - **Do you have enough straws for the juice boxes? How could we find out?**

You may wish to continue, **How do you know? Show me how you know that.**

- In situations in which a group of children are involved in play, e.g., a bus scene, you might use any of these questions to initiate discussion:
  - **Do you have the same number of passengers as seats? How could we find out?**
  - **Do you have enough seats for your passengers?**
  - **Give each passenger a ticket. Do you need more tickets than you have now?**
  - **Give each passenger 2 (or more) tickets. Are there more tickets or more people?**

Number: Sets to 10

- When appropriate, take advantage of situations that the children create or set the scene yourself so that the children are considering number. For example:

  - **There are 4 people coming for dinner. Please set the table.**
  - **How many cookies are in the cookie jar?**
  - **There will be 6 people at the party. Are there enough napkins (glasses, forks, plates) for everyone?**
  - **Susan and James just phoned to say they were sick and couldn't come for dinner. How should we change the table?**
  - **How many socks are there in your pile? How many pairs do you think that will be? Match them up and see.**
  - **How many cookies will you give to each person? Then how many will you still have to make?**
  - **There are only these 5 tickets left. Do we have enough for everyone to go to the movies?**
  - **Give each doll 2 pieces of fruit. How many pieces of fruit do you need?**

- As the children place a set of objects on a table, e.g., 5 glasses, you could use this as an informal opportunity to assess their understanding of number concepts. For example, you might ask, **How many glasses do you have on the table?** Move the glasses further apart or arrange them differently and ask, **How many glasses are there now?** A similar process can be used for removing a glass or adding a glass.

Geometry: Geometric Figures

Provide play dough or Plasticine and cookie cutters for making various shapes. As the children make their cookies, you might ask:

- **What shape cookies have you made?**
- **May I have your round cookies?**
- **How many square cookies did you make?**
- **I wonder which cookie cutter would make a cookie shaped like a penny?**

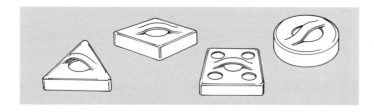

Measurement: Capacity

- Post make-believe recipes or have a recipe file for the children to use in conjunction with different substances in their play.

Some children will enjoy creating their own recipes to add to the collection. Similarly, parents may have easy no-cooking recipes that they would contribute to the class recipe box.

- As the children create different situations and act out various experiences, you may find appropriate opportunities to challenge some children. For example, you could initiate an investigation by asking any of these questions:
  - **Which of these 2 (or more) teapots would be better for making your cups of tea?**
  - **How many glasses of juice do you think you could pour from that jug?**
  - **Do you think you will have enough milk in there to fill 4 glasses?**
  - **How can you make sure that each person will get the same amount of cereal?**

Measurement: Area

Use the children's play or stage simple situations to engage the children in estimating and determining area. For example:
- Indicating a shelf and a collection of soup tins, ask the children to predict how many cans they think will fit on the shelf. Then have them find out. Ask, **Do you think more tin cans will fit on the second shelf?**
- Have the children predict and find out how many rug samples it will take to cover the kitchen area of the center.

Measurement: Time

Use a real or homemade clock to set the scene for the children's play. For example:
- **It's 3:00 in the afternoon. What might be happening?**
- **It's about 7:30 in the morning. What will you be doing?**

Free Exploration with Collection B

Allow the children to engage in imaginative and imitative play with the various store materials in a variety of roles, e.g., clerk, customer. Continue to watch for opportunities to extend the child's play into a mathematical experience.

Suggested Materials: Collection B

- A store setting with materials, e.g., coins, shopping bags, a variety of merchandise, receipts, cash register, store coupons, wallets and purses, shopping list pads, hats, and shopping carts.

Observations

Daniel is taking an order from a group of people who have come for lunch at his restaurant. Bruce and Lori are cooking the special of the day. They are following a posted recipe.

Patricia and Dianne are pushing the shopping buggy along in the grocery store. Their conversation is focussed on the food preferences of their "children." They are sorting the food into categories of those their children like and those they do not like.

Jimmy drew up a shopping list at the writing table. He is now examining the shelves for the items he needs. Sara, the storekeeper, has just offered to help. They are matching the items on the list to those on the shelf in a systematic fashion.

Activities with Collection B

Sorting

- Have the children sort the items to be sold in the store. They could create a display of each group and include an advertisement as a label, e.g., breakfast foods, canned foods.

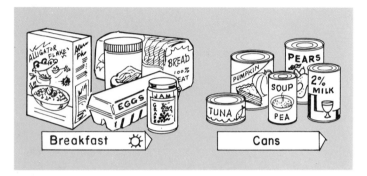

- Place a collection of coins in wallets or containers. Suggest to the storekeeper or banker that the coins be sorted and placed in the cash register.
- Store coupons can be placed in a collection bin in the store for the children to use in a variety of sorting experiences. For example, the children could:
  - sort and re-sort the coupons by a variety of different criteria
  - use the coupons as sorting labels for sets of products purchased or arranged on shelves

Patterning

Some children may enjoy making signs with a patterned border for the store.

Seriation

The children can order the items for sale in many different ways, e.g., from largest to smallest, tallest to shortest, or most expensive to least expensive.

Number: Sets to 10

- Have the children complete an inventory of the items in the store. Each child could select a type of item to count. A pictorial record of the inventory could be kept.
- Some children will enjoy taking numeral cards (cut from Line Masters 11 to 13) as their shopping list. These children select a set of items from the shelves to correspond with each numeral.

Geometry: Geometric Solids

- Maps of different products can be drawn on paper and used to line the store shelves. When the children are stocking the shelves, they match the product to the shape outlined.

- Some children may enjoy going on a shopping spree using a geometric solid as their shopping list. The child purchases any product that has a similar shape.

Measurement: Money

- Have the children role play buying and selling at the store. Provide a dish of pennies or wallets containing different collections of pennies. After obtaining their money, the children select an item and pay the sales clerk. To tidy up, items may be returned and money refunded. Encourage the children to assume different roles.

- Provide the children with wallets or envelopes containing a collection of pennies or mixed coins. Have them match the wallet to an item priced of equal value.

- Have the children select a wallet of pennies. Ask them to isolate all the items that cost that amount. You may wish to challenge some children by asking an open-ended question. For example:

  - **What could you buy with your 7 pennies?**
  - **What costs more than what you have?**

- The children can select store coupons and create a set of pennies to match the amount indicated.

Measurement: Mass

Place the balance scale in the store with small objects, such as plastic fruit, nuts, or raisin boxes. At times, you may have the children select an item to act as a standard measure, e.g., a block. The children determine how many blocks it takes to balance the item for sale.

The Water Center

Mathematics at the Water Center

The Water Center provides many opportunities for children to explore a variety of mathematical concepts. The children investigate and compare capacity as they fill, pour, and empty various containers. Once they have had an opportunity to explore the materials, the children should be encouraged to make predictions and estimates. When you encourage the children to offer a possible answer, you create an opportunity to gain further insight into their thinking and perceptions. Opportunities for sorting and classifying also arise at the Water Center as the children observe materials floating and sinking.

This center can also provide a comfortable, informal setting to reinforce counting and comparison of quantity. To initiate discussion, you might ask questions such as:

- **How many objects did you use?**
- **If we add this one to your collection, how many will we have?**
- **Did more (less) objects float or sink? How do you know?**
- **Show me (5) things that float.**

The following list will help you find activities for specific strands:

- Observation Skills, page 160
- Sorting, pages 157, 160-161
- Problem Solving, pages 157, 161-162
- Number: Sets to 10, page 162
- Graphing, page 162
- Measurement: Capacity, pages 154-155, 157-158
- Measurement: Time, page 158

There will be times when you will want to introduce a display, a problem or an activity to all or some of the children. You might gather a small group of children about the water table for the introductory discussion, then leave them to pursue the task independently. Remember to plan some follow-up time with these children. Alternatively, you may wish to bring a small tub of water and other appropriate materials to the circle for discussion and a group investigation.

This section on the Water Center provides a wide variety of ideas and suggestions to act as a springboard for your planning and interaction with the children. In order to facilitate the learning and development of mathematical concepts, you will need to select, adapt, repeat, and extend activities based on the needs, abilities, and interests of your children. Many activities can be introduced and maintained over an extended period of time. By adding to or changing the materials, you can create a new context for a familiar activity. This allows the children to focus on their activity and observations rather than procedures and routines.

Due to similarities between the Sand and Water Centers, many of the ideas and discoveries that evolve in one of these areas can be tested and verified in the other. From time to time, stimulate the children's senses, discussion, and discovery further by adding different materials to the water, e.g., soap flakes, food coloring, or salt, or by adding warm water or ice to change the temperature.

Vocabulary

- Pour in, Pour out, Through, Around, Inside, Outside
- Float, Sink, Drift, Pull, Push, Down, Up
- Pouring, Blowing, Shaking, Spilling, Holding, Filling, Splashing, Bubbling, Emptying, Melting, Flowing, Tipping, Squeezing, Dropping, Squirting, Sprinkling, Pushing, Pressing, Spraying, Squirting, Dripping, Mixing
- Too much, As much as, How much; More than, Less than; Not enough, Enough; Left over; More, Most; Less, Least; Between; Exactly
- Wet, Damp, Dry, Soaking, Soggy
- Shallow, Deep; Full, Empty; Smooth, Rough; Wide, Narrow; Heavy, Light; Fast, Slow; Over, Under; Up, Down; Different, Same; High, Low
- Spoonful, Cupful, Tubful, Mugful, Bowlful, Ladleful, Lidful, etc.
- Quickly, Slowly, Spills over, Fills up
- Bubbles, Disappears, Keeps water in, Keeps water out, Soaks up, Spreads out, Ripples, Waves

Suggested Materials

Collection A

- A collection of containers of various sizes and shapes, such as plastic cups, plastic jars, plastic tubs, plastic bottles, pails, mugs, and lids

Collection B

- Containers as listed in Collection A
- A variety of implements for pouring and squeezing substances, e.g., plastic tubing, funnels of various sizes and shapes, colanders, sieves, watering cans, eye droppers, straws, food basters, a shower head, plastic bottles of different sizes and shapes, some with holes punctured in the sides and/or bottom

Collection C

- A variety of items of different sizes and shapes that float, e.g., corks, lids, a plastic soap dish, bottles, elastic bands, twigs, plastic boxes
- A variety of items of different sizes and shapes that sink, e.g., keys, paper clips, stones, Plasticine, interlocking cubes, coins

Setting up the Water Center

When selecting an area for the Water Center, you might consider these questions:

- If I have to change the water 2 or 3 times a week, where is the easiest place to empty and fill the water table?
- If I want to have at least 2 or 3 children working at the Water Center at one time, where do I have enough space for them to move around freely?
- If I add a table on which to set up displays or place small tubs of water for presenting some investigations, will there still be enough space for the children to work?
- If I want some of the materials and activities of the Water Center to be shared with the Sand Center and Science Center, how can I best arrange these 3 centers?
- If I want the children to talk and share ideas, where can I locate the Water Center so as not to disturb those at the quieter centers?
- When spills or floods occur, where is the easiest place to clean up?

Once you have identified your area for the center, you may wish to cover and secure to the floor plastic sheeting. You will need to determine the size of water tub, pool, or table. The tub, by its size, limits the number of children using it at one time. It should be large enough for at least 2 or 3 children to work easily with an assortment of materials. Position it at a comfortable working height for the children, and fill it with at least 10 cm of water.

If you store all of your Water Center materials in this area, establish a list of materials and post it on the appropriate bin or cupboard for your reference. Isolate and label the materials that the children may select for current use. This pre-planning facilitates an easier clean up. Making other materials accessible is important as the children pursue ideas.

Establish clean up routines.

- Sponges, paper towels, and mops placed at the center can be used by the children to clean up any spills that occur. A pile of newspaper should be kept close by for larger spills.
- Materials should be dried with a dish towel and sorted into the appropriate storage containers or matched to their map outline.

Establish general routines.

- The children should wear a plastic apron, a large shirt, old raincoats, or a covering made from large plastic garbage bags.
- The children should be reminded to roll up their sleeves.

- Establish a method of identifying how many children may work at the center at one time, e.g., number of aprons provided, a sign, etc.
- You may wish to close the Water Center from time to time. A lid can be placed over the table to transform it into a display or work area.

Recording at the Water Center

These photographs show some ways that the children could record their selected discoveries.

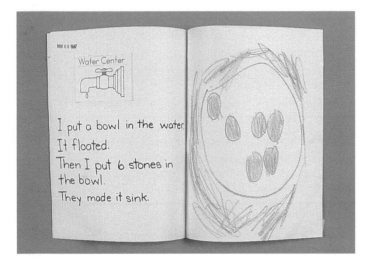

The children can keep a record in their scrapbook with your help or that of a parent volunteer.

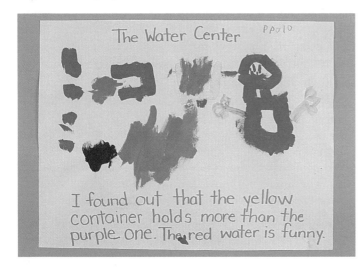

The children can draw a picture of what they discover. You can assist some children in printing their descriptions to accompany their work.

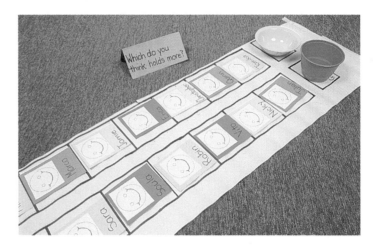

Name cards can be used to record predictions as well as discoveries.

Displays can be set up to show the children's discoveries.

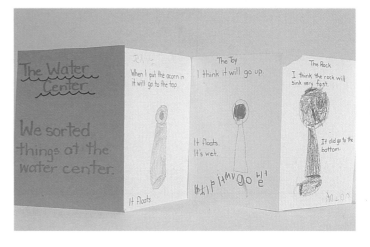

A cooperative booklet can be compiled to reflect the children's activities, ideas, and discoveries.

Free Exploration with Collection A

Allow the children frequent opportunities to explore these materials. Encourage them to pour, empty, and fill the various containers. The children will discover a good deal about the capacity of the containers during this exploratory time. They need to talk about what they are doing among themselves. At times you might invite a group of children at the Water Center to share their discoveries. This discussion might help you in deciding on future activities as well as help the children to verbalize their learning. This opportunity to express observations and thinking helps clarify and formulate concepts and ideas.

Suggested Materials: Collection A

- A collection of containers of various sizes and shapes, such as plastic cups, plastic jars, plastic tubs, plastic bottles, pails, mugs, and lids

Observations

Alessandra and Cecilia filled the ice cream tub with water. They added a large shell from the Science Center and watched the water level rise and the water overflow. As they repeat this action with different shells, they observe the same effect each time. They have added and counted 6 shells so far.

Brian is pouring the water back and forth from the margarine tub to the clear container. He notices that the margarine tub fills up but the clear container does not.

Melvin filled several different containers with water and placed them on the side table. He is now emptying the containers into the bowl. He has discovered that it takes 2 glasses, 1 tub, and 1 mug to fill the bowl. He has 2 containers filled with water that he didn't use.

Extending Free Exploration

Free exploration is a time for children to discover relationships. It is also a time for you to gather information about the children's interests, learning styles, knowledge, and attitudes. This profile of the child, in conjunction with program objectives, affects the planning of each learning experience. It is this knowledge of child and program that will allow you to observe and recognize an opportunity to use a child's natural play to initiate a learning experience aimed at a specific program objective. The decision as to how and when to engage a child in discussion or further activity rests with you.

Brian's pouring experience could act as a springboard for initiating discussion or further activity. You might present one of these activities to Brian during free exploration to see if he is interested in pursuing the investigation.

Measurement: Capacity

Many of the activity suggestions presented in this section could form the basis for extending Brian's water play. The following questions reflect a sampling of some gentle challenges:

- **If your favorite soup could be served in either the margarine tub or the container, which would you choose? Why?**
- **What happens when you pour the water from the margarine tub into the container?**
- **Why doesn't the container fill up as the margarine tub does?**
- **Do you think there is another container here that would fill up the margarine tub? Why do you think the pail will fill it?**
- **Do you think the margarine tub will hold another container of water?**

Observation Skills

- If you wanted to engage Brian in a discussion about what he observes about the water as it pours, you might ask any of these questions:
    - **What do you notice about the water as it pours?**
    - **Where else have you seen water being poured?**
    - **What does the water feel like if you pour it over your hand?**
    - **When might you feel water pouring over you?**
- You could also ask, **If we leave the water in the margarine tub overnight, where could we leave the tub?** Alternatively, you may suggest to Brian that he place the tub of water in the refrigerator, in the freezer, or by the window and observe the changes the next day.

Problem Solving

You might want to engage Brian in searching for different possibilities. You could ask:

- **How could you get the water from the container to the margarine tub without touching the container?**
- **What are some of the different things you can do with water besides pouring it?**

Activities with Collection A

Measurement: Capacity

- Some children will enjoy comparing the capacity of different containers. Identify 2 containers of different volume and shape, e.g., a jug and a bowl, and have the children tell whether they think the jug of water will fill the bowl. Then have them find out.

  To clarify how the child approached the task and the thinking involved, you might ask:

  - **Does all the water from the jug fit in the bowl? Do the 2 containers hold the same amount of water?**
  - **Was there any water left over in the jug? Does the jug hold more?**
  - **Is there room to spare in the bowl? Does the bowl hold less?**
  - **Do you think the water from the bowl will fit back into the jug? Try and see.**

  Repeat this activity many times using different containers.

- Attach a different color or shape of label to each container. Have the children select 2 containers to compare. Ask them to predict which one holds more (less) and check to find out. You may want the children to keep a record of their discoveries by displaying their work.

From time to time, you may wish to pursue a child's approach to this task. You might ask some children questions such as:

- **What are you trying to find out?**
- **Which one do you think holds less (more)? Why do you think that?**
- **How are you trying to find out which one holds more (less)?**
- **What did you do first? Next? And after that? What did you find out?**

Repeat this activity over a long period of time. Add to the collection of containers periodically.

- Present a small collection of containers. Include 2 containers of equal capacity but different shape. Identify 1 of these containers, e.g., a paper cup, to the children. Have the children determine which container holds the same amount as the paper cup. If you would like to engage a child in discussion, you might ask any of the following questions:

  - **What were you trying to find out?**
  - **How did you go about finding the container that held the same amount of water as the paper cup?**
  - **Which containers did you try before you found the (small yogurt container)? Why do you think this one holds the same amount?**

  Repeat this activity several times, changing the pair of containers and adding to the collection.

- Display small containers, some with the same capacity but different shapes and some with different capacities and shapes. Have the children identify several containers that they think will hold the same amount as a specified container, e.g., the yogurt cup. Then have them find out. You may wish the children to display the results of their discovery.

Repeat this activity many times using different containers as a reference. Change the containers in the collection from time to time.

- Present 3 containers: 1 large container that is equal to the combined capacity of 2 identical smaller ones. Have the children investigate the capacity of the 3 containers by filling the containers and pouring water from one to the other. As the children work with this type of investigation, you will have many opportunities to observe their approach to the task. There will be times when you may want to pursue a child's thinking or initiate further investigation. You might like to keep these questions in mind to use selectively.

  - **What can you tell me about the containers?**
  - **Why were you able to pour the water from the jug into the 2 cups?**
  - **How many of the cups did you fill with the jug of water?**
  - **Can you pour the 2 cups of water into the jug? Why do you think that?**
  - **What do you think will happen when you pour the water from the jug into the cups?**
  - **Does the jug hold as much water as the 2 smaller cups? How do you know?**
  - **What would you see if you poured all the water from this cup into this cup? Why do you think that?**
  - **What do you think would happen if you poured all of the water from the jug into this cup? How do you know?**

Repeat this activity several times using different containers.

- Present a small collection of containers that have different capacities and shapes. Include a pair of containers of different shape but equal capacity. Have the children determine which 2 containers hold the same amount of water.

  Repeat this activity often using different containers. Encourage the children to prove their discovery by pouring the water from the first container into the second container.

- Present different shaped containers, some with different capacities and some with equal capacities. Identify one container, e.g., a juice can, to act as a standard. Have the children select a few containers and identify whether they think each one will hold more than, less than, or the same as the juice can. Ask the children to test their predictions and label the results.

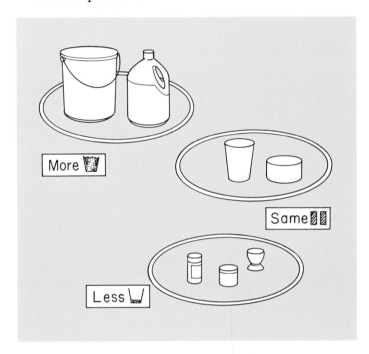

Repeat this activity many times over the course of the year. From time to time, change the standard container as well as the selection of containers.

If you continue this type of activity, over time you will have many opportunities to observe the children's approach as well as to engage them in discussions. These questions can serve as a resource for pursuing a child's thinking or for initiating further activity.

- **What is the same about these containers? What is different about them?**
- **How many containers do you have that hold less than the juice can? Can you find another one?**
- **Which containers held more than (less than, the same as) the juice can? How do you know?**
- **Does the ice cream cup hold more than the juice can? Does the juice can hold less than the ice cream cup? What could you do to make sure?**
- **Would you choose a juice can or an ice cream cup filled with your favorite drink? Why?**
- **What do you notice about all of the containers that hold less than the juice can? Is there anything the same about them? Anything different?**

Free Exploration with Collection B

Free exploration of containers should continue. The shape of a container is often deceptive. Children need to fill, empty, and compare containers many times to see that the capacity of a container is not necessarily what it appears to be. Investigating the various ways water can be poured from different containers and openings can provide much enjoyment to the children. This is a valuable time for incidental learning.

As the children explore the materials, you may observe an opportunity for teaching. Keep your objectives and the child's experiences and interests in mind when utilizing these opportunities.

Suggested Materials: Collection B

- A variety of containers of all shapes and sizes, e.g., pails, plastic food tubs, bottles, cups, spoons, jugs, bowls, lids, mugs
- A variety of implements for pouring and squeezing substances, e.g., plastic tubing, funnels of various sizes and shapes, colanders, sieves, watering cans, eye droppers, food basters, a shower head, plastic bottles of different sizes and shapes, some with holes punctured in their sides and/or bottoms

Observations

Earl and Jason are filling containers with water and watching the streams of water pour out of the holes on the sides. They noticed that the first streams of water to stop were from the holes near the top of the container.

Ricky and Joey are using the stream of water from their squeeze bottles to aim at the center of the floating plastic rings. As they comment to each other, they are talking about speed, position, and distance.

Simon has been pouring water into the rubber tube. He has placed the tube at different angles and watched the results. After placing one end of the tube in the water, he is now pouring water into the other end. Children's curiosity will often motivate them to experiment with materials in different situations.

Christina and Kelly are working cooperatively to fill the containers. Christina enlisted Kelly's help to hold the funnel over the yogurt container as she poured a mugful of water into it. She is adding more water because the mugful did not quite fill the yogurt container. Christina was able to verbalize that the yogurt container held a bit more than a mugful of water when asked by her teacher.

Activities with Collection B

Sorting

You might display some containers and some implements for pouring and say, **Look at these things. Which could you use to catch and hold water as it flows out of the funnel? Which of these things will water pour through?**

Problem Solving

Display several labelled containers. Pose different problems for some children to investigate. For example:

- **You are going to serve 5 children a Dixie cup filled with juice. In which containers do you think you could make the juice?**
- **In which container would you choose to make this recipe?**
- **Which container do you think holds the most mugfuls of water? How could you find out?**
- **Which container do you think you could use to fill these 3 yogurt cups?**
- **Which of these containers would you give to Papa Bear? Which container would you give to Baby Bear? Why did you choose those containers?**

Encourage the children to describe their approach to the task and explain their discoveries.

Measurement: Capacity

- Display a food baster and clear plastic glasses. Have the children investigate whether the baster always takes in the same amount of water by emptying it into a different glass each time and comparing the water level. You might ask:

  - **Which container shows the most water that was taken in? The least?**
  - **How could you order these containers? Show me.**

- Display a container, e.g., a margarine tub. Have the children tell how many spoonfuls they think it will take to fill the margarine tub. Ask them to find out. Working in pairs, one child can count or keep a tally (by snapping cubes together or placing counters in an egg carton) while the other child pours the spoonfuls into the tub.

  Repeat the activity using cupfuls, ladlefuls, or mugfuls. Later change the container to be filled. You might ask some children one of these questions:

  - **How many spoonfuls did you need to fill the tub?**
  - **Did you need more (or less) spoonfuls than you thought?**
  - **Do you think it would take more (less, same) ladlefuls than spoonfuls to fill the margarine tub? Why do you think that?**

- Display 2 labelled containers. Have the children identify which of the 2 containers holds more mugfuls of water. Ask them to find out. You might ask:

  - **About how many mugfuls did it take to fill this container? And this one?**
  - **How did you keep track of the number of mugfuls you used?**
  - **Which container held less water? How do you know that?**
  - **If you had to make juice for many children at Snack Time, which container would you use? Why?**

Repeat this activity many times. Change 1 container each time the task is presented.

Measurement: Time

- Present 2 different funnels or containers. Have the children identify which funnel they think will empty a Dixie cup of water the fastest (slowest, first, last). You may want some children to record their predictions before they pursue the task.

- Place a sand clock or non-standard timer beside the water table. Ask the children to select containers with holes that they think will empty before the timer stops. Have them test the containers to find out. Then have the children work with a partner to find out.

Free Exploration with Collection C

The children should have many opportunities for uninterrupted play with different sets of materials that float and sink. This time allows the children to freely explore these and other properties and relationships of the objects and water.

You may wish to circulate among the children to silently observe their actions and listen to their comments.

Suggested Materials: Collection C

- A collection of small items that float and sink, e.g., corks, lids, soap dishes, plastic bottles, elastic bands, twigs, plastic boxes, keys, paper clips, stones, Plasticine, interlocking cubes, coins

Observations

Ercole and Lori placed a few nuts and bolts in the middle of the red lid to make a barge. They found that if they piled the metal objects at one end of the lid, that end would submerge as the water poured into their boat. Now they are loading the cargo into the middle of the boat.

Damien has made his own boat at the Art Center and is sailing it in the water. An interplay of materials between centers should be encouraged.

Young children come to school having had many experiences with water. Due to the relaxing nature of this center, the children are often found sharing experiences and observations, an activity that is important to their social development. Sometimes the conversation is unrelated to the water play, as observed in this situation with Benny and Gabriel. They are talking about a television program they watched last evening.

Angela and Deborah are having boat races. Each child selected a floating item from the collection of materials to act as a boat. On the count of 3, the race begins as each child pushes the boat with a stir stick. In the previous race, Angela's boat came in first and Deborah's boat was second. They are watching to see which boat will be first this time.

Activities with Collection C

Observation Skills

You might have some children isolate from a collection those items that float. Have them create a display by placing each item in a clear plastic glass or container half-filled with water.

You may wish to guide some children's observations by asking any of these suggested questions:

- **What do you notice about the floating things?**
- **Which ones seem to be deeper in the water? Why do you think they are like that?**
- **Which ones are not floating very deep in the water? Why?**
- **Do you notice anything the same (different) about some of them? All of them?**
- **What happens if we tap the container lightly?**
- **What happens if you poke the object lightly with your finger?**
- **What happens when we put this object in the water another way? Do you think all the objects would do that?**

Sorting

- The children can work with a collection of small objects to create a set of objects that float. If you are observing selected children and wish to find out more about their thinking, you might ask any of these questions:
  - **How are these floaters the same? How are they different?**
  - **What else do you think might belong in your set? Why do you think that?**
  - **What could you name this set?**
  - **Why do you think these float? Do you think all small, light plastic things float? What else could you try to see if that is true? Try it.**

  The children may wish to bring in items from home to test and add to the collection.

- Have the children determine which items in the collection sink. If you wish to engage some children in discussing their activity and discoveries, you might ask any of these questions:
  - **What is the same about these sinkers? What is different about them?**
  - **What could you call your set?**
  - **Did all these things sink to the bottom in the same way? Would you show me and tell me about one that you found interesting?**
  - **Do you think all heavy (big, metal, ...) things sink? What else could you try to see if that is true? What do you think now?**

- Present a collection of sinking (or floating) items. Have the children sort this collection in many different ways. They could sort the items according to fast and slow sinkers, material, size, mass, or floaters that can be made to sink easily.

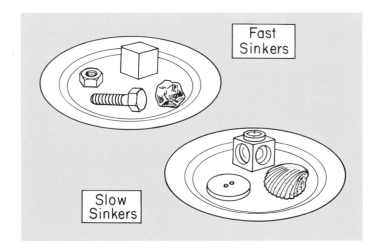

- The children can sort objects according to whether they float or sink. If you would like to find out more about a child's thinking, you might ask any of the following questions:

  - **How did you sort these?**
  - **Why does this belong here?**
  - **Why doesn't this belong?**
  - **What could you name the sets?**
  - **Tell me about the objects that float. The ones that sink.**
  - **Why do you think some things float and others don't?**
  - **Do all (small) objects float? Do all (large) ones sink? Try and see.**
  - **What types of things float? Sink?**
  - **What else do you think will float? Sink? Show me.**
  - **What objects float in your bathtub at home? What objects sink?**

This activity should be repeated many times. Add to and change the collection of items from time to time.

Problem Solving

- Set up a display beside the water table or tub. Invite the children to meet there. Tell them that all of the displayed objects have been sorted according to whether they float or sink. One object (or more) does not belong where it has been placed. Have them guess which one it is. You may list the children's predictions at that time. Encourage the children to test their predictions when they go to the Water Center. To maintain the center, encourage the children to either return the mystery item to the wrong set after they have found it or place it in the correct set and pick a new mystery item. If the children are working independently on this task, you might ask them to make a record of their discoveries.

The children can trace the objects they test onto a large piece of paper.

The children can make a tally of the number of items tested before the mystery item is discovered. A cooperative record can be made, if desired.

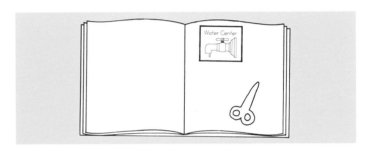

The children can draw a picture of their discovery in their scrapbook.

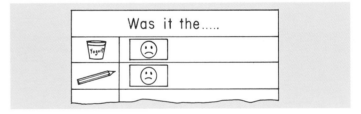

A recording sheet can be prepared. The children place a happy or sad label card beside the objects that they tested.

- Some children may enjoy the challenge of finding different ways to make a toy boat and/or plastic container sink. You may wish to silently observe the children as they investigate the situation. If you would like to engage some children in discussion, you might ask any of these suggested questions:

  - **How did you make the boat sink?**
  - **Why do you think it sank when you did that?**
  - **What other ways did you try?**
  - **Can you think of another way to make the boat sink? Show me.**
  - **Can you think of something else you could put in the boat to make it sink? Show me.**
  - **Do you think it would take more (less) stones or paper clips to sink the boat? Why do you think that? Would you like to try and see?**

- The children can investigate how many different ways they can make an object float, e.g., a bolt. The process a child goes through in pursuing this task can provide you with further insight into her or his thinking. If you would like to discuss a child's activity, you might ask:

  - **How did you make the bolt float?**
  - **Show me one way. Why do you think that made it float?**
  - **Can you think of another way? Show me.** Or, **What do you need to do that?**

- You might gather all or some of the children around the Water Center and observe whether a ball of Plasticine floats or sinks. Have the children suggest how they can make the Plasticine float. When the children return to the Water Center independently, have them investigate the possibilities. You might wish to challenge some children further by asking, **What is the smallest boat of Plasticine you can make that will float? The longest? The shortest?**

- Present a chain of paper clips in a jar of water. Have the children investigate how they can get a chain of paper clips out of the water without getting their hands wet.

Number: Sets to 10

Have the children identify how many stones they think it will take to make a boat sink. Invite them to find out. You may wish to ask some children to identify the results of their investigation.

- **How many stones did you think you would need to sink the boat?**
- **How many did you find out you needed?**
- **If you used these bigger stones, do you think it would take more or less to sink the same boat? Why? Show me.**

Graphing

You may wish to work with a small group at the Water Center to create a graph. You could ask, **Do you think there are more (less) items in this collection that float or more (less) items that sink?** After the children identify their predictions, invite them to test the items at the water table and to place each item on a plastic graph in the appropriate column.

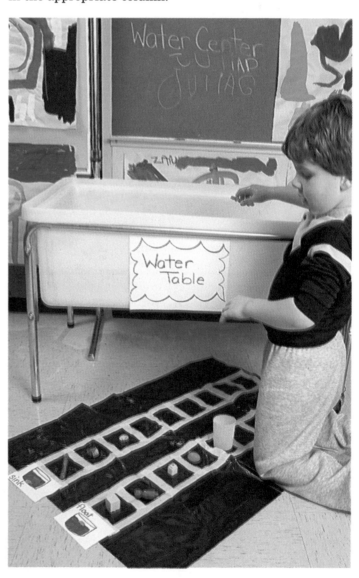

These questions may be used to initiate discussion with an individual or small group.

- **Show me the column with more.**
- **Show me the column with less.**
- **Do the columns have the same number of things?**
- **Are there more (less) things that floated or sank?**

The Science Center

Mathematics at the Science Center

The Science Center is an area that will spark curiosity and exploration. It is most effective if the materials displayed at the Science Center directly reflect the children's interests, experiences, or questions. At times, materials that demonstrate a specific property should be featured.

Since the activities suggested represent only a sampling of the ideas and topics that could be presented, you should look to your children and to your program expectations for further guidance in your planning decisions.

Many skills developed in mathematics are also developed in science as both subjects deal with observing, measuring, and quantifying the environment. Therefore, the Mathematics and Science Centers can support and enrich each other. The children can experience an idea at one center and have the same idea confirmed and reinforced at the other. Observation, classification, seriation, and measurement are the main mathematical skills featured and reinforced in this section. For those children who require further experience with number, the Science Center can provide a comfortable setting to encourage set recognition and comparison. The Science Center also offers an ideal setting for children to explore and compare the mass of various objects. This is particularly important since the Circle Activities do not focus on the comparison of mass.

You will find activities for each of these topics as listed here:

There will be times when you will want to introduce a problem, materials, or an activity to the children. This can be accomplished through a circle activity by gathering a small group around the Science Center. The children should be encouraged to share their observations, predictions, or the results of an investigation during circle activity time.

Vocabulary

- Heavy, Heavier, Heaviest; Light, Lighter, Lightest
- Mass, Weigh, Balance
- Overflow, Full, Empty
- Same, Different
- Waterproof
- Cold, Colder, Coldest; Warm, Warmer, Warmest
- First, Second, . . . Fifth; First, Last
- Long time, Short time
- Shortest, Tallest, Longest, Broadest, Narrowest
- Young, Old

Suggested Materials

Collection A

- A variety of collections to be gathered and displayed. To initiate a collection, you might go on a field trip, take a class walk, ask the children to bring in materials from home, or write letters requesting information or samples. Some examples of things that could be collected are:

  - materials from nature: plants (leaves, seeds, fruits, vegetables) shells, rocks
  - toys
  - small machines
  - materials that demonstrate specific properties. For example:

    - materials that absorb liquid: fabric, paper towelling, tissue, bandages, cotton
    - materials that do not absorb liquid: vinyl, rubber, plastic, metal
    - objects that are attracted and repelled by magnets
    - substances that dissolve in liquid, e.g., sugar, flour, soap flakes
    - substances that do not dissolve in water, e.g., rice, macaroni, corn

- Science equipment. For example:

  - balance scales
  - magnifying glass
  - magnets
  - prisms
  - thermometers

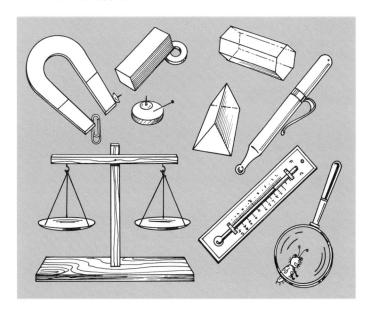

Collection B

- A variety of seeds, plant cuttings, and materials for planting

- A class pet and materials for its care and feeding

Setting up the Science Center

A small table can be set up as the focal point of the Science Center. This space can be used to house science equipment and current collections and displays. Other areas of the classroom may also feature aspects of science, e.g., plants on a windowsill, the water/sand tables, and the pet corner. At times, appropriate science equipment should be displayed in these locations to promote further observation and comparison.

Select an appropriate number of materials for current display and investigation. It is important not to overwhelm the children nor to distract them from the features or purpose of the materials. Change the materials frequently to maintain interest. Encourage the children to contribute to these collections and displays. Materials can be collected on class walks, on field trips, at home, or at school.

Science equipment should be introduced gradually so as to allow time for explaining the care and handling of these materials.

Recording at the Science Center

There may be occasions when you would like some children to make a recording of their activity, observations, predictions, or discoveries. There are many different ways children can make a record on their own or collectively. The following ideas represent only some of the potential outcomes of mathematical experiences at the Science Center.

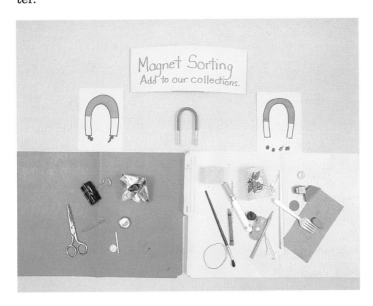

Displays can be made and maintained for a designated period of time.

The children can make their own records in a variety of ways. Guide and assist them when it seems appropriate.

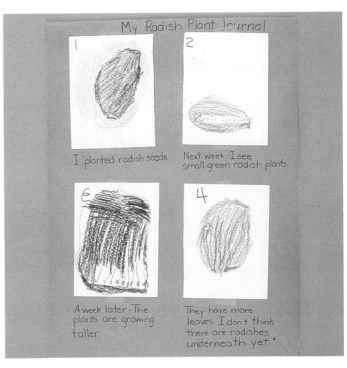

The children can record some observations on a continuous basis.

Picture collections created by the children and others can be displayed at the Science Center and possibly used for recording.

Free Exploration with Collection A

Over the course of the year, as topics are discussed and interests are pursued, collections of materials can be gathered and displayed. There will also be collections of materials you may wish to present that demonstrate specific properties. Each time a new collection is presented, the children should be given opportunities to manipulate and explore these materials. Interesting collections can be gathered from class walks, field trips, home, or school. The children should be encouraged to examine and talk about the materials and add to the display when appropriate.

Introduce the care and handling of science equipment as each new piece is made available at the science table.

Suggested Materials: Collection A

- Collections of interest and/or collections of materials that demonstrate a specific purpose; science equipment such as magnifying glasses, different magnets, balance scales, prisms, and a thermometer

Observations

Christina is discovering how a balance scale works. She is commenting on which objects she has found to be lighter than the large rock. Adrian has found a bolt that fits the hole. He discarded several that were too small.

Gabriella is looking through a book on magnets that accompanied the science table display. She is comparing a picture in the book to an experience she had. Toni is continuing with her own exploration.

Kristen is placing a variety of shells on the balance scale. There appears to be no plan or problem that she is pursuing. However, she is interested in watching the movement of the scale in response to her additions and deletions.

Andy and Sarah have been placing the toys on the ramp and watching them race down. Sarah added another book under the ramp in response to her teacher's comment, **I wonder if it would make any difference to the cars' speed if you placed another book at the top to make the ramp steeper?**

Brian is examining the collection of nature items with the magnifying glass. His teacher focussed his attention on certain features through a general comment. Brian is now checking to see which objects in the collection the teacher's comment relates to.

Extending Free Exploration

Free Exploration is not only a time for the children to discover relationships, but it is also a time for you to reinforce routines and gather information about the children's interests, learning styles, knowledge, and attitudes. This profile of the child, in conjunction with program objectives, affects the planning of each learning experience. It is this knowledge of child and program that will allow you to observe and recognize an opportunity to use a child's natural play to initiate a learning experience aimed at a specific program objective. The decision as to how and when to engage a child in discussion or further activity rests with you.

Kristen's observations of the balance scale could act as a starting point for developing several mathematical ideas. You might present one of the suggested activities to Kristen during free exploration to see whether she is interested in pursuing the investigation.

Measurement: Mass

- You might direct Kristen's attention to the movement of the balance scale pans by asking any of these questions:

  - **Why do you think one arm of the balance scale is hanging lower (higher)?**
  - **Can you find a way to make this arm change its position?**
  - **Can you find something that is heavier (lighter) than this object?**
  - **What do you think the balance scale will look like when you put these 2 things on the pans? Why do you think that?**

- If Kristen is ready for measuring with non-standard units, you might ask these questions:

  - **How many pebbles do you think you would need to balance this stone? Would you like to find out?**
  - **If you put 4 pebbles in this pan and 4 stones in this pan, what do you think will happen? Why? Would you like to try it and find out?**

Activities with Collection A

Observation Skills

- Create a display area by placing the same amount of different types of material in clear plastic bags, e.g., dry fine sand, wet sand, aquarium gravel, flour, salt, cinnamon, sugar, sawdust, rice, cereal, oatmeal. Place the same materials in open containers. Provide a magnifying glass. Encourage the children to take time to observe the displayed materials.

- Have the children look, feel, smell, and shake each material. If you would like to find out more about the child's thinking, you could ask any of these questions:

  - What can you tell me about the material in this container?
  - What does the material feel like? (Look like? Smell like? Sound like?)
  - I wonder what the material is.
  - How are these the same? Different?
  - Which material do you like feeling the most? Why?

To provide a further challenge for some children, you might select one of the following questions:

  - Which material would you use to build a castle? Why would you use this one?
  - What could you do with this material?
  - On which material would you draw a picture with your finger? Why?
  - Which bags do you think would lose material if they had a very small hole? Why?
  - Which materials do you think would pour easily into a bag? Why? Which ones would be hard to pour? Why?

Sorting

- Have the children sort and re-sort the collections of interest. The collections that are presented at the Science Center offer a wonderful opportunity to initiate sorting experiences. Place picture labels on sorting mats with the materials to act as a resource for some children in sorting by a given criterion.

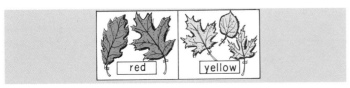

- Display some mystery sets at the center. Encourage the children to identify the sorting rule and add a new member to the set. To keep the original set distinct, you might have the children place new members of the set on a small piece of paper with their name printed on it. In this way, you can follow up with individuals if you wish.

- Place a variety of different types of materials in clear plastic bags or jars, e.g., dry fine sand, wet sand, aquarium gravel, flour, salt, cinnamon, sugar, sawdust, rice, cereal. Have the children compare the materials using their different senses and make observations. They sort and re-sort the bags of materials to make sets that are similar in some way.

- Have the children experiment with the magnets to determine which materials in a collection are attracted. Encourage the children to describe their observations and discoveries.

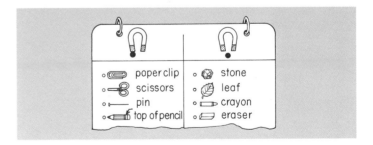

- Present clear plastic containers of water along with a collection of different substances: some that dissolve, such as sugar, flour, baking soda, or soap flakes, and some that do not dissolve, such as sand, rice, macaroni, or corn. Have the children observe the materials as they put a spoonful of each substance into different containers of water. You could have them sort the containers by whether the materials dissolved in water or remained intact. Over time, the children can add a variety of different substances, e.g., liquids and solids of different materials, to containers of water. Discuss their observations and have them sort the containers according to similarities and differences.

• Present a tub of water and a collection of different materials: some that absorb water and some that do not absorb water. Have the children dip items into the water and sort them according to whether they absorb or do not absorb water.

If you would like to guide a particular child's observations or pursue an individual's thinking, you might ask any of these questions:

- **What happened when you dipped the cloth into the water? The vinyl strip?**
- **What was different about these 2 things? How does the cloth feel (look) now that it is wet? How is it different from the dry piece of cloth?**
- **What happens when you squeeze the cloth? The vinyl strip?**
- **Which other material soaked up some water when you dipped it in the tub? Which one didn't?**
- **What is the same about the things in this group? And this group? Where will you put the cotton ball?**

Measurement: Mass

• Place the balance scale at the center with a collection of materials. Have the children explore the mass of the materials in a collection. Encourage them to use the balance scale to describe their discoveries. When appropriate, you may wish to offer an occasional question to initiate further exploration. For example:

- **What happened to the balance scale when you put the pine cone and the stone in the pans?**
- **Why do you think the arm of the balance scale that has the stone on it is hanging lower?**
- **Which object is heavier? Lighter?**

- **Can you find something else that you think might be heavier (lighter) than the stone?**
- **Is there anything the same about the things that make the arm of the balance scale go lower?**
- **What would happen to the balance scale if we kept adding pine cones?**

• Have the children select 2 items from a collection and compare their mass. Encourage the children to look at the items and predict which is heavier (or lighter). After the children have held the items, allow them to change their prediction if they like. Then have them compare the 2 items on the balance scale. You may wish to provide picture labels and have children keep a displayed record of their discoveries.

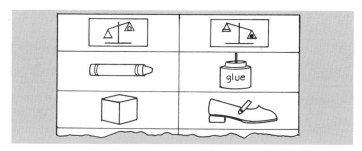

• Place a balance scale at the center with a collection of materials. Have the children select an object and place it on one pan of the scale. Encourage the children to add objects to the other pan to make the pans balance. For example, a child might place a large shell in one pan and a set of 12 smaller shells in the other pan to balance the scale.

• When children are working with the balance scale, you might present a container of Plasticine. Have the children place an object from a collection in one pan of the scale. Encourage the children to add Plasticine to the other pan to make the pans balance.

If you would like to use this situation to assess whether a child is conserving mass, you might ask the child to change the shape of the Plasticine or break it into smaller bits, and have her or him predict whether it will still have the same mass as the selected object. It is important to remember that conservation of mass cannot be taught; it is a result of development and experience.

• Have the children select an object as a standard. Encourage them to sort items from the collection that they think might be heavier, lighter, and/or the same mass as the standard. You may wish them to use picture labels to name their set(s). Then have the children test their predictions on the balance scale. Encourage them to describe their discoveries.

Measurement: Temperature

- At the center, place several containers filled with water of different temperatures. Encourage the children to compare the temperatures and order the containers from coldest to warmest or warmest to coldest.

- At the center, place several partially filled containers of water, a thermometer, and a bucket of ice. Have the children place the thermometer in the water and observe any changes. Encourage them to add varying amounts of ice to each container and observe what happens to the thermometer when placed in each container.

Measurement: Capacity

- You could have the children experiment and observe what happens to a partially filled container of water when small items from the science collections are added.

  You may wish to silently listen to children's comments and discussions as they perform this task. If you would like some children to verbalize your thinking, you might ask any of these questions:

  - **What did you notice as you added the stones to the container of water?**
  - **Would the same thing happen if you added these cubes?**
  - **Can you make the level of one container higher than another? How would you do it? Try it.**

- You might wish to present a challenge to a group of children or an individual. For example, you could provide 2 similar containers filled to the same level with water. You might ask, **If you add (5) pebbles to this container and the same number of these bottle caps to this container, what do you think will happen to the level of water in each?**

When you follow up on the investigation, encourage the children to talk about their observations. At times, you may wish to challenge some children further by asking any of these questions:

- **How many stones do you think will need to be added to make this glass of water overflow? Add them and see.**
- **How many did you need? Did you need more or less than you thought?**
- **Look at this container of water. Do you think it will need more, less, or the same number of stones to make it overflow? Would you like to try and see?**

- Present a collection of material scraps that are about the same size, several clear plastic glasses, and a bowl or tub of water. Have the children soak the materials in water for the same length of time. Then have them squeeze the water into the glasses to determine which material absorbed the most (least) amount of water. You might ask any of the following questions:

  - **Which item soaked up the most water? How can you tell?**
  - **Which item soaked up the least water?**
  - **Where do you think a piece of wet newspaper would fit in this order? Would you like to try and see?**
  - **Can you put the containers in order from most to least (least to most) water?**

Children will bring their own language to experiences dealing with absorption, evaporation, and the dissolving of substances. There will be times when you need to use the child's words to communicate effectively. It is also important for the children to hear the correct terminology in context.

Free Exploration with Collection B

Have a variety of plants and cuttings displayed in the classroom for the children to observe, compare, and care for. You may wish to provide a magnifying glass for the children to examine the plants more closely.

Suggested Materials: Collection B

- Plants, a variety of seeds, bulbs, plant cuttings, and planting materials
- A class pet and material for its care and feeding
- Science equipment such as a magnifying glass and a balance scale

Observations

This class has developed a gardener's work schedule to identify the pairs of children who are responsible for tending to the different plants. Vito is watering the plants. While Pamela turns the green plants to expose their other side to the direct light, she comments on the differences in their height.

Alissa loves to watch and care for the class pets, the new ducklings. As Jerett and Melissa walked by, she asked them if they'd like to watch the ducklings wake up. She has noticed a routine to their day. The ducklings usually wake up just after the children come in from recess. The 3 continue their observations, commenting on the different characteristics of the ducklings.

Shallen and Carol have been comparing the bugs that they found on their nature walks. They have identified many similarities and differences. The children are now talking about returning the bugs to their natural habitat.

Activities with Collection B

Sorting

Have children sort and re-sort leaves, seeds, or pictures of plants.

Patterning

- Plant different seeds in a pattern in a shallow tray. Label each seed with the corresponding fruit or vegetable. Encourage the children to describe the pattern in different ways at different stages of growth.

- The opportunity may arise as a child is observing the plants to discuss and identify different leaf patterns.

Seriation

When a child is caring for the different plants, you may wish to take advantage of this opportunity to reinforce a graduated sequence. There are a variety of ways the child could order the plants, e.g., shortest to tallest or broadest leaves to narrowest leaves.

Number: Numeral Recognition

Some children may enjoy planting fast-growing grass seed in a tray of soil. Have the children form a numeral in the soil with their finger, e.g., 3, and sprinkle grass seed within the lines created. The seeds should be gently covered with soil and watered daily.

Some children may wish to keep a tally of how many days it takes for their "3" to grow.

Measurement: Mass

- If the class has a hamster or gerbil, you may wish the children to use a balance scale to compare the mass of the pet to other objects.

- Some children may wish to compare the mass of different bulbs displayed at the center. Encourage the children to talk about their observations and discoveries.

Measurement: Time

- During your circle time, present the pictures cut from Line Master 41, which show the sequence of planting seeds. Have the children discuss and order these pictures. Display them at a center with the appropriate materials, and have the children use the sequence cards as a guide to plant their own seeds or bulbs.

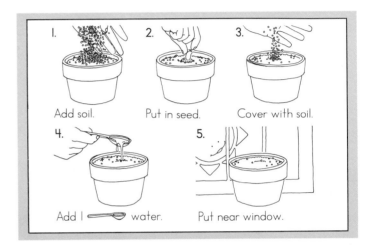

Sequence cards can be prepared to guide children in a variety of tasks. For example, the cards can illustrate:

- the steps to follow in caring for the plants
- the steps to follow in planting bulbs or seeds in different materials
- the steps to follow in caring for the class pet
- the steps for cleaning a pet's cage

- The children will enjoy planting different types of seeds. Marigold, radish, grass, and pumpkin seeds produce gratifying results. The children can observe and discuss the different rates of growth. Encourage them to identify which types of seeds sprouted first, second, third, etc. Some children may enjoy making a gardener's diary to show the sprouting sequence.

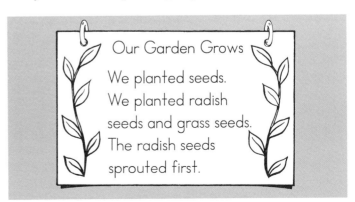

- Guide the children in placing a variety of different seeds between dampened paper towels and the side of a clear jar. Label the types of seeds. Have the children observe the seeds and record the sequence in which they sprout.

- You may wish to gather a group of children together to plant different seeds and bulbs in trays of soil. Encourage these children to observe the trays daily. A record can be made of how long it takes to see the different sprouts appear. Encourage the children to describe what they see and the changes that take place.

  Number can be incorporated into this activity by presenting a numeral or dot card to specify how many bulbs or seeds are to be planted.

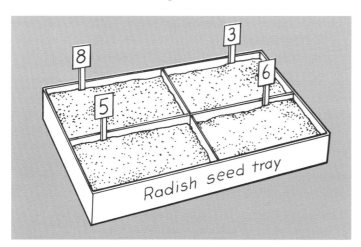

- Some children may enjoy observing the habits and routines of the class pet. These observations can be drawn by the children or recorded by a volunteer to make a timetable of the pet's day.

- The care of the plants and animals provides opportunities to develop a helper's schedule with the children. These schedules could focus on the days of the week. Post the schedule, and guide the children in remembering their responsibilities as needed.

Measurement: Linear

- Some children may enjoy observing and recording the growth of their seedlings or bulbs. This can be achieved in different ways. For example:
  - A popsicle stick or tongue depressor can be placed in the soil. The children mark the growth of the seedling on the stick at regular intervals, e.g., every other day or once a week.
  - String can be used to measure the plant and cut to represent the height. The children can measure the height at regular intervals, e.g., once a week. The strings can be posted each time to keep a permanent record of the growth pattern.

- If the class pet is acquired when it is a baby, the children may enjoy keeping a record of its growth. You might consider working with a group of children to measure the height or length of the pet with strings or strips of adding machine tape. These strips can be posted in sequence to represent the pet's growth.

Theme Activities

Themes are a wonderful vehicle for presenting activities, initiating discussions, and introducing concepts and skills. Not only do they appeal to the children's natural interests, but they provide an opportunity to integrate the various subject areas. Often theme activities have a language arts or social studies focus. This unit suggests ways to integrate and highlight mathematics in your theme work. We have selected 5 themes that are often introduced in early childhood programs to illustrate how mathematics can be developed and reinforced through theme studies. The themes are entitled All About Me, Special Days, Colors, Seasons, and Animals. The activities included here are samples of the many kinds of activities you might choose to include when planning a thematic unit. In selecting a theme, it is important to be sensitive to the needs and interests of your children and your community. For example, in the Special Days theme, mathematical experiences related to Hallowe'en have been suggested with the focus on the secular aspects of this special day. You may prefer to focus on other special days that are integral to the cultural or religious beliefs of your community, using our Hallowe'en activities as a model.

The suggested activities can be presented to individual children, small groups, or the whole class. Not all children will be interested in doing the same thing at the same time. Often, however, an activity introduced to a small group will quickly motivate other children to become involved. The length of activities will also vary. For example, the children may work for several days on creating a model of their homes using geometric junk objects, whereas a discussion of whether the children could fit under, travel over, or go around certain objects might take only 5 to 10 minutes.

ALL ABOUT ME

Number: Booklets of personal numbers can be made. Phone numbers, addresses, birth dates, and ages are only a few possible entries.

Sorting: After the children draw pictures of their families, they can sort them according to the number of family members.

Number: Baby pictures and recent photographs can be used to create a matching display. The children match the pictures one-to-one.

Sorting: Personal belongings such as books, mittens, shoes, hats, and scarves can be sorted and re-sorted.

Measurement: The children can find things that are smaller or larger than their handspans.

Sorting: The children can be sorted according to different criteria, e.g., length, type, or color of hair; eye color; or clothing.

ACTIVITIES

Graphing: The children can stand in the appropriate column of a large floor graph to answer questions such as: Are there more children wearing striped shirts than plaid shirts?

Sorting: Create a mystery set of children, e.g., children wearing blue pants. Call out the names of children wearing blue pants, and have them stand together. Ask the others to guess your mystery rule. Invite a volunteer to lead the activity.

Seriation: Have the children trace one of their shoes and cut it out. They can then trace and cut out 2 other objects. The cutouts can then be glued in order of size on a large sheet of paper.

Graphing: Photocopied photographs or children's self-portraits can be used to form an age graph. The pictures can be glued to the appropriate large cutout number.

Number: The children can identify body parts that come in 2s. Once a small group of children is standing, the class can count their (hands) by 1s then by 2s.

Geometry: The children can discuss and explore things that they could hide in or behind; stand on, in, or under; jump over, or climb under.

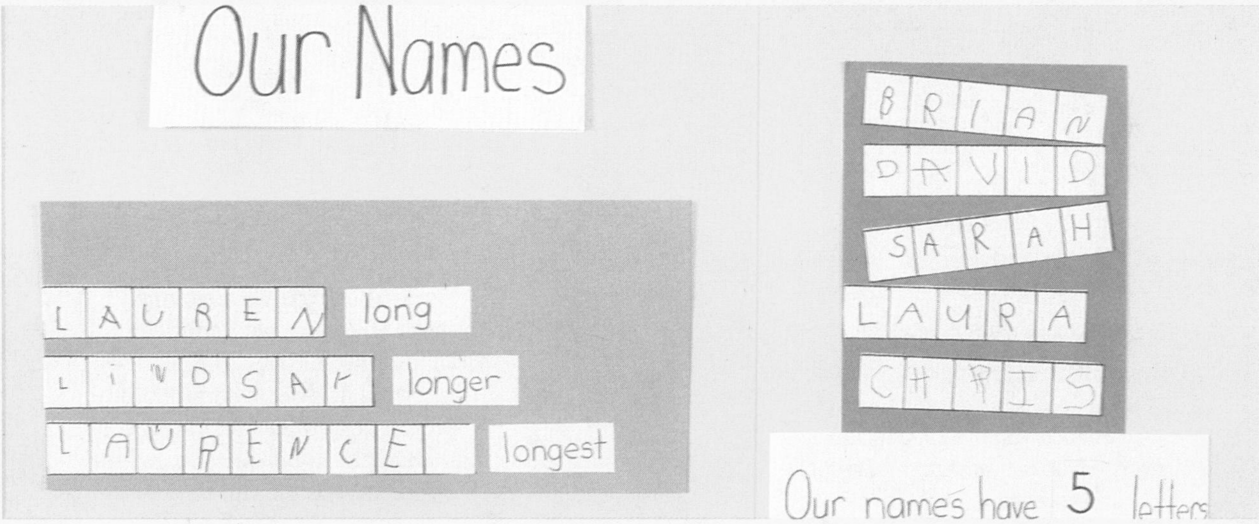

Our Names

L A U R E N long
L I N D S A Y longer
L A U R E N C E longest

B R I A N
D A V I D
S A R A H
L A U R A
C H R I S

Our names have 5 letters

Erin Sal

April Tooth Pillow

Louis Laura Joey

May Tooth Pillow

In April 2 children
lost a tooth.

In May 3 children
lost a tooth.

We Sorted
Ourselves

green eyes

brown eyes

blue eyes

Monika's Family

ERIKA

MOM

MONIKA

DAD

Monika's family

This is my family. There's my mommy and my daddy and Erika and me. That makes 4 of us.

My daddy is tall. My mommy is tall too. I am almost as tall as Erika.

How Old Are You?

Happy Birthday

5

Mark
Janine
Maria
Milo
Jake

Ryan
Erin
Ian
Chris
Alice

We are 5!

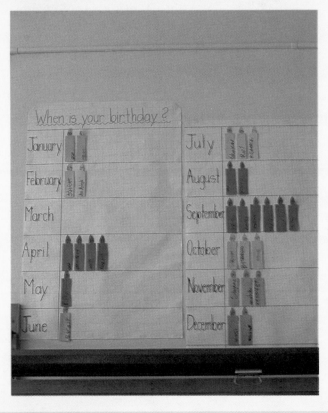

When is your birthday?

January	July
February	August
March	September
April	October
May	November
June	December

tall   taller   tallest

SPECIAL DAY

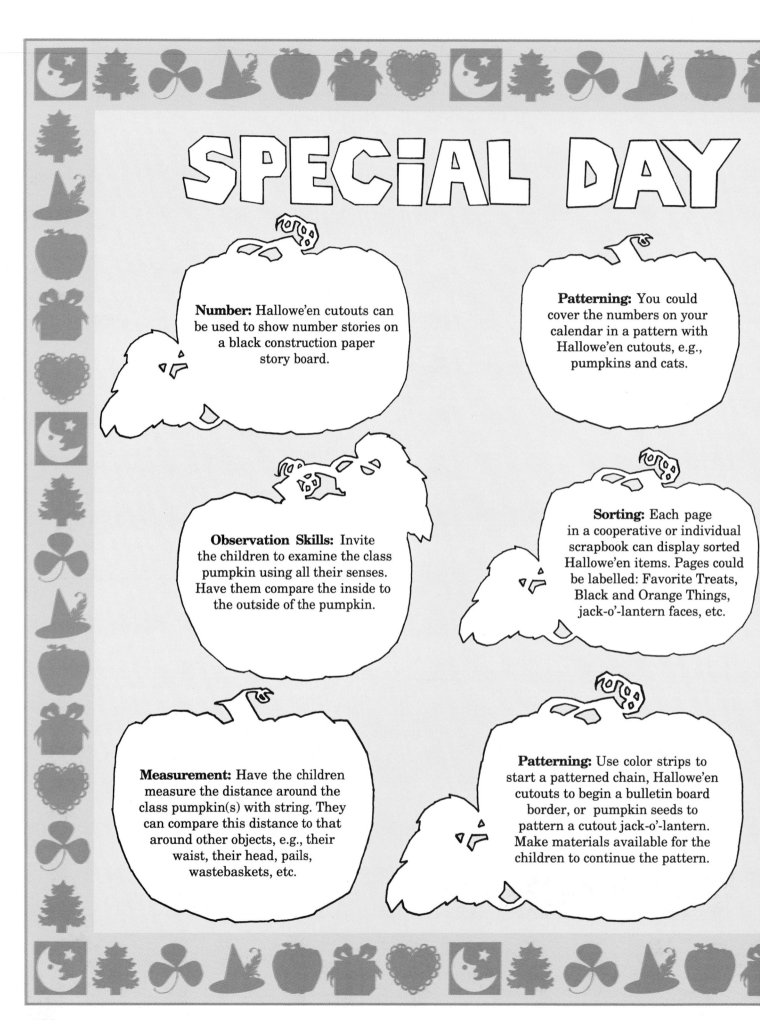

Number: Hallowe'en cutouts can be used to show number stories on a black construction paper story board.

Patterning: You could cover the numbers on your calendar in a pattern with Hallowe'en cutouts, e.g., pumpkins and cats.

Observation Skills: Invite the children to examine the class pumpkin using all their senses. Have them compare the inside to the outside of the pumpkin.

Sorting: Each page in a cooperative or individual scrapbook can display sorted Hallowe'en items. Pages could be labelled: Favorite Treats, Black and Orange Things, jack-o'-lantern faces, etc.

Measurement: Have the children measure the distance around the class pumpkin(s) with string. They can compare this distance to that around other objects, e.g., their waist, their head, pails, wastebaskets, etc.

Patterning: Use color strips to start a patterned chain, Hallowe'en cutouts to begin a bulletin board border, or pumpkin seeds to pattern a cutout jack-o'-lantern. Make materials available for the children to continue the pattern.

ACTIVITIES

Sorting: Treat wrappers or cutouts from advertising flyers can be sorted according to type, preference, chocolate/not chocolate, flavor, etc.

Graphing: On a graph, use name labels, pictures, or the children themselves to answer questions such as:
- Are you wearing the costume of a friendly or scary creature?
- Do you think we should carve a happy or sad jack-o'-lantern face?

Number: Place pumpkin seeds in a container. Invite the children to estimate whether there are more than or less than 10 seeds before a volunteer counts.

Number: Prepare treat bags containing 1 to 10 items. The children sort the bags according to whether they contain more than, less than, or the same amount as a displayed treat bag.

Measurement: The children can compare the mass of the class pumpkin to other classroom objects.

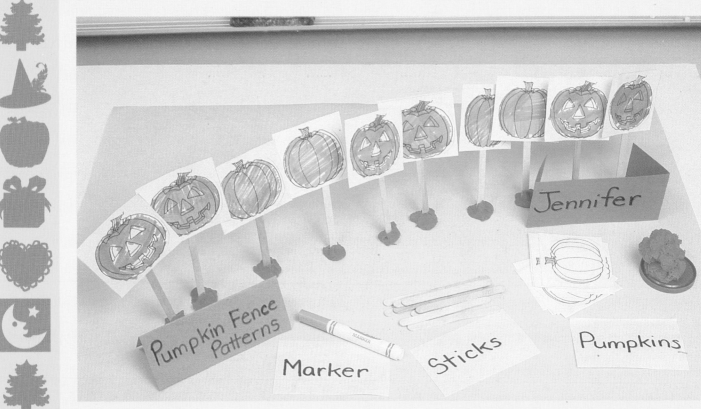

Pumpkin Fence Patterns

Marker

Sticks

Jennifer

Pumpkins

There are 6 witches ready for Hallowe'en. 4 have black hats. 2 have orange hats.

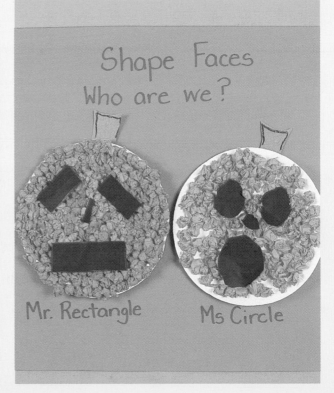

Shape Faces
Who are we?

Mr. Rectangle

Ms Circle

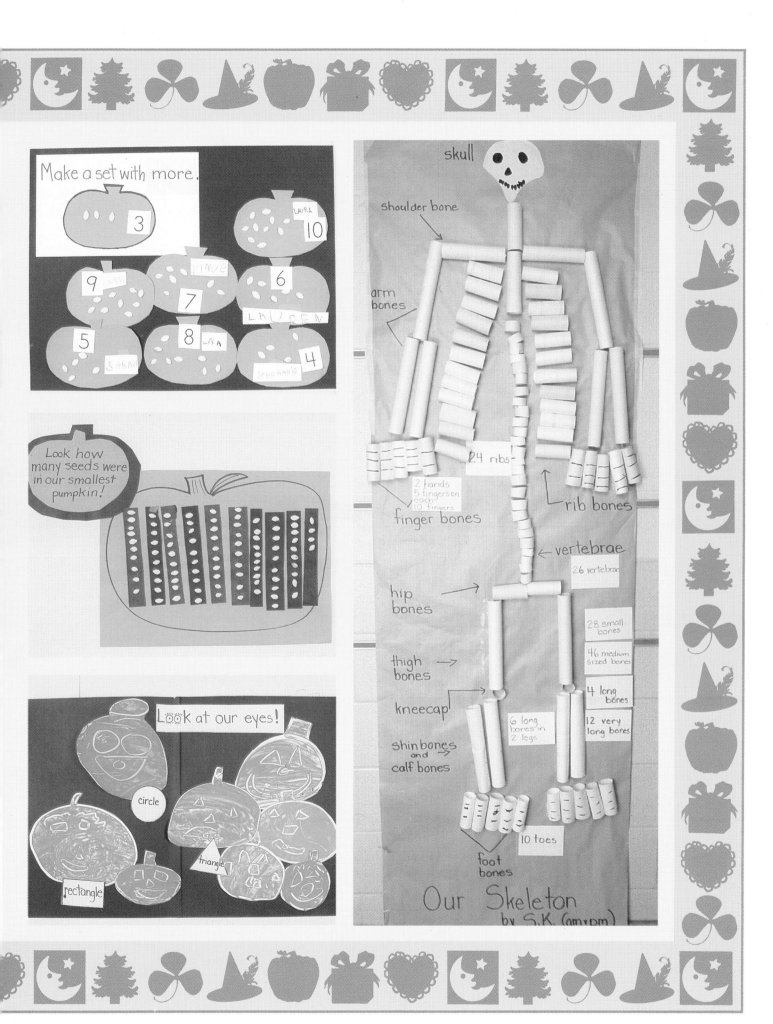

Make a set with more.

Look how many seeds were in our smallest pumpkin!

Look at our eyes!

circle

triangle

rectangle

skull

shoulder bone

arm bones

24 ribs

2 hands 5 fingers on each 10 fingers

finger bones

rib bones

vertebrae

26 vertebrae

hip bones

thigh bones

kneecap

6 long bones in 2 legs

28 small bones

46 medium sized bones

4 long bones

12 very long bones

shin bones and calf bones

10 toes

foot bones

Our Skeleton
by S.K. (am+pm)

COLOR

Seriation: Place colored construction paper in the sunlight for different lengths of time. The children can order the papers from lightest to darkest.

Patterning: Stamps and different colored ink pads, paper cutouts, stickers, and Pattern Block stamps can be used to create color patterns.

Seriation: The children can order fabric swatches, wallpaper samples, paint chips, or construction paper from lightest to darkest.

Seriation: Encourage the children to experiment with chalk on the chalk board. Using 1 color, they can try to draw a line from lightest to darkest.

Sorting: Have the children sort colored leaves onto the branches of a large tree branch placed in a basket.

ACTIVITIES

Sorting: Each section of a mural can be drawn to show what the world would look like if it were 1 color.

Observation Skills: The children will enjoy observing and describing the effects of sunlight passing through a prism.

Observation Skills: Add food coloring a drop at a time to a glass of water. Ask the children to describe the color changes.

Sorting: Paint chips can be sorted according to light and dark colors.

Patterning: Record the numbers on the calendar using different colored markers in a pattern. Have the children identify the pattern.

Patterning: Interlocking cubes can be snapped together in a color pattern. The children can glue colored paper squares or color squared paper to record their pattern.

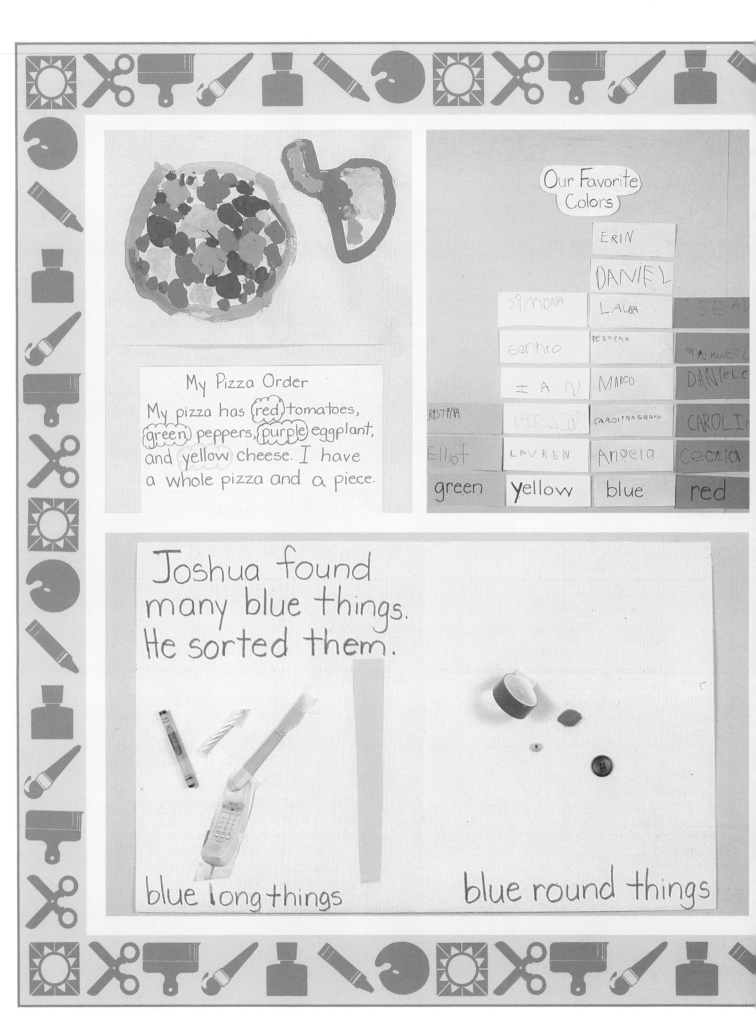

My Pizza Order

My pizza has (red) tomatoes, (green) peppers, (purple) eggplant, and (yellow) cheese. I have a whole pizza and a piece.

Our Favorite Colors

green	Yellow	blue	red

Joshua found many blue things. He sorted them.

blue long things   blue round things

A group of RED things

Red is Best

CAROLYN

I made 3 rainbows. I used 8 colors in each rainbow. I think rainbows are beautiful.

Color Pattern Necklaces

yellow green yellow green yellow green...

green yellow yellow red green yellow yellow red green yellow yellow red...

red green red green red green...

green blue yellow green blue yellow green blue yellow...

SEASON

Observation Skills: Sightings of different birds visiting the bird feeder can be recorded with photos or drawings of the birds.

Sorting: Mittens, boots, hats, or scarves can be sorted and re-sorted according to color, texture, material, and features.

Seriation: Containers of snow can be ordered from heaviest to lightest, fullest to emptiest, or dirtiest to cleanest.

Number: Have the children wear their mittens. Ask, **If I ask 3 of you to stand, how many mittens will we see?**

Graphing: You can create a graph using the children themselves, pictures, or name cards to display favorite winter activities.

Seriation: Discuss the steps in different sequences, e.g., how to make a snowman or how to dress for skating.

Sorting: Calendar pictures, post cards, and pictures from magazines can be sorted and re-sorted according to season.

ACTIVITIES

Observation Skills: The children can compare seasonal items, such as a mitten and a glove, a skate and a ski, or a hat and a scarf.

Measurement: The children can compare the mass of a cup of snow to a cup of water or ice.

Seriation: The children's snowman drawings can be ordered from tallest to shortest or fattest to thinnest.

Observation Skills: The children can examine a tree outside and then create a similar class tree by making and attaching leaves to a large branch secured in a pail.

Seriation: Snow that has melted in clear containers can be ordered by height of the water level.

Patterning: Boots can be lined up in a pattern, e.g., heels out, toes out, heels out, toes out, heels out, toes out,....

Story Board
Number Stories

Snowmen Numbers

7

There are 7 snowmen. There are
7 hats and 7 brooms. There are
7 small snowballs and 7 large
snowballs. But there are 14 eyes.
Angela

8 Snowflakes

6 snowflakes
falling.

2 snowflakes
on the ground.
Shawna S.

Patterned Winter Clothing

white, red, purple, white, red, purple,....

white, red, white, red, ...

line dot line dot line dot line dot line dot

blue   line
yellow   dots
blue
red   line
blue   dots
yellow   line
blue   dots
              line

Winter

Spring

Fall

Summer

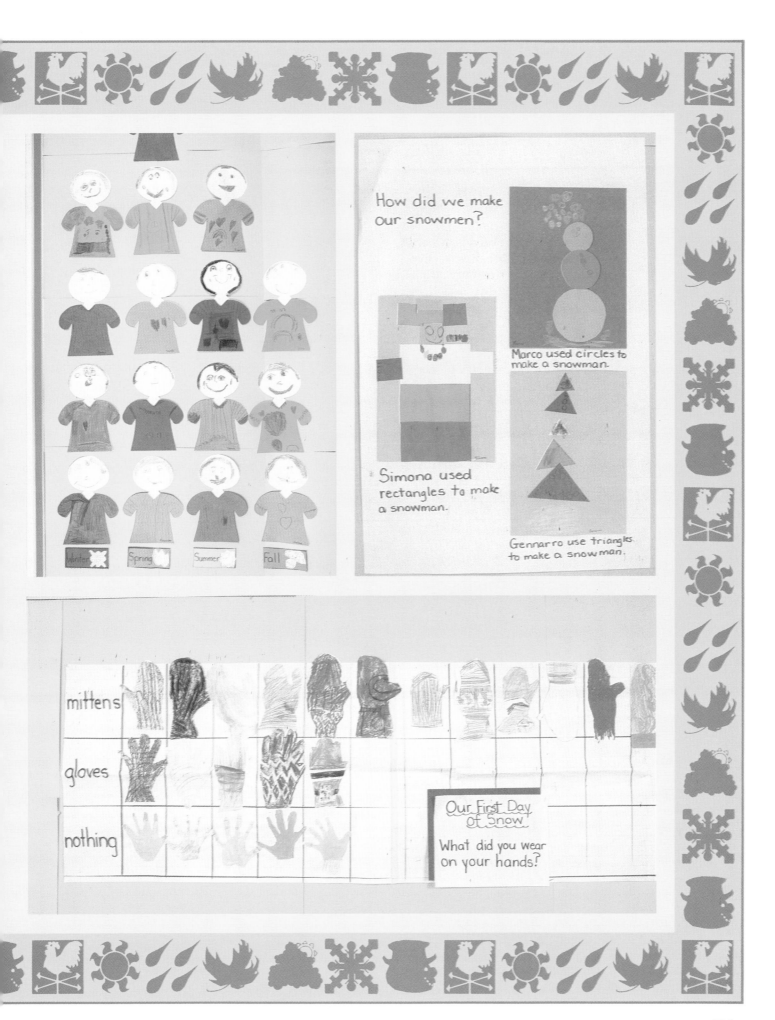

How did we make our snowmen?

Marco used circles to make a snowman.

Simona used rectangles to make a snowman.

Gennarro use triangles to make a snowman.

Winter   Spring   Summer   Fall

mittens

gloves

nothing

Our First Day of Snow

What did you wear on your hands?

ANIMAL

Geometry: Discarded boxes and paper towel rolls can be used to create a real or imaginary animal.

Number: The children can select a number up to 10 and then create an animal using that number of pipe cleaners, straws, or other material.

Observation Skills: The children can compare 2 animals and create a list of likenesses and differences.

Seriation: Have the children bring in a series of photographs to show how a pet dog or cat has grown.

Geometry: The children can try to create an animal of their choice using various geometric figures or using only 1 type of figure.

ACTIVITIES

Sorting: Animal models and pictures can be sorted and re-sorted according to body covering, where they live, type of home, color, way they travel, etc.

Seriation: With the children, discuss and order the developmental stages of a butterfly, robin, frog, or other animal of interest.

Patterning: The children can create a pattern parade of animals with their animal models or flannel board cutouts.

Seriation: Cut mural paper to the size of animals, and have the children paint them. The cutouts can be ordered according to size.

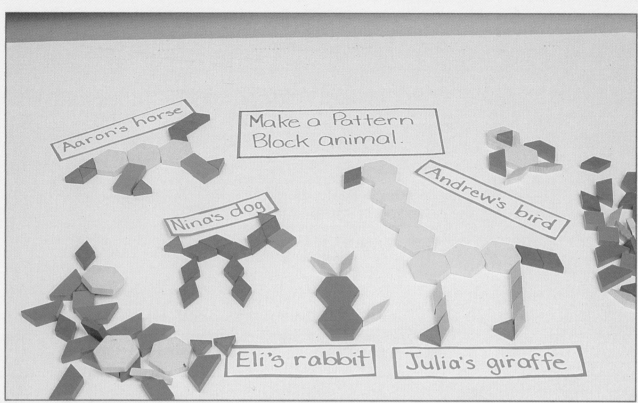

Aaron's horse

Make a Pattern Block animal.

Andrew's bird

Nina's dog

Eli's rabbit

Julia's giraffe

Animals sorted by Chloe

zoo

farm

What kind of pet would you like?

fish
rabbit
bird
dog
cat

What should we name our goldfish?

Goldy — Justin, Vito, Christopher, Soula, Beth, Erin, Sara

Lucky — Shallen, Julian, Nicky, Erica, Marco

Swimmer — Michael, Tamika, Quinn, Robin, Jamie, Alison

Monday we went to the zoo.

This is the tallest animal we saw.

This is the shortest animal we saw.

Giraffe

Animal Patterns

black gray stripes

blue black dots

red green yellow stripes

blue red stripes

purple blue red dots

Make an Animal

Use:
3 ●●●
4 ▲▲▲▲
5 ▬▬▬▬▬

Martin's camel

Angela's cat with a bow tie

Daily Routines

Often incidental experiences and daily routines can be used to reinforce mathematical ideas and concepts. By highlighting and labelling these experiences as mathematics, you can help the children to increase their awareness of the relevance and enjoyment of mathematics. You may wish to consider these experiences as part of your mathematics instruction for the day. Two routines often found in early childhood classrooms have been featured in this unit: Snack Time and Calendar Time. The sample activities represent only a few of the numerous mathematical ideas that can be presented during these times. Many of these ideas can also be adapted for use during other daily routines.

Snack Time

In many early childhood classrooms, some time is allotted for children to have a snack. Snack Time can offer an opportunity for mathematical discussion and activity. You may wish to join the children with your cup of coffee or snack and initiate an activity based on your observations of the children's snacks, actions, and comments. If the snack is provided by the school, you may wish to assign monitors and incorporate mathematics into the preparation and distribution of the snack.

The activities described in this section suggest only a few of the many ways Snack Time can be used to reinforce mathematical ideas or concepts.

Calendar Time

Many early childhood classrooms have a permanent display area devoted to the calendar. The children often start their day gathered in this area to discuss attendance, special events, news, the weather, and/or the date. This calendar time can be used to reinforce many mathematical ideas and concepts.

The activities and display boards featured in this section offer some suggestions on how to highlight different aspects of the calendar to develop a sense of the sequence and cyclical nature of the days of the week. Patterning, numeral recognition, sequencing, and printing can also be reinforced by the children's participation in calendar time. Involving the children in the attendance procedures engages them in a practical counting situation.

You will notice that the calendar displays are headed by a specific month. This is not indicative of a predetermined pacing model but offers you a sample display method and a possible sequence for developing calendar awareness.

Snack Time

Calendar Time

Snack Time Activities

Observation Skills

The snacks that the children bring or that are provided for them can form the basis of observation activities. For example, volunteers may offer parts of their snacks or you can use an extra portion from a class snack for exposure to air and/or water over a period of time. Interesting changes can be observed by placing fruits and vegetables on a plate to dry. Alternatively, expose bread or crackers to the air and have the children observe and describe the changes over time.

This class had celery for Snack Time. There were 2 extra pieces. One was immersed in a glass of water, and the other was placed in a glass of water tinted with red food coloring. The children have been observing and comparing the 2 pieces of celery.

Sorting

- In some early childhood classrooms, children bring their own snacks to school. Before Snack Time, you could provide each child with a paper plate labelled with her or his name. The snacks can be placed on the plates and sorted into plastic hoops or loops made with string or yarn. From time to time you may wish to extend these sorting experiences and graph each set in response to a question. For example, **Did more children bring a drink or something to eat?**

- A Snack Time theme can be suggested to parents, e.g., fruits, vegetables, grains, dairy products, or a specific flavor. After discussing the similarities and differences, the children can sort the snacks accordingly.

These children have been asked to bring a fruit for their snack for the entire week. After they observe and sort the fruits, a record of their sorting rule is made.

- Seeds from fruit, sections of fruits and vegetables, and packaging from the children's snacks can be used for sorting. For example:

  - Wrappers and packages from the children's snacks can be collected over time and used for sorting. A record of a child's sorting groups can be made by gluing the wrappers to cardboard or stiff paper.

  - Mystery seed sets can be made by gluing sets of seeds, e.g., pumpkin, watermelon, grapefruit, orange, or apple, to cardboard. Pictures of the fruits can be placed with the mystery sets. The children can label the seeds with the pictures.

Seriation

- The preparation of a class snack provides an ideal situation to reinforce sequencing. Individual instruction cards illustrating the steps to follow in preparing a snack can be posted at a snack preparation table or at the Dramatic Play Center. You may wish to have "chefs of the day" prepare the snacks for the class or have each child prepare her or his own. Line Masters 36 to 40 can be used for this purpose.

- The children can make butter for their Snack Time. Since the jar of cream needs shaking for 30 minutes, the children take turns. Once a child is tired of shaking, he or she passes it to another child or to you. There may be times when the class will engage in cooking experiences to prepare a snack. Presenting an illustrated recipe provides an opportunity for the children to discuss and follow a sequence.

Measurement: Linear

The children can identify the parts of fruit and vegetable snacks that grow. Have them plant the seeds or vegetable tops and observe, describe, and compare the growth of their plants. For example:

- The children can place the seeds from different snacks, e.g., grapefruits or oranges, between a damp paper towel and the side of a clear plastic glass. Have them keep the towel wet. Seeds that sprout can be transplanted into soil. The children can mark the growth of their plant on a popsicle stick placed in the soil.

- If an avocado is sampled during Snack Time, the pit can be stuck with toothpicks so that it is partially immersed in a dish of water. The growth of the avocado can be measured by cutting lengths of string or marking a posted strip of cardboard.

These children ate carrots during their Snack Time. They placed the tops of the carrots in shallow dishes of crushed pebbles with some water. They plan to measure the growth of the carrot tops every Tuesday before Story Time.

Number: Sets to 10

Snack preparation by a few individuals or by the class can provide an opportunity to reinforce number. For example:

- If the children are sitting in groups for Snack Time, you could ask volunteers to put out enough cups for each person in their group.
- If there is a chef of the day, you can ask her or him to set out enough plates for each child to have one.
- The children preparing the class snack might be asked to give the same number of raisins to each child.
- A numeral card or dot card can be placed at the snack preparation table identifying how many crackers can be taken by each child.
- You might want to present a clear container of peanuts and ask, **Do you think there are enough peanuts in this jar for each person to have one? Let's find out.**
- A chef preparing the plates for Snack Time might be asked to give each person 1 more slice of apple.

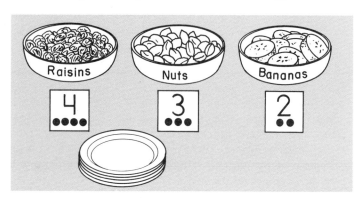

A snack preparation table can be set up. The number of raisins, peanuts, and banana slices each child can take is identified on a card.

Recipes that include number can be posted or used during snack preparation to make individual portions.

Measurement: Capacity

When a beverage is being served to the children during Snack Time, it provides a wonderful opportunity to explore capacity. For example, if 13 children wanted apple juice and 6 children wanted orange juice, you could present 2 different sizes of juice containers. You could then discuss with the children which juice container would be suitable for making the appropriate amount of the 2 kinds of juices. To extend the experience further, you might ask a volunteer to pour the juice into the appropriate number of cups. Alternatively, you might present 3 different beverage containers and ask volunteers to determine which one would be best for serving 15 paper cups of juice.

Jennifer and Nils are chefs for the day. They are preparing the drinks for Snack Time. Their teacher told them to each pour 7 glasses of milk and to fill them about half full. The 2 chefs have filled their glasses and are now discussing if the first glass is about half full.

Geometry: Geometric Figures

If the children are provided with a snack, you may wish to select snacks that focus the children's attention on shape. Or you may wish to highlight the shape of snacks brought by the children. For example, you might ask:

- **What other snacks have the same shape as John's orange?**
- **Does anyone else have a square snack today?**
- **Do you see anything in our room that has the same shape as Cindy's cracker?**

Graphing

There are many possible investigations that could use concrete graphing as an organizer for the children's snacks. These suggested questions are only a few of the many that could be asked as the basis for constructing a graph:

- **Which shape of cracker did you get?**
- **Is your snack wrapped?**
- **Did you bring a fruit or a vegetable?**
- **Did you like the apple cider we made?**
- **Which type of snack would you like tomorrow?**
- **Do you have a sticky snack?**
- **Does your snack have a smell to it?**

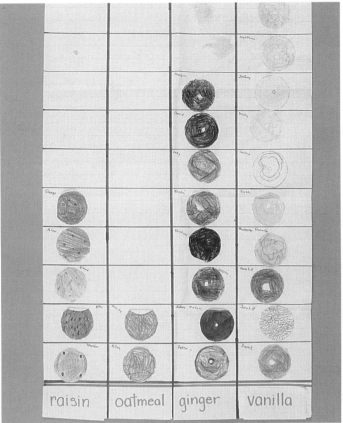

raisin | oatmeal | ginger | vanilla

This pictograph shows which cookies the children chose for their snack.

Calendar Time Activities

Measurement: Time

- Calendar Time provides an opportunity to introduce and reinforce the days of the week and the concepts today, yesterday, and tomorrow. For example, each day a card can be posted that identifies the day of the week.

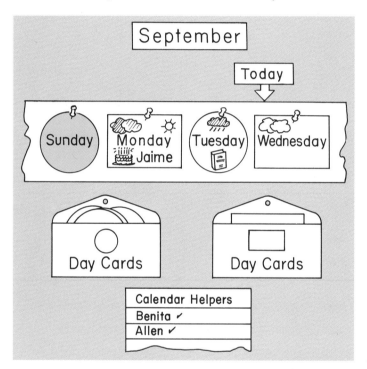

Special events, weather observations, and news can be recorded as well. You may wish to use a different color to represent Saturday and Sunday so that the children recognize them as non-school or weekend days. You may wish to initiate discussion by asking any of these questions:

- **What is the day today?**
- **How many Wednesdays have we had in September?**
- **What day comes before Wednesday?**
- **What did you enjoy doing yesterday?**
- **What would you like to do tomorrow? What day will that be?**
- **Let's say the days of the week out loud.**
- **How many cards have we posted? How many days have we had in September?**
- **What day comes after Wednesday?**
- **What is something you are looking forward to doing tomorrow?**

- To reinforce the repetitive nature of the days of the week, a circular wheel labelled with the days of the week can be used for Calendar Time. Each day, the children identify the day of the week and clip a clothespin to the wheel. You may wish to use another color to represent Saturday and Sunday.

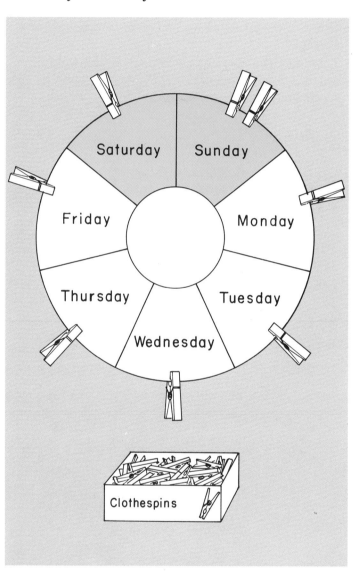

To initiate discussion, you might ask any of these questions:

- **What day is it today? How do you know that?**
- **How many Mondays have we had in November?**
- **What day was it yesterday?**
- **What day will it be tomorrow?**
- **How many days have we had in November?**
- **How many of those days were we in school? At home?**

- To introduce the traditional form of a calendar and to assist the children in interpreting a grid, you could post the days of the week on a bulletin board. Each day, as the day is identified and discussed, a volunteer can be guided to post the appropriate day of the week card on the calendar display.

January

Sunday	Monday	Tuesday	Wednesday	Thursday	Friday	Saturday
	Monday holiday	Tuesday holiday	Wednesday Mark	Thursday ✳✳✳	Friday	Saturday
Sunday	Monday	Tuesday	Wednesday	Thursday		

Sunday	Monday	Tuesday	Wednesday	Thursday	Friday	Saturday

As part of your calendar discussion, you might like to ask any of these questions:

- **What is happening today?**
- **What day is it today?**
- **How many days have we had in January? How do you know?**
- **What was special about the first 3 days of this month?**
- **What happened yesterday?**
- **What day will it be tomorrow? How do you know that?**
- **What was our first day back at school after the holidays?**

Number: Numeral Recognition

- A calendar can be used to reinforce numeral recognition. Prepare a calendar on stiff paper or chart paper with the numerals printed in place. Post a second set of numerals beside the calendar. As part of your calendar discussion and activity, have the children identify the date and ask a volunteer to locate and post the appropriate numeral on the calendar.

March						
Sunday	Monday	Tuesday	Wednesday	Thursday	Friday	Saturday
			1	2	3	4
5	6	7	8	9	10	11
12	13	14	15	16	17	18
19	20	21	22	23	24	25
26	27	28	29	30	31	

15 18 17 20 22 25 27

26 23 21 16 24 28

30 31   19 29

Calendar Helpers	
Jason	✓ ✓ ✓
Allison	✓ ✓ ✓
Yarsha	✓ ✓ ✓

- The children can locate the numerals on the calendar in response to questions such as:

- **What happened on the 19th?**
- **When were there birthdays this month?**

Number: Numeral Printing

The calendar can offer an opportunity to reinforce numeral printing. For example:

- A volunteer can be asked to print the numeral on the class calendar to represent the date.

JUNE						
Sunday	Monday	Tuesday	Wednesday	Thursday	Friday	Saturday
						1
2 🎂 Kyle	3 🥛☕	4	5	6	7 🚌	8
9	10 🎂 Mandy	11	12 🌂☂			

- The children can be given a blank calendar on which to record the numerals in order to create their own calendar. This can be posted at home or given as a gift. You may wish to laminate the blank calendars so that they may be used each month. The children can print the numerals on the calendars with a water soluble marker or on paper shapes or cutouts that are then posted on the calendar.

May						
Sunday	Monday	Tuesday	Wednesday	Thursday	Friday	Saturday
🌼1	🌼2	🌼3	🌼4	🌼5	🌼6	🌼7
🌼8	🌼9	🌼10				

Roses 🌹   Daisies 🌼

Number: Counting

- Counting opportunities can be incorporated into Calendar Time on a daily basis or interspersed over time. Recording special events and birthdays on the calendar can initiate counting. You might use questions such as these:

  - **How many days until we go to the park?**
  - **Susan's birthday is on Thursday. How many more days does she have to wait?**
  - **What did we do 4 days ago?**
  - **What will we be doing 6 days from today?**
  - **Michael is playing soccer in 5 days. Show me 5 with your fingers.**
  - **How many children have birthdays this month?**

- The weather observations recorded on the calendar can provide a reference for counting. For example:

  - **How many sunny days have we had this month?**
  - **How many days has it been raining this week?**
  - **How many days has it been since we saw the sun shining?**

- You may wish to keep an ongoing record of the number of days the children are in school. For each school day, a bean or small object can be placed in a clear jar and the number printed on a cumulative record. From time to time, you might have the children count the collection of small objects to confirm how many days they have been in school.

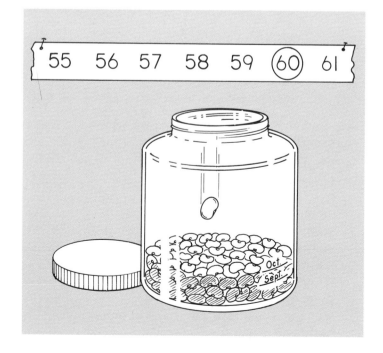

- If you would like to focus the children's attention on how many days there are in each month, you can establish a monthly counting jar. Each day, as children identify and discuss the day and date on their calendar, a small object can be added to the "October jar" to represent another day in the month.

- Daily attendance provides an opportunity for counting. You might do any of these suggested counting activities:
  - Encourage the children to count aloud to determine how many children are present. To help keep track, you might have the children stand. As a volunteer lightly taps them on the head, the children are counted and then sit down.
  - A magnetic board can be posted as shown. The children move their name card or photograph from "At Home" to "At School" when they arrive in the classroom. The display can then be used to count the number of children present and the number of children absent.

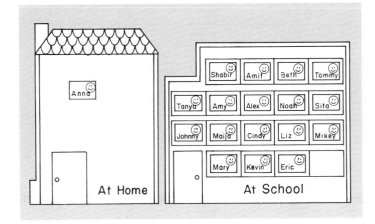

  - The children can sort themselves into boys and girls. The number of children in each group can be counted and recorded on a daily news board.

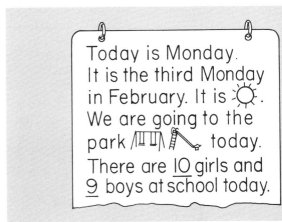

Patterning

Patterns can be created on the calendar as the date is printed or posted. Numeral or day-of-the-week cards can be created to represent a variety of patterns, e.g., color, shape, size, or cutout figures that correspond to a current theme. Encourage the children to read the pattern and to predict what will come next.

Sorting

At the end of each month, the children can count and identify how many days there were in the month. A month card can be posted in the appropriate group of an ongoing display showing the number of days in each month.

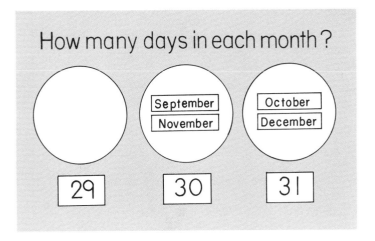

Observation Skills

Encourage the children to make observations about the weather. These observations and comments can be recorded on the calendar.

Sunday	Monday	Tuesday	Wednesday
		1	2
3	4		

Home Projects

This unit features activities and sample letters that are intended to facilitate communication between home and school and encourage parental involvement. Discretion should be used when planning and presenting Home Projects. Be sensitive to the needs of your community and the children as you select and adapt Home Projects for use throughout the year.

It is wise to introduce and discuss the rationale and potential of Home Projects on a Parents' Night. Ensure that the parents understand that these are *optional* tasks and that children should never be pressured to participate if they do not appear eager to do so.

This discussion should be followed up with a letter to the parents outlining once again the nature and purpose of the projects. The sample letter provided here can serve as a guide in preparing your own letter to parents. Then, at appropriate intervals throughout the year, Home Project Newsletters can be sent home describing activities in which the parents and children can participate together. Line Master 46 has been provided to help you create attractive newsletters. In this unit, we have included samples of several possible newsletters, each containing a number of activities. Select those that seem most appropriate for your children. It is important that these newsletters be inviting and not overwhelming. Your first newsletter might suggest only 1 or 2 activities. If there is a positive response, the next newsletter might include a few more suggestions. Remember that the parents will be receiving many notes from the school. Try to send the Home Project Newsletter on days when there are no other notes going home so that it does not get overlooked.

There may be occasions when you feel it is appropriate to have a follow-up discussion or activities in response to a Home Project. For example, when the children bring in materials to contribute to the class collections, you could do any of the following:

• Play Tell Me About It, page 39.
• Sort the materials.
• Count the materials brought in that day.
• Graph the materials.
• Discuss possible uses for certain items.

You might also generate a Home Project Newsletter to accompany a special piece of work which the children are bringing home. For example, if the children are taking home vegetable print patterns, you might describe the process used and the mathematics involved.

Dear Parent or Guardian:

I am sure you have on occasion asked your child what he or she did in school that day. I am also sure you have heard your child respond "Nothing", "Just play", or perhaps even "I don't remember". Don't be alarmed. Often, what the child thinks is "just play" is in fact an activity designed to develop important skills in mathematics and/or language.

This year, we are using an activity-based mathematics program called Explorations for Early Childhood. As part of this program, I will periodically be sending home newsletters intended to keep you informed about what your child is doing at school.

These newsletters will also describe activities in which you can participate with your child, if your child is interested. Please keep in mind that these activities are completely optional. If your child does not appear interested in an activity, simply do not do it. You might want to file the newsletter and try again at a later date. The most important thing always is that you and your child enjoy the activity, that you have fun.

If you have any questions about these newsletters or about our mathematics program, please call. I would also be interested in hearing about any mathematics activities or games you have enjoyed with your child.

Sincerely,

Home Project 1

Collecting materials for your mathematics program can become a community project by involving the parents and children. If you ask the children to contribute junk materials to the classroom collections, they will feel that they have an important role in setting up and organizing the classroom. The sample Home Project Newsletter below can be used as a model for requesting materials.

HOME PROJECT NEWSLETTER

I would like to ask for your help in collecting some items for our mathematics program. Often what you consider junk can be put to good use in the classroom for sorting, counting, building, patterning, graphing, sculpting, and so on. I have included a general list of items that we could use. Thank you for your help!

Materials We Could Use

- Natural objects: sticks, pebbles, shells, acorns, chestnuts, pine cones, dried beans, seeds

- Containers: boxes, plastic food tubs, plastic jars and bags of various shapes and sizes, egg cartons, washed milk cartons, shampoo bottles, plastic spray and pump bottles

- Lids from containers of various shapes and sizes, e.g., toothpaste tubes, shampoo bottles, plastic bottles, spice jars

- Fasteners: buttons, bread tags, twist ties, nuts, bolts, screws, clips

- Paper things: cups, napkins, envelopes, towelling, plates, magazines, advertising flyers, ends of wrapping paper and wallpaper, post cards, photographs, sandpaper, odd puzzle pieces, cardboard cylinders, empty food and household packages

- Odds and ends: keys, odd pieces of jewellery, toy cutlery, wigs, hats, old clothing. Nearly anything will do!

Thank you.

Home Project 2

It is important to help young children become aware of the relevance and presence of mathematics throughout their world. One way of achieving this is by asking the children to search their environment for examples of concepts you have introduced at school. Activities described in the Home Project Newsletter below will help to involve the parents in this search for mathematics. Please note that you will likely not want to include all the activities described here in one newsletter for fear of overwhelming the parents. Select the ones that appeal to you.

HOME PROJECT NEWSLETTER

Mathematics surrounds us! At school we have been working together to look for mathematics inside and outside our classroom. We had a wonderful time sorting and labelling our supplies and toys. Each day we take time to see who is wearing a patterned piece of clothing and then we chant the pattern in as many different ways as we can. Today we matched children to Home Project Newsletters to see if we had as many as we needed. Similar activities can be done at home. I have tried to explain briefly what we have done at school and then suggested how you might want to continue the activity at home. Remember that my suggestions are just that — suggestions. If your child is not interested, do not try to force the activity.

- We have looked in our classroom to find all the things that come in twos. We found that there are 2 panes of glass in each window, 2 shelves in each bookcase, and 2 boots in each pair, to name only a few discoveries. Your child might like to continue this search for things that come in twos at home.

- Our list "We Spy Numbers" is growing longer every day. You can continue a search for numbers at home with your child. Each time your child spies a number, you might add it to a "Numbers at Home" list.

- We are comparing the number in different sets during daily routines. For example, we match juice cups to children to see if there are as many cups as we need. Matching is an activity that occurs naturally each time you set the table. Your child can help you and acquire prenumber skills at the same time. Casual conversation, such as discussing if there are as many knives as forks, or enough napkins for each person, can bring our classroom experiences into your home.

- Today we discovered that the tiles on our floor were placed to form a pattern. We chanted the pattern we found as black, white, black, white, black, white, black, white. Later we made our own floor patterns with small tiles. Your child might enjoy looking for patterns in your home. It is always fun to try and think of ways to chant the patterns you find.

- We have discovered that not many things have the same shape as a triangle. But our list of things with shapes the same as squares, circles, and rectangles grows daily. You child may be curious to see if our school list is similar to one you can make together at home.

- The children naturally compare the size of objects to themselves. Often, however, they only use the words "bigger" and "smaller" to describe their observations. We are now talking about objects that are taller or shorter than ourselves, longer or shorter than our feet, and wider or narrower than our handspan. If your child wants to measure to find such things at home, encourage her or him to tell you about the discoveries.

Home Project 3

It is worthwhile for young children to have opportunities to identify and describe mathematical experiences that occur incidentally throughout their day. This labelling of experiences helps the children realize that mathematics is fun and meaningful.

You may wish to send home a Home Project Newsletter asking the parents to enlist their child's help in a variety of different jobs that will reinforce specific mathematical skills.

Our children are discovering that mathematics is relevant and can be fun! Children who enjoy mathematics are likely to be successful students. To most of us, mathematics meant only arithmetic. To our children, it means much more. I am always trying to make sure that our math program involves the children in activities that are meaningful. Often I say things like: **We are doing a lot of math when we make our cookie dough.** Comments like these help the children to see that they are involved in mathematics activity often that is important and fun. The suggestions that I have included today highlight the mathematics in activities that take place naturally at home. Your child might enjoy doing some of them with you. The extent of your discussions should depend on your child's interest. Don't continue a discussion if your child does not seem eager.

- Sorting is a basic thinking skill. There are many things we sort at home, e.g., dishes, cutlery, clothes, toys, laundry, and groceries. You might involve your child in any of these sorting activities. Some children may enjoy explaining the decisions they make, e.g., why a shirt belongs in a particular drawer or which load of laundry the tablecloth belongs in.

- Matching and counting is at the heart of setting the table. Your child might respond quite eagerly to a comment such as: **Let's use our math to set the table.** If your child responds enthusiastically you might continue with a comment similar to this: **We have a guest tonight. How many places must we set?**

- Children are usually quite keen to solve problems, and kitchens usually are settings for a variety of problems!

Any of the following situations might interest your child:

- pouring the milk so that each glass has the same amount
- measuring baking or cooking ingredients
- giving each person 6 tablespoons of cereal
- tidying a cupboard by arranging all the boxes from tallest to shortest
- deciding if there are enough hamburger patties for everyone to have 2
- choosing the best sized bowl for the leftovers
- setting the table for the family and 2 guests

- We have been paying quite a bit of attention to the sequence of our day. We talk about what happened before and after our snack and also try to use the words "first", "second", "third", etc., when describing a sequence of activities. Your child might enjoy a similar activity at home. For example, the child could describe in order everything he or she does before school or on a Saturday morning.

Home Project 4

There may be times throughout the year when you would like to inform the parents of a current theme or topic of interest. This information could be given in the form of a Home Project Newsletter that describes some of your activities as well as provide some ideas for home activity. The sample newsletter below offers suggestions related to a Hallowe'en theme.

Hallowe'en is quickly approaching. Since the children are so excited about this special day, we are using a Hallowe'en theme as a focus for many of our circle discussions and mathematics activities. We have already made several graphs, created patterns on our treat bags, and talked about our Hallowe'en safety rules. There are many Hallowe'en activities involving mathematics that can be completed at home. You and your child might like to try 1 or 2 of the following:

- We have made many interesting designs and pictures using circles, triangles, rectangles, and squares. Your child might like to help plan the family jack-o'-lantern by arranging shape cutouts on a large orange circle. At school I always encourage the children to try many different arrangements before they decide on the one that they want to glue down.

- The gooey insides of a pumpkin are usually very appealing to young children! Your child might be interested in guessing how many handfuls are needed to empty the pumpkin. Or your child might like to try and take out 10 seeds in a scoop.

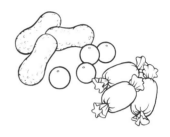

- I dry and clean the seeds from our class pumpkin. We use these seeds for counting and patterning activities. If you dry your pumpkin seeds, your child might like to show you how we use them at school.

- Children are always interested in examining their treats. Ask your child to explain to you how he or she sorted the treats. Your child might then enjoy thinking of another way to sort the treats.

- At school we have done a lot of work with patterns. If your child is planning on wearing a homemade costume, you might provide materials for creating patterns on the costume. A patterned sheet would make a more interesting and unconventional ghost than a plain white one.

- Shopping for our class pumpkin was quite an event! The children wanted the biggest one. It was most interesting to hear them discuss which one they thought was actually the biggest. When we got it to class, we each cut a piece of string to show how far we thought it was around the pumpkin. We then checked. Your child might enjoy introducing this activity to your family.

Home Project 5

There may be times when a particular material catches the interest of the children. It may be possible to send a sample of this their child might be interested in doing at home. Two examples are given in the newsletter below: one for colored pasta and one for a small piece of colored paper. Of course, you might have made other materials that you would prefer to send home.

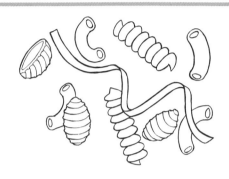

HOME PROJECT NEWSLETTER

Your child has brought home some colored pasta that we made in school. We have been using this material in many of our mathematics activities. These are just a few of the activities we did:

- We sorted the pasta many different ways, e.g., by color, shape, size, texture, and type.

- We made patterns with the pasta. One of the activities was to make a pattern necklace.

- We graphed the pasta and found out that we made more red pasta than orange or blue.

If you would like to make colored pasta with your child, the recipe is as follows:

Put pasta of different sizes and shapes in a plastic bag. Add several drops of red food coloring and about 15 mL of rubbing alcohol. Shake gently. Check that all pieces are colored. Add more coloring and alcohol, if necessary. Spread on newspaper to dry. Repeat the same process to make pasta of other colors.

We have been talking about color in class for several weeks now. Today was a special color day when each child wore a colored piece of paper pinned to her or his clothing. This little piece of paper was the focus of many of our mathematics activities throughout the day. Your child is bringing home this special colored piece of paper. You may wish to use it to pursue other mathematical activities at home. You might have your child look around your house or garden for other objects that are:

- the same color as the piece of paper

- made of the same material as the piece of paper

- larger than the piece of paper

- smaller than the piece of paper

- the same shape as the piece of paper

Have fun!

Home Project 6

You might suggest to the parents some enjoyable activities that can turn routine moments in the child's day into very enjoyable learning times. For example, bath time at home can be an ideal time to pursue many of the same experiences the children have had at the Water Center. The boredom of a long car or bus ride can be filled with number and observation games. If you think your parents would be interested in investigating these ideas and others, you might select several of the following activities to include in a Home Project Newsletter.

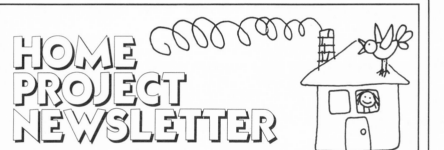

Many situations arise in a child's daily home routine that can be linked to our mathematics program. I am sending home suggestions for a few mathematics activities that could occur at bath time, bed time, in the store, or in the car. These ideas are only suggestions for you to consider. Your child may not be interested in pursuing an activity when you suggest it. Don't force the task, but consider raising the same idea again at a later point. If you have some favorite learning game you play with your child, I'd like to hear from you. Thank you again for your support and assistance.

Car Rides

Long car rides provide an ideal opportunity to play games. You might make a travel game kit to keep in the car. A box can be used to store materials. The lid can act as a lap board. You might place books, a notepad, crayons, and favorite toys in this kit. There are many activities that can be played in the car that will reinforce mathematical skills and ideas. You might consider any of these ideas.

- Provide your child with different shaped road signs cut from an old map. Encourage your child to watch for signs en route that have the same shape.

- License plates on passing cars or the scenery can initiate these number games:

  - Have your child look at the first number on the license plates. Ask the child to find 0, then 1, then 2, and so on, until he or she has seen the numbers 0 to 9 in order.

  - Have your child look at the license plates and clap every time he or she sees 3 numbers printed in order, e.g., 1, 2, 3 or 4, 5, 6 or 2, 3, 4.

  - Say, **Count the number of fire hydrants you see between now and the next time we stop for a red light.**

  - Say, **I need to turn right 8 streets from now. Would you please count the streets as we pass them.**

- Before you leave home, you can make scavenger hunt lists by securing pictures to a piece of paper. Each player watches for the various objects on her or his list. Each item is checked off after it has been sighted.

- Bingo cards can be prepared before a long car ride. In each square of the grid, record a different picture, sign, numeral, or letter. Each player watches for the different items on her or his card and then marks off the item when it is spotted. A player calls "Bingo" when he or she has marked off a row, 2 diagonals, a full card, or whatever you decide.

Shopping Time

The store provides many opportunities for mathematics activities. You might consider initiating all or any of these suggested activities with your child.

- Talk about how the products have been sorted on the shelves. Many grocery stores have labelled the sorting groups with signs above the aisles. Encourage your child to identify the different sorting rules.

- Have the child help you sort the items onto the check-out counter, e.g., tinned goods, produce, and breakables.

- You might consider initiating a measurement activity by asking one of these questions:
  - **Please find me the largest box of detergent.**
  - **Would you carry the lightest bag for me, please?**
  - **Which box of cereal would give us the most? Why do you think that?**
  - **Look at the scale. Which is heavier, the bag of potatoes or the bag of apples?**

- As you are walking through the store, you might suggest that your child help you with some counting. For example:
  - **How many items are on my list?**
  - **How many items are in the cart?**
  - **We can only have 8 items to line up at this check-out counter. Can we stay here?**
  - **Please put 10 potatoes into the bag.**

- The packaging of many products provides a wonderful opportunity to talk about and compare geometric shapes. You might like to suggest any of these activities to your child:
  - **Would you please get me the potato chips that are in a container the same shape as this soup can.**
  - **Please put all the packages that are the same shape as this cereal box on the counter first.**
  - **Watch for 5 things in this aisle that are the same shape as this package of butter.**

Bath Time

Children enjoy examining and playing with different bath toys. A variety of materials such as spoons, sieves, empty squeeze bottles (puncture holes in some of them), funnels, plastic food tubs, and plastic toys allows children to explore the properties of water, learn about relationships, and discover mathematical ideas. You might consider initiating an investigation by asking one of these questions at any given time:

- **I wonder which of these things float and which sink. Would you like to find out?**

- **I wonder which containers hold water and which ones allow the water to flow through. Would you like to find out?**

- **Which containers can't I use to rinse your hair? Why not?**

- **Can you make this plastic tub sink? How?**

- **I want to rinse your hair. Please hand me the rinsing tub that holds the most water.**

- **Can you put your pajamas on and brush your teeth before the bathtub drains?**

Bed Time

If you read to your child at bed time, you might be interested in looking for some of these books at your local library. Children's stories and literature are wonderful ways of representing mathematics in a practical context, whether it be real or fantasy. These books will allow you to initiate some discussion about mathematics as part of the talk that might arise from hearing the story.

- Anno's Counting Book by Mitsumasa Anno
- The Shopping Basket by John Burningham
- The Most Amazing Hide-and-Seek Counting Book by Robert Crowther
- The Doorbell Rang by Pat Hutchins
- Over in the Meadow by Ezra Jack Keats
- One Duck, Another Duck by Charlotte Pomerantz

Finger Plays

Finger plays and rhymes have always delighted young children. Many of the rhymes that children typically listen to and recite reflect mathematical ideas and language. It is not expected that children will develop a greater understanding of mathematics by performing these rhymes and finger actions. After all, a child will not likely learn more about number concepts simply by reciting, **One, two, buckle my shoe.** However, if we are aware of the mathematical potential of the rhymes, we can use them in 2 ways. First, by reciting and discussing rhymes during Mathematics Circle Activities, we can help the children to associate another enjoyable experience with mathematics. Second, the children can sometimes represent mathematical vocabulary inherent in the rhymes using concrete objects, thus exploring mathematical ideas in another context. Care must be taken not to make such situations so contrived as to detract from the enjoyment of the rhyme itself. There are many different rhymes and finger plays. Included here are several that are part of our English speaking heritage. Suggestions on how to use them are offered.

There are many rhymes that can be used to expose children to the counting sequence. These same rhymes can be used to reinforce numeral recognition. Provide each child with a numeral card cut from Line Masters 11 to 13 to represent the numbers you wish to reinforce. As the rhyme is being recited, the children can hold up the appropriate numeral card. Following are 2 rhymes that lend themselves well to this activity.

Four Little Pussy Cats

One, two, three, four, one, two, three, four,
These little pussy cats come to my door.
(The children with numeral card 4 hold it up;
the other children hold up 4 fingers.)
They just stood there and said, "Good day,"
(Make fingers bow.)
And then they tiptoed right away.
(Walk fingers away over the front of the body and
behind a shoulder.)

This Old Man

This old man, he played one,
(The children with numeral card 1 hold it up;
the others raise 1 finger.)
He played knick-knack on my thumb.
(Touch thumb.)
With a knick-knack,
(Pound left thumb with right hand.)
Paddy-whack,
(Pound right thumb with left hand.)
Give the dog a bone.
(Toss imaginary bone over right shoulder.)
This old man
(Pull imaginary beard with right hand.)
Comes rolling home.
(Roll hands over each other.)

Other verses follow as:
two: on my shoe; three: on my knee;
four: on my door; five: on my hive;
six: with his sticks; seven: up to heaven;
eight: on my gate; nine: on his spine;
ten: all again

There are many rhymes that can be used to represent different number concepts through concrete experiences. The children can act out the situations through role playing. Alternatively, you could have the children act out the situation with counters or cutout characters (Line Masters 33, 34, and 47) on a story board. This allows all children to be actively involved in the experience. An appropriate scene for the rhyme can be created by using the story board line masters (Line Masters 15 to 21), the children's drawings, or colored paper to represent the sky, water, ground, etc. Some of the following rhymes provide an opportunity for the children to create sets, while others emphasize the removal of items to represent 1 or 2 less than a given set. For the rhyme "Ten Galloping Horses," the children represent a set in different ways. Any of these rhymes can be adapted to represent different numbers, characters, or settings.

Two Little Boats Are on the Sea

Two little boats are on the sea,
(Put 2 counters or 2 boat cutouts [Line Master 47] on a story board, or hold up 2 fingers.)
All is calm as calm can be.
(Move hands slowly left to right.)
Gently the wind begins to blow,
(Cup hands to mouth and blow.)
Two little boats rock to and fro.
(Move the 2 counters, 2 boat cutouts, or 2 fingers back and forth.)
Loudly the wind begins to shout,
(Cup hands to mouth.)
Two little boats are tossed about.
(Wave the 2 counters, cutouts, or fingers about.)

This rhyme can be adapted to suit any number of boats.

The Beehive

Here is the beehive,
(Clasp hands together.)
Where are the bees?
Hidden away where nobody sees.
Soon they come creeping out of the hive,
(Slowly bring thumb out of clasped hands.)
One – two – three, four, five!
(Bring out other fingers as you count, or have the children place counters or bee cutouts [Line Master 47] on a story board.)

This rhyme can be adapted for other numbers.
For example:
three: Soon they come creeping out of the tree
four: Soon they come creeping out of the door
six: Soon they come creeping out to play tricks

Little Brown Rabbits

A little brown rabbit popped out of the ground,
(Right index finger pops up.)
Wriggled his whiskers, and looked around.
(Right index finger wriggles.)
Another wee rabbit who lived in the grass
(Left index finger pops up.)
Popped his head out and watched him pass.
(Right hand hops over left and wrists cross.)
Then both the wee rabbits went hoppity hop,
Hoppity, hoppity, hoppity hop,
(Crossed hands, with index fingers extended, hop up and down.)
Till they came to a wall and had to stop.
(Both hands stop suddenly.)
Then both the wee rabbits turned themselves round,
(Hands uncross.)
And scuttled off home to their holes in the ground.
(Right and left index fingers hop in opposite directions and finish in pockets.)

If story boards are used, the children can move counters or rabbit cutouts (Line Master 34), representing the rabbits, on the boards as they recite the rhyme.

Peter

Peter taps with one hammer,
One hammer, one hammer;
(Tap lightly with 1 finger or hold
up numeral card 1.)
Peter taps with one hammer
This fine day.

Peter taps with two hammers, etc.
(Tap lightly with 2 fingers or hold
up numeral card 2.)
Peter taps with three hammers, etc.
(Tap lightly with 3 fingers or hold
up numeral card 3.)
Peter taps with four hammers, etc.
(Tap lightly with 4 fingers or hold
up numeral card 4.)
Peter taps with five hammers, etc.
(Tap lightly with 5 fingers or hold
up numeral card 5.)
Peter goes to sleep now,
Sleep now, sleep now;
(Place palms of hands together,
and rest head on hands.)
Peter goes to sleep now
This fine day.

Alternatively, the children can place counters on a story
board to show the number of hammers.

One Little Brown Bird

One little brown bird, up and up she flew.
(Raise 1 finger.)
Along came another, and that made two.
(Raise a second finger.)
Two little brown birds, sitting in a tree.
(Hold up 2 fingers.)
Along came another one, and that made three.
(Raise a third finger.)
Three little brown birds, here comes one more.
(Hold up 3 fingers and raise a fourth.)
What's all the noise about? That made four.
(Show 4 fingers.)
Four little brown birds, and one makes five.
(Raise a fifth finger.)
Singing in the sun, glad to be alive.
(Wiggle 5 fingers.)

Alternatively, children can place bird cutouts from Line
Master 34 on a story board.

Peas

Five little peas in a pea pod pressed,
(Clench fingers on 1 hand.)
One grew, two grew, and so did all the rest.
(Uncurl 1 finger at a time.)
They grew and grew and did not stop
(Raise hand in the air.)
Until one day the pod went POP!
(Clap loudly.)

Five Little Sparrows

Five little sparrows sitting in a row;
One said, "Cheep, cheep, I must go!"
One little, two little,
Three little, four little,
Five little sparrows – Oh.

Four little sparrows sitting in a row, etc.
Three little sparrows sitting in a row, etc.
Two little sparrows sitting in a row, etc.

One little sparrow left in the row
Said, "Oh, dearie me, what shall I do?"
One little, two little,
Three little, four little ...
"Cheep! I'll fly away too."

The children can use the fingers of one hand, counters,
or bird cutouts (Line Master 34) to indicate the number
of sparrows. Repeat the song, having the children use the
other hand.

Five Little Dancing Leaves

Five little leaves so bright and gay
Were dancing about on a tree one day.
The wind came blowing through the town
Oooooo ... oooooo ...
One little leaf came tumbling down.

Four little leaves so bright and gay, etc.
Three little leaves so bright and gay, etc.
Two little leaves so bright and gay, etc.
One little leaf so bright and gay, etc.

The children can hold up fingers to represent the leaves
and blow hard to make the noise of the wind. Alternatively,
they can place counters or leaf cutouts (Line Master 47) on
a tree story board (Line Master 16) and remove them 1 at
a time.

Five Little Monkeys Swinging from the Tree

Five little monkeys swinging from the tree,
(Hold up 5 fingers of right hand.)
Teasing Mr. Alligator, "You can't catch me."
Along comes Mr. Alligator, sneaky as can be.
SNAP!
(Left hand moves over to right hand and snaps over 1 finger.)

Four little monkeys swinging from the tree, etc.
(Hold up 4 fingers of right hand, and snap 1 finger with left hand.)
Three little monkeys swinging from the tree, etc.
(Hold up 3 fingers of right hand, and snap 1 finger with left hand.)
Two little monkeys swinging from the tree, etc.
(Hold up 2 fingers of right hand, and snap 1 finger with left hand.)
One little monkey swinging from the tree, etc.
(Hold up 1 finger of right hand, and snap it with left hand.)
No little monkeys swinging from the tree.

Alternatively, the children can place and remove the appropriate number of counters or monkey cutouts (Line Master 47) on a story board.

Jelly Fish

Three jelly fish, three jelly fish,
Three jelly fish – sitting on a rock.
One fell off!

Two jelly fish, two jelly fish, etc.
One jelly fish, one jelly fish, etc.
No jelly fish, no jelly fish, etc.

One jelly fish, one jelly fish,
One jelly fish jumped on. Hooray!
Another jumped on.

Two jelly fish, two jelly fish, etc.
Three jelly fish, three jelly fish, etc.

The children can either use fingers or counters on a story board to show the number of jelly fish.

Four Scarlet Berries

Four scarlet berries
Left upon the tree.
"Thanks," said the blackbird,
"These would do for me."
He ate numbers one and two,
Then ate number three.
When he'd eaten number four,
There were none to see.

The children can use 4 fingers on right hand for berries and use the left hand for the blackbird. Alternatively, they can place 4 counters on the tree story board (Line Master 16) and remove them 1 at a time.

Five Seeds

Five little seeds a-sleeping they lay,
A-sleeping they lay.
A bird flew down and took one away.
How many seeds were left that day?

Four little seeds a-sleeping they lay, etc.
Three little seeds a-sleeping they lay, etc.
Two little seeds a-sleeping they lay, etc.
One little seed a-sleeping it lay, etc.

The fingers of one hand can represent the number of seeds, while the other hand can act as the bird. If seeds or counters are placed on a story board, the children can use a bird cutout (Line Master 34) to move the seeds away.

Five Ducks

Five little ducks went swimming one day,
Over the pond and far away.
Mother Duck said, "Quack, quack, quack, quack!"
But only four little ducks came back.

Four little ducks went swimming one day, etc.
Three little ducks went swimming one day, etc.
Two little ducks went swimming one day, etc.

One little duck went swimming one day,
Over the pond and far away.
Mother Duck said, "Quack, quack, quack, quack!"
And five little ducks came swimming back.

The children can wriggle the fingers of one hand to represent ducks swimming. Alternatively, they can use the duck cutouts from Line Master 33 on a story board.

Five Frogs

Five little froggies sitting on a well,
One looked up and down he fell;
Froggies jumped high,
Froggies jumped low,
Four little froggies dancing to and fro.

Four little froggies sitting on a well, etc.
Three little froggies sitting on a well, etc.
Two little froggies sitting on a well, etc.
One little froggy sitting on a well,
She looked up and down she fell.

The children can use fingers to represent the frogs, reducing the number held up for each verse. The fingers can be wriggled high or low to suit the words. Alternatively, the children can use counters or frog cutouts (Line Master 47) on a story board.

Five Little Speckled Frogs

Five little speckled frogs
(Show 5 fingers.)
Sat on a speckled log
(Place 5 fingers on other arm.)
Eating a most delicious bug. Yum! Yum!
(Hold fingers together and make eating motion.)
One jumped into the pool
(Hold up 1 finger and have it dive onto open palm of other hand.)
Where it was nice and cool.
(Fan face with hand.)
Now there are four little speckled frogs. Glug! Glug!
(Show 4 fingers.)

Four little speckled frogs, etc.
Three little speckled frogs, etc.
Two little speckled frogs, etc.
One little speckled frog, etc.

The children can use counters or frog cutouts (Line Master 47) to act out this rhyme.

Five Little Monkeys

Five little monkeys jumping on the bed,
(Have 5 fingers of one hand jumping on open palm of other hand.)
One fell off and bumped his head.
(Hold up 1 finger; put fist of other hand against head.)
Mama called the doctor and the doctor said:
(Cup one hand to ear and pretend to dial the telephone with the other hand.)
"No more little monkeys jumping on that bed."
(Point and shake a finger.)

Four little monkeys jumping on the bed, etc.
Three little monkeys jumping on the bed, etc.
Two little monkeys jumping on the bed, etc.
One little money jumping on the bed, etc.

No little monkeys jumping on the bed,
None fell off and bumped their heads.
Mama called the doctor and the doctor said:
"Put those monkeys right to bed!"

The children can use counters or monkey cutouts (Line Master 47) on a story board to act out this rhyme.

Ten Little Candles

Ten little candles on a chocolate cake.
(Hold up 10 fingers.)
Wh! Wh! Now there are eight.
(Blow twice and hold up 8 fingers.)
Eight little candles on candlesticks.
(Hold up 8 fingers.)
Wh! Wh! Now there are six.
(Blow twice and hold up 6 fingers.)
Six little candles and not one more.
(Hold up 6 fingers.)
Wh! Wh! Now there are four.
(Blow twice and hold up 4 fingers.)
Four little candles – red, white, and blue.
(Hold up 4 fingers.)
Wh! Wh! Now there are two.
(Blow twice and hold up 2 fingers.)
Two little candles standing in the sun.
(Hold up 2 fingers.)
Wh! Wh! Now there are none!
(Blow twice and turn palms face up.)

The children could use counters or small birthday candles to show 10 candles, blow on them, and remove 2 each time.

Ten Galloping Horses

Ten galloping horses came through the town:
Five were white and five were brown.
They galloped up and galloped down;
Ten galloping horses came through the town.

Use fingers, counters, or horse cutouts (Line Master 33) to act out the rhyme.

Following are some rhymes and finger plays that can be used in conjunction with your theme activities. At times, the children may wish to act out these rhymes using finger puppets or counters and a story board. They may also enjoy role-playing the characters in the rhymes themselves. For some of the rhymes that follow, the children show the ordinal position of each character; for other rhymes, they create the sets described.

Five Little Goblins

Five little goblins on a Hallowe'en night
(Hold up 5 fingers.)
Made a very, very spooky sight.
The first one danced on his tippy-tip-toes.
(Dance fingers on opposite arm.)
The second one tumbled and bumped her nose.
(Touch hand to nose.)
The third one jumped high up in the air.
(Raise arms high in the air.)
The fourth one walked like a fuzzy bear.
(Swing arms slowy at sides.)
The fifth one sang a Hallowe'en song.
(Cup hands around mouth.)
Five goblins played the whole night long!
(Wiggle 5 fingers in the air.)

Jack-o'-Lanterns

Five little jack-o'-lanterns sitting on a gate.
(Hold up 5 fingers.)
The first one said, "My, it's getting late."
(Point to thumb.)
The second one said, "Who goes there?"
(Point to index finger.)
The third one said, "There are ghosts in the air."
(Point to middle finger.)
The fourth one said, "Let's run! Let's run!"
(Point to ring finger.)
The fifth one said, "Isn't Hallowe'en fun?"
(Point to baby finger.)
Puff went the wind and out went the light.
(Blow on extended fingers.)
And off ran the jack-o'-lanterns on Hallowe'en night.
(Run fingers behind your back.)

The children might enjoy making jack-o'-lantern finger puppets using cutouts from Line Master 43.

Finger Plays   **221**

Valentines

Five little valentines, pretty with lace,
Standing in a row, in their own place.
The first one says, "Will you be mine?"
The second one says, "Be my valentine!"
The third one says, "I love you."
The fourth one says, "I'll be true."
The fifth one says, "Let's all run away
And find a little friend today."

The children hold up 5 fingers and wiggle each one as it is mentioned. They can use the valentine cutout from Line Master 43 to make finger puppets.

Five Little Snowmen

Five little snowmen, happy and gay,
The first one said, "What a beautiful day!"
The second one said, "We'll never have tears."
The third one said, "We'll stay here for years."
The fourth one said, "But what will happen in May?"
The fifth one said, "Look! We're melting away!"

The children hold up 5 fingers and wiggle each one as it is mentioned. The snowman cutout from Line Master 43 can be used to make finger puppets.

Little Witches

One little, two little, three little witches,
(Hold up 3 fingers 1 at a time.)
Flying over haystacks, flying over ditches,
(Fly 3 fingers through the air.)
Sliding down the moonbeam without any hitches,
(Slide 3 fingers down opposite arm.)
Hi, ho! Hallowe'en's here!
(Wave 3 fingers.)

The children might enjoy making witch finger puppets using cutouts from Line Master 43.

Ten Witches

One little, two little, three little witches,
Four little, five little, six little witches,
Seven little, eight little, nine little witches,
Ten witches in the sky.
Ten little, nine little, eight little witches,
Seven little, six little, five little witches,
Four little, three little, two little witches,
One little witch, "Bye, bye!"

Hold up fingers to show counting sequence. The children might enjoy using witch cutouts (Line Master 43) as finger puppets.

Annotated Bibliography of Children's Literature

Counting

Adams, Pam. *There Were Ten in the Bed*. Sudbury, Massachusetts: Playspace International, 1979.

Each time the 10 children in the story roll over, 1 more falls out of the bed until all are on the floor. The children in your class will enjoy turning the cardboard wheel that makes the children in the story fall out of bed. The illustrations promote counting backwards from 10.

Anno, Mitsumasa. *Anno's Counting Book*. New York: Harper and Row, 1977.

This book is the story of the seasons and how the landscape changes from day to day. The beautiful illustrations show how a land is altered by the people and animals who come to live there. The children will enjoy counting the objects in the pictures and finding all the sets of a number.

*Barber, Lois. *The Twelve Days of Christmas North*. Terrace, British Columbia: Northern Times Press, 1984.

This version of the famous Christmas song uses animals of the Canadian North rather than turtle doves, lords, and ladies. The children will enjoy illustrating sets of their favorite objects to create their own version of this song.

Burningham, John. *The Shopping Basket*. New York: Crowell Junior Books, 1980.

Steven sets off for the store to buy a number of items for his mother. Even though he encounters a bear, a monkey, and various other out-of-the ordinary animals, he manages to get his purchases home. The children will enjoy re-enacting this story, as well as counting the items on the shopping list.

*Carle, Eric. *The Rooster Who Set Out to See the World*. New York: Franklin Watts, Inc., 1972.

This is the story of a rooster who sets off on a journey to see the world. He is joined on his trip by groups of animals. As each new group joins the caravan, it is recorded in symbolic form. The children will enjoy counting the number of animals in the procession.

Crowther, Robert. *The Most Amazing Hide-and-Seek Counting Book*. New York: Viking-Penguin, 1981.

This pop-up picture book holds many counting surprises for the reader as bees, bugs, and worms appear. Objects are counted from 1 to 20 and then by tens to 100. The children might enjoy creating their own pop-up cards.

Hutchins, Pat. *The Doorbell Rang*. New York: Greenwillow Books, 1986.

Each time the doorbell rings, there are more children to share the dozen cookies that Ma just baked. The concept of division as sharing is introduced.

*Keats, Ezra Jack. *Over in the Meadow*. New York: Scholastic Book Services, 1971.

Told in rhyme, this is a story of creatures that inhabit a meadow. Each family of creatures has a different number of offspring, from 1 to 10.

*Kitamura, Satashi. *When Sheep Cannot Sleep*. London: A & C Black (Publishers) Ltd., 1986.

This is the story of a sheep that cannot sleep. What does he do? He goes for a walk at night and counts up to 22! The children will enjoy role playing their own sleepwalking adventures and counting sets of objects to 22.

*Lottridge, Celia Barker. *One Watermelon Seed*. Toronto: Oxford University Press, 1986.

Max and Josephine plant their garden with a variety of seeds. Their planting takes the reader from the numbers 1 through 10. Their harvesting takes the children from 10 to 100 and beyond.

Petty, Kate and Lisa Kopper. *What's That?* New York: Aladdin Books Ltd., 1986.

From the time Amy awakes to the time she goes to bed, she finds a number of things to count. This book shows how counting can be done in a simple, everyday way by just looking around your environment.

Pomerantz, Charlotte. *One Duck, Another Duck*. New York: Greenwillow Books, 1984.

Danny counts for his grandmother using the words "and another," until he learns to count by rote. Once he catches on though, there is no stopping him, and he ends his day by counting the stars.

Schenk de Regniers, Beatrice. *So Many Cats*. New York: Houghton Mifflin Company, 1985.

This is the story of how 1 cat can easily turn into 12. The reader is invited to count the cats along the way.

Testa, Fulvio. *If You Take a Pencil*. New York: Dial Books, 1982.

This drawing book turns into a counting book which hides many puzzles within the pictures. The readers are led to count from 1 to 12.

Geometry

Fisher, Leonard E. *Boxes! Boxes!* New York: The Viking Press, 1984.

Told in rhyme, this picture book shows over 80 types of boxes that can be found in the everyday environment. This book can provide the inspiration for a box shape scavenger hunt.

Hoban, Tana. *Circles, Triangles, and Squares*. New York: Macmillan, 1974.

Circle, triangles, and squares can be found within the book's photographs of everyday objects. Children enjoy identifying these shapes by name and sorting the geometric figures.

Hoban, Tana. *Shapes and Things*. New York: Macmillan, 1970.

This collection of black and white photographs shows various geometric shapes. Children enjoy identifying the figures.

Hutchins, Pat. *Changes, Changes*. New York: Macmillan, 1973.

Geometric solids are manipulated to form easy-to-recognize structures. Children will enjoy identifying what has been made as well as the shapes used.

Pienkowski, Jan. *Shapes*. New York: Harvey House, 1975.

Colorful illustrations are used to show various shapes. Children enjoy recognizing these shapes and manipulating Pattern Blocks to match the pictures in the book.

*Reit, Seymour. *All Kinds of Signs*. New York: Western Publishing, 1970.

This book is a collection of different kinds of signs. The children will enjoy naming the geometric figure that is the same shape as the sign. They may wish to make cut-and-paste collections of signs having the same shape which they find in magazines.

Testa, Fulvio. *If You Look Around You.* New York: Dial Books for Young Readers, 1983.

This picture book shows how points and lines can be combined to form triangles, cylinders, cubes, and spheres. Each figure is described in everyday language. The children will enjoy searching for these shapes in their own environment.

Wildsmith, Brian. *The Little Wood Duck.* Toronto: Oxford University Press, 1983.

The little wood duck is different from the other ducklings. He can only swim in circles because one of his legs is shorter than the other. Despite the ridicule he receives he still manages to save the day. The children will enjoy sorting geometric solids and other 3-dimensional objects to show which ones move the same way as the little wood duck.

Number Concepts

Marzollo, Jean. *Three Little Kittens.* Toronto: Scholastic Inc., 1985.

In this story version of a favorite nursery rhyme, the kittens wear and lose their mittens because they spend a day outside in the snow. The children will enjoy finding sets of 3 in the pictures and making sets of 3 for the kittens.

*Melville, Heather. *Four Pigs and a Bee.* England: Dinosaur Publications Ltd., 1974.

This simple country rhyme gives examples of 4 things combining naturally in the everyday world. Children will enjoy looking for natural sets of 4 in their own environment.

Ordering Objects and Events

Adams, Pam. *There Was an Old Lady Who Swallowed a Fly.* Sudbury, Massachusetts: Playspace International, 1973.

This is the favorite song told in pictures of a lady that not only swallows a fly, but 6 other animals as well. The children will enjoy retelling the story by referring to pictures of the things that she swallowed.

Burningham, John. *Mr. Gumpy's Outing.* Markham, Ontario: Penguin, 1984.

Mr. Gumpy sets off down the river on his raft. One by one his animal friends beg for a ride. Despite warnings, they are unable to sit still and they all end up in the river. The children will enjoy retelling this story at the Water Center using a toy boat and plastic animals.

Carle, Eric. *The Very Hungry Caterpillar.* New York: Putnam Publishing Group, 1969.

A hungry caterpillar nibbles his way through larger and larger bits of food. The children will enjoy using finger puppets to retell the order of his meals.

Coleridge, Sarah. *January Brings the Snow.* New York: Dial Books for Young Readers, 1986.

This book of months tells the story of the seasons through a young child's eyes. Each month is described in terms of a special moment. The children will enjoy telling the story of the months using calendar pictures that depict other special moments.

Keats, Ezra Jack. *The Snowy Day.* Toronto: Scholastic, Inc., 1962.

Peter wakes up to find it's snowing. He tries to save a snowball for indoors but is disappointed to find it gone from his pocket. The children will enjoy re-enacting the events that make up Peter's day.

*Zolotow, Charlotte. *Over and Over.* New York: Harper & Row Publishers, 1957.

The little girl in the story remembers the passing of time in terms of special events. After her recollections, she wishes that it will all happen again. Her mother assures her it will happen "over and over again." The children will enjoy sequencing items that represent special events, such as a pumpkin, a valentine, Christmas tree, etc.

Patterning

*Batherman, Muriel. *Some Things You Should Know Abo[ut] [a] Dog.* New Jersey: Prentice Hall Inc., 1976.

The author of this story describes his dog using a phrase and a descriptive word. This pattern of description demonstr[ates] simple cause and effect can easily be modelled by the childre[n].

*Gilman, Phoebe. *Jillian Jiggs.* Richmond Hill: Scholastic-T[AB] Publications Ltd., 1985.

Jillian Jiggs has the messiest room around. Her mother repeat[ed]ly tries to get her to clean it up, but Jillian is too busy creating new adventures and accompanying props to actually perform the task. The children will enjoy chiming in with Jillian's mother during her repeated pleas for a tidy room.

*Hazby, Nancy and Condy, Roy. *How to Get Rid of BAD DREAMS.* Richmond Hill: Scholastic-TAB Publications, Ltd., 1983.

This book reveals secrets for getting rid of bad dreams. Based on a simple pattern, the story offers all kinds of solutions for dealing with nightmares. The children might like to come up with their own solutions and express them using a similar pattern of speech.

Hutchins, Pat. *Don't Forget the Bacon.* Toronto: Clarke Irwin and Co. Ltd., 1970.

The easiest way to remember a shopping list is to repeat it over and over again. After a series of unsuccessful purchases, the little boy in the story finally remembers what he has been sent out to buy. The children will relish repeating the pattern and inventing new shopping list patterns.

Martin, Bill, Jr. *Brown Bear, Brown Bear, What Do You See?* New York: Holt, Rinehart, & Winston, 1983.

The pattern in this book is simple and quickly learned by young children. The children could easily adapt the pattern to suit other themes and make up their own verses.

Mayer, Mercer. *Just for You.* New York: Golden Press, 1975.

Everything this little fellow wants to do for his mother turns out badly. Identifying quickly with this simple cause-and-effect pattern, young children will be able to relate their own version of this pattern using examples from their own life.

Robart, Rose. *The Cake That Mack Ate.* Toronto: Kids Can Press, 1986.

This story, told in the pattern of "The House That Jack Built," has a surprise ending. The children will enjoy creating patterns of their own following this traditional model.

Sorting

Ahlberg, Janet and Allan. *The Baby's Catalogue.* Boston: Little Brown & Co., 1983.

This picture book is modelled on the format of a simple catalogue. The categories reflect the types of people, places, and things in a baby's daily life. The children could suggest other items to be added to the categories. A class catalogue could be created.

Carlson, Nancy. *Harriet's Hallowe'en.* Minneapolis: Carolrhoda Books, 1982.

After collecting Hallowe'en candy, Harriet sorts the candy first by color, then by size, and then by preference. She shares her candy with her brother only after she has made herself sick from eating it. Children enjoy contributing to a class collection of candy wrappers and sorting them according to their own criteria.

Hoban, Tana. *Is It Red? Is It Yellow? Is It Blue?* New York: Greenwillow Books, 1978.

This colorful collection of photographs introduces children to the concept of color. The children will enjoy creating sets of objects that are the same color.

Spier, Peter. *CRASH! BANG! BOOM!* New York: Doubleday & Company Inc., 1979.

An assortment of groups of objects that make sounds are listed in this book, e.g., kitchen appliances, machines, musical instruments. The children will enjoy classifying objects according to the sound that they make.

* These books are out of print but will be available at many school and public libraries.